DARK PSYCHOLOGY SECRETS & MANIPULATION TECHNIQUES

THE ULTIMATE GUIDE TO LEARN THE ART OF MIND CONTROL. SUBLIMINAL PERSUASION TACTICS, NLP, ANALYZE & INFLUENCE PEOPLE, READ BODY LANGUAGE & HYPNOSIS

Darren Brown

DARREN BROWN

© Copyright 2020 - All rights reserved.

The content contained within this book may not be reproduced, duplicated or transmitted without direct written permission from the author or the publisher.

Under no circumstances will any blame or legal responsibility be held against the publisher, or author, for any damages, reparation, or monetary loss due to the information contained within this book. Either directly or indirectly.

Legal Notice:

This book is copyright protected. This book is only for personal use. You cannot amend, distribute, sell, use, quote or paraphrase any part, or the content within this book, without the consent of the author or publisher.

Disclaimer Notice:

Please note the information contained within this document is for educational and entertainment purposes only. All effort has been executed to present accurate, up to date, and reliable, complete information. No warranties of any kind are declared or implied. Readers acknowledge that the author is not engaging in the rendering of legal, financial, medical or professional advice. The content within this book has been derived from various sources. Please consult a licensed professional before attempting any techniques outlined in this book.

By reading this document, the reader agrees that under no circumstances is the author responsible for any losses, direct or indirect, which are incurred as a result of the use of information contained within this document, including, but not limited to, — errors, omissions, or inaccuracies.

Table of Contents

Part 1: Dark Psychology Secrets 6

Introduction 8
Chapter 1: Dark Psychology Traits 14
Chapter 2: Nlp 20
Chapter 3: How To Analyze People 28
Chapter 4: Nonverbal -Verbal Communication 34
Chapter 5: Manipulation 40
Chapter 6: Subliminal Manipulation Techniques 44
Chapter 7: Favorite Victims Of Manipulators 50
Chapter 8: Dark Seduction 56
Chapter 9: How To Defend Yourself From Manipulators 60
Chapter 10: Ways To Put An End To Your Manipulation 64
Chapter 11: Hypnosis 68
Chapter 12: Brainwashing 76
Chapter 13: Famous Dark Psychology Case Studies 82
Chapter 14: Profiling A Sociopath 86
Chapter 15: Subconscious Mind Suggestions 94
Chapter 16: Using Dark Psychology To Manipulate A Man 100
Chapter 17: Power Techniques On Reading People 106
Chapter 18: Confidence And How It Is Displayed 114
Chapter 19: Spot The Lie 118
Chapter 20: Understanding Psychopaths 126
Chapter 21: Mind Control Tactics 130
Chapter 22: Dark Psychology Steps 134
Chapter 23: Conversational Skills Techniques 140

Chapter 24: Psychological Warfare 148

Chapter 25: Psychology And Self-Improvement 152

Chapter 26: The Dark Side Of Marketing Psychology 156

Chapter 27: Body Language And Dark Psychology 160

Conclusion 166

Part 2   Manipulation Techniques 168

Introduction 170

Chapter 28: Manipulation 172

Chapter 29: Psychological Manipulation 176

Chapter 30: Manipulation And Emotions 180

Chapter 31: Manipulation In Business 186

Chapter 32: Manipulation In Relationship 190

Chapter 33: Manipulation In Friendship 194

Chapter 34: Manipulation Techniques 198

Chapter 35: Nlp 204

Chapter 36: Mind Control 208

Chapter 37: Difference Between Manipulation And Influence Or Persuasion
.... 214

Chapter 38: Persuasion Tactics 218

Chapter 39: Tips And Tricks 224

Chapter 40: Developing Manipulative Behavior 230

Chapter 41: Identifying Hidden Manipulation 236

Chapter 42: Consequences Of Remaining In Manipulative Relationships .. 240

Chapter 43: Convincing Your Parents 246

Chapter 44: Things You Need To Do To Manipulate People 250

Chapter 45: Manipulation Games 254

Chapter 46: Reading Personality Types 260

Chapter 47: Strategies In Seduction Through Manipulation 266

Chapter 48: Social Manipulation 270

Chapter 49: Manipulation And Moral Question: Why Is Manipulation Important In Life 278

Chapter 50: Negative Manipulation, Tactics And Recognizing 284

Chapter 51: How Psychology Is Tied To Manipulation 290

Chapter 52: What To Do If You Get Caught 296

Chapter 53: Employing Manipulation And Persuasion To Get What You Want 302

Chapter 54: Knowing Yourself 308

Chapter 55: Why Is Manipulation Important In Life 312

Chapter 56: Financial Statement Manipulation 318

Conclusion 324

PART 1:

DARK PSYCHOLOGY SECRETS

Introduction

Psychology is the study of the mental process of humans. It seeks to investigate the thought process of humans by looking critically at the reason why people do what they do and the way they do it.

When it comes to dark psychology, the focus is on the human condition in relation to the nature of the psyche of humans, which propels them to prey on other people with the aim of influencing them. This is driven by criminal or deviant tendencies that lack purpose, as well as other general assumptions of both social science and instinctual drives.

All the members of humanity have the tendency to victimize other people, as well as every living creature on Earth. For some people, these tendencies are restrained and very minimal, while others easily fall for the instinct and act upon these impulses.

Typically, what dark psychology strives to achieve is the understanding of the thoughts, feelings, and perceptions that lead to the predatory behavior of a human being. However, it assumes that the production of this feeling and quest to influence others has a purpose and some rational, goal-oriented motivation about 99% of the time. The remaining 1% falls under dark psychology, characterized by a brutal victimization of other people with an intent devoid of purpose or a logical definition with either evolutionary science or religious dogma.

According to dark psychology, every human has a bank of malevolent intentions geared towards other people, and these intentions range from fleeting thoughts to minimally obtrusiveness to pure psychopathic deviant characters that are devoid of any form of cohesive rationality. This is described with a term known as the Dark Continuum.

Also, there is another term known as the Dark Factor, which refers to the mitigating factors that act as accelerants or attractive factors to every form of approaching Dark Singularity, which indicates the point where a person's heinous actions fall on the radar of the Dark Continuum.

Michael Nuccitelli (2006) states that dark psychology isn't only the dark side of the moon, but the dark side of the combination of all the moons. It is a combination of everything that makes an individual who they are in relation to their dark sides. It is a trait that is present in every religion, culture, faith, as well as every race of humanity.

From the point of birth to the point of death, there is an inherent not-so-pleasant side within everyone, which some have described as evil, while others call it deviant, criminal, and/or pathological.

With dark psychology, there is an introduction of a third philosophical construct, which looks at these behaviors from a different angle aside from religious dogmas and contemporary theories of social science. To be successful, every individual must take an interest in their fellow humanity. It is from the lack of interest in others that every failure in life springs, and this causes great injury to others. All human failures arise from this type of individual (Alfred Adler, n.d.).

According to the tenets of dark psychology, some of those who commit these acts do not do so for the love of money, power, sex, retribution, or any other known motivation. They just merely commit these horrid acts without any goal at all. They easily simplify their ends and do not justify their means.

Some other people just violate or cause injury to other people for the sake of doing so, and the potential for this lies within the core of everyone—a drive to harm other people without any reason, explanation, or purpose.

According to dark psychology, this is a complex potential that is hard to define. It states that the potential to become a predator, which is present in everyone, has access to people's thoughts, feelings, and even their perceptions. The good thing is that it is only a few people that act on this potential.

At one point or the other, every human will have had thoughts or feelings of acting towards another person in a brutal manner and many times would have had thoughts or feelings of hurting someone else without mercy. To be honest with oneself is to accept the fact that at a certain point in time, there has been a feeling of wanting to commit some heinous acts.

As a result of the fact that humans consider themselves to be a benevolent species, it isn't surprising that most times humans want to believe and convince themselves that these thoughts and feelings are non-existent, but the truth is that these thoughts are always present in everyone.

In dark psychology, it is believed that this predatory side of human nature is of a certain purpose. Several fields of religion, psychology, and other dogmas have attempted to give a solid definition to dark psychology.

Although it is true that most areas of human behavior related to evil actions have a purpose and a goal, when it comes to dark psychology, the aspect that is concerned with goal-oriented and purposive motivation seems to become very indistinct.

There exists a continuum of dark psychology victimization which ranges from thoughts and spans all the way to pure psychopathic deviance. However, this contributes to helping in conceptualizing the philosophy of dark psychology.

The aspect of the human psyche which dark psychology addresses is that which makes room for these predatory behaviors. In many cases, these behavioral tendencies are characterized by a lack of obvious rational motivation, which is universal and lacks predictability.

In dark psychology, it is assumed that the universal human condition is quite different, or it can be said to be an extension of human evolution. However, to give a critical look at this concept, it is important to study the tenets of evolution. This means that one will first consider that the evolution of man started from the life of other animals, and now man has become the paragon of all other animal life.

This is thanks to the frontal lobes of the brain, which make room for the human to be the apex creature. Therefore, it is valid to assume the fact that man as the apex creature does not make him completely isolated from both his animal instincts and his predatory nature.

If there is any truth in this evolutionary theory, and if you belong to the league of those who believe in the theory, you will agree with the fact that every behavior has something to do with three instincts: aggression, sex, and self-sustenance. These are the primary instincts that drive humans.

In the evolutionary theory, there is a tenet of the survival of the fittest, which is replicated in other species. In other to survive and reproduce, there is a similarity between humans and all other life forms. To be able to mark one's territory, there must be a show of aggression. This also goes a long way in protecting these marked territories, as well as gaining the right to procreate.

Although this may seem to be a rational process of thoughts and actions, it is not a part of the human condition in the purest sense of it. Therefore, it is important to note that dark psychology is not applicable when it comes to other animals on the planet, as it is only humans that are prone to exhibiting the tenets of dark psychology. However, a critical look at the human condition will dissolve the theories of natural selection, evolution, and animal instincts as humans are the only species that are able to prey on themselves without any apparent reason for procreation in order to survive and sustain humanity.

Humans prey on one another for reasons that are not clear and cannot be sustained. It is this part of the human mental state, or what is known as the universal human condition, that dark psychology aims at addressing, the part that makes humans impel this predatory attitude.

In dark psychology, it is believed that there is an intrapsychic part of human nature that makes people do what they do in terms of preying on others, and this part of human nature goes against the tenets of evolution. Humans are also the only other creatures on the planet that will kill one another for reasons other than the want of food, survival, territory, or procreation.

For ages, philosophers and other ecclesiastical writers have made several attempts at looking at this phenomenon in order to explain it. What has only been discovered is the fact that it is only human beings that harm themselves without any form of rational motivation.

It is assumed in dark psychology that there is a part of the human psyche that gives life to these dark and vicious characters, and this part within all human beings is universal. At this point, in the past or in the future, there hasn't been any human creature that did not possess this dark side.

Chapter 1: Dark Psychology Traits

Dark psychology is not a single, universally applicable medical diagnosis that can be applied across all cases of deviant personalities. There are, in fact, a wide variety of ways that dark psychology may manifest itself in someone's psychological and behavioral makeup.

There is no absolute division of one deviant personality type from another, and many deviant personalities with prominent features of dark psychology may display elements of more than one manifestation of dark psychology.

Psychopathy

Psychopathy is defined as a mental disorder with several identifying characteristics that include antisocial behavior, amorality, and an inability to develop empathy or to establish meaningful personal relationships, extreme egocentricity, and recidivism, with repeated violations resulting from an apparent inability to learn from the consequences of earlier transgressions.

Antisocial behavior, in turn, is defined as behavior based upon a goal of violating formal and/or informal rules of social conduct through criminal activity or through acts of personal, private protest, or opposition, all of which is directed against other individuals or society in general.

Egocentricity is the behavior when the offending person sees himself or herself as the central focus of the world, or at least of all dominant social and political activity.

Empathy is the ability to view and understand events, thoughts, emotions, and beliefs from the perspective of others and is considered one of the most important psychological components for establishing successful, ongoing relationships.

Amorality is entirely different from immorality. An immoral act is an act that violates established moral codes. A person who is immoral can be confronted with his or her actions with the expectation that he or she will recognize that his or her actions are offensive from a moral, if not a legal, standpoint.

Amorality, on the other hand, represents a psychology that does not recognize that any moral codes exist, or if they do, that they have no value in determining whether or not to act in one way or another.

Thus, someone displaying psychopathy may commit horrendous acts that cause tremendous psychological and physical trauma and never understand that what he or she has done is wrong.

Worse still, those who display signs of psychopathy usually worsen over time because they are unable to make the connection between the problems in their lives and in the lives of those in the world around them and their own harmful and destructive actions.

Machiavellianism

Strictly defined, Machiavellianism is the political philosophy of Niccolò Machiavelli, who lived from 1469 until 1527 in Italy. In contemporary society, Machiavellianism is a term used to describe the popular understanding of people who are perceived as displaying very high political or professional ambitions. In psychology, however, the Machiavellianism scale is used to measure the degree to which people with deviant personalities display manipulative behavior.

Machiavelli wrote The Prince, a political treatise in which he stated that sincerity, honesty, and other virtues were certainly admirable qualities, but that in politics, the capacity to engage in deceit, treachery, and other forms of criminal behavior were acceptable if there were no other means of achieving political aims to protect one's interests.

Popular misconceptions reduce this entire philosophy to the view that "the end justifies the means." To be fair, Machiavelli himself insisted that the more important part of this equation was ensuring that the end itself must first be justified.

Furthermore, it is better to achieve such ends using means devoid of treachery whenever possible because there is less risk to the interests of the actor.

Thus, seeking the most effective means of achieving a political end may not necessarily lead to the most treacherous.

In addition, not all political ends that have been justified as worth pursuing must be pursued. In many cases, the mere threat that a certain course of action may be pursued may be enough to achieve that end. In some cases, the treachery may be as mild as making a credible threat to take action that is not really even intended.

In contemporary society, many people overlook the fact that Machiavellianism is part of the "Dark Triad" of dark psychology and tacitly approve of the deviant behavior of political and business leaders who are able to amass great power or wealth.

However, as a psychological disorder, Machiavellianism is entirely different from a chosen path to political power.

The person displaying Machiavellian personality traits does not consider whether his or her actions are the most effective means to achieving his or her goals, whether there are alternatives that do not involve deceit or treachery, or even whether the ultimate result of his or her actions is worth achieving.

The Machiavellian personality is not evidence of a strategic or calculating mind attempting to achieve a worthwhile objective in a contentious environment. Instead, it is always on, whether the situation calls for a cold, calculating, and manipulative approach or not.

For example, we have all called in sick to work when we really just wanted a day off. But for most of us, such conduct is not how we behave normally, and after such acts of dishonesty, many of us feel guilty.

Those who display a high degree of Machiavellianism would not just lie when they want a day off; they see lying and dishonesty as the only way to conduct themselves in all situations, regardless of whether doing so results in any benefit.

What's more, because of the degree of social acceptance and tacit approval granted to Machiavellian personalities who successfully attain political power, their presence in society does not receive the kind of negative attention accorded to the other two members of the Dark Triad—psychopathy and narcissism.

Narcissism

The term "narcissism" originates from an ancient Greek myth about Narcissus, a young man who saw his reflection in a pool of water and fell in love with the image of himself. In clinical psychology, narcissism as an illness was introduced by Sigmund Freud and has continually been included in official diagnostic manuals as a description of a specific type of psychiatric personality disorder. In psychology, narcissism is defined as a condition characterized by an exaggerated sense of importance, an excessive need for attention, a lack of empathy, and, as a result, dysfunctional relationships. Commonly, narcissists may outwardly display an extremely high level of confidence, but this façade usually hides a very fragile ego and a high degree of sensitivity to criticism.

There is often a large gulf between a narcissist's highly favorable view of himself or herself, the resulting expectation that others should extend to him or her favors and special treatment, and the disappointment when the results are quite negative or otherwise different.

These problems can affect all areas of the narcissist's life, including personal relationships, professional relationships, and financial matters.

As part of the Dark Triad, those who exhibit traits resulting from Narcissistic Personality Disorder (NPD) may engage in relationships characterized by a lack of empathy.

For example, a narcissist may demand constant comments, attention, and admiration from his or her partner but will often appear unable or unwilling to reciprocate by displaying concern or responding to the concerns, thoughts, and feelings of his or her partner.

Narcissists also display a sense of entitlement and expect excessive reward and recognition, but usually without ever having accomplished or achieved anything that would justify such feelings.

There is also a tendency toward excessive criticism of those around him or her, combined with heightened sensitivity when even the slightest amount of criticism is directed at him or her.

Thus, while narcissism in popular culture is often used as a pejorative term and an insult aimed at people like actors, models, and other celebrities who display high degrees of self-love and satisfaction, NPD is actually a psychological term that is quite distinct from merely having high self-esteem.

The key to understanding this aspect of dark psychology is that the narcissist's image of himself or herself is often completely and entirely idealized, grandiose, and inflated and cannot be justified with any factual, meaningful accomplishments or capacities that may make such claims believable.

As a result of this discord between expectation and reality, the demanding, manipulative, inconsiderate, self-centered, and arrogant behavior of the narcissist can cause problems not only for himself or herself but for all of the people in his or her life.

Chapter 2: NLP

NLP is the act of seeing how individuals compose their reasoning, feeling, language, and conduct to deliver the outcomes they do. NLP furnishes individuals with a system to display remarkable exhibitions accomplished by prodigies and pioneers in their field. NLP is additionally utilized for self-improvement and for achievement in business

A key component of NLP is that we structure our one of a kind inside mental maps of the world as a result of the manner in which we channel and see data retained through our five faculties from our general surroundings.

Neuro

Every individual has set up their own special mental separating framework for handling a great many bits of information being assimilated through the faculties.

Semantic

We, at that point, dole out close to home importance to the data being gotten from the world outside. We structure our second mental guide by doling out language to the inside pictures, sounds, and sentiments, tastes, and scents, therefore framing regular cognizant mindfulness. The second mental guide is known as the Linguistic Map (at times known as Linguistic Representation)

Programming

The conduct reaction that happens because of neurological sifting forms and the resulting etymological guide

Neurolinguistic Programming (NLP) was created by Richard Bandler and John Grinder in 1975. Neuro identifies with the cerebrum and the manners by which we process data from our five detects. Phonetic identifies with language or correspondence, and how we use images to compose and offer significance to our encounters, how we speak to our encounters in our internal world. Programming alludes to the manner in which we code our encounters and program our subliminal with practices, channels, convictions, and so forth. On and when we were PCs, NLP would be the investigation of our programming, and this thing that makes up our elucidation of life and decides our encounters. It's exceptionally emotional. Every one of us has our own projects, the vast majority of which were found out at a very young age. Since it endeavors to see how we do what we do, it likewise uncovers the methods for changing or reconstructing our subliminal. It enables us to comprehend brain science in a manner that is anything but difficult to apply to day by day life.

Essential Suppositions of NLP

The guide isn't the region. Representation is at the core of NLP. What your involvement with the world depends on your observation, not what is genuine.

Experience has a structure, the manner in which we experience the world, channel, and example reality, and how we code things into our psyches are organized. When you see how somebody structures their world, you can assist them with making changes. Changes to the structure will bring about another experience.

The importance of correspondence is the reaction it gets. On and when you are speaking with somebody, attempting to express what is on your mind, the importance is controlled by the audience, not the talker. Regardless of how you state it, the message the audience gets depends on how they translate it. It really is great to consider who you're conversing with and how they decipher their reality in the event that you truly need to get your significance crosswise over to them

In the event that what you're doing doesn't work, accomplish something other than what's expected. NLP is about adaptability. Too often, we continue saying very similar things to ourselves and playing out similar practices, yet anticipate that things should change. All change starts inside.

The individual with the most adaptability has the most power in a circumstance. Living stuck gives you the groove's eye to see.

You can't NOT impart, you're continually speaking with your voice, your eyes, your signals, your vitality. In any event, saying nothing has meaning. You have every one of the assets you have to accomplish your ideal result. It's simply a question of arranging them in an unexpected way.

Each conduct has a positive goal. All practices are the aftereffect of your intuitive, attempting to accomplish something positive for you. Individuals precede with negative behavior patterns for one reason - there is a reward included. Regardless of whether there are practices you don't care for, the aim behind them is certain. It is conceivable to accomplish a similar positive expectation with another, progressively attractive conduct.

The mind and body and interlinked and influence one another. Contemplations make feelings; feelings change our bodies down to the sub-atomic structure. Your inner discourse is leading the entire show.

Individuals are substantially more than their conduct. You can adore somebody. Sincerely, a kid, for example, dislikes their conduct. The kid isn't 'awful'; the conduct is. Having a decision is superior to not having a decision. Try not to get tied up with an injured individual mindset. You generally have a decision. Demonstrating fruitful execution prompts greatness. In the event that another person can do it, you can do it. You can figure out how to display greatness by focusing on how specialists do it - how would they think, feel, inhale, what are their qualities and convictions.

NLP is something that you see best once you begin to utilize it. All things considered, you are your very own research facility. You can search inside and perceive your considerations, the pictures you make, the sensations you feel, investigate how your convictions constrain you, and what could occur on, and when you transformed them. NLP gives its clients numerous systems and apparatuses for personal growth, constructive change, and self-awareness. You can do a significant number of techniques on yourself and start evolving today. Working with a professional is unquestionably simpler; however, as a prepared master can see things we don't enable ourselves to see. In any case, you can change, and you can change quickly with NLP.

NLP (the abbreviation for Neurolinguistic writing computer programs) is a self-awareness situated methodology, completely investigating every human response and communications to inward or outside improvements. NLP intrigue centers around unlimited potential outcomes of emotionally encountering a typical reality. A similar aptitude or capacity is distinctively created because of individual experience; hence, people should discover advantageous intends to interrelate, convey, and coordinate. Modifying our sensorial mindfulness while interrelating and mingling, we may effortlessly see that noteworthy enhancement rises up out of a progressively adaptable way to deal with a genuine world.

A constructive rebuilding of individual observations may change your everyday life.

For example, cutoff times are a bad dream for everybody, you can't leave each time you feel under strain, and certainly, you can't change time passing. Possibly you should search for the appropriate response inside, hence, attempt first to coordinate your own qualities with explicit necessities inside your profession ventures. Before long, you'll see that things are truly showing signs of improvement, and you may feel urged to continue. Nothing has changed except for an alternate methodology of a similar issue when you diversely coordinated your perspective, acting, and communicating.

Correspondence depends fundamentally on a pre-set upset of shows and on a typical multicultural foundation. Ambiguities and mistaken assumptions are inadequacies of significant social associations. In this way, NLP distinguishes the satisfactory methods through the misuse of every single human sense (for both speaker and audience) for a proficient correspondence grouping. At the point when you send or get a message, you actuate by methods for sensorial mindfulness various ideas, and consequently, you prevail with regards to relegating sense to your message. In view of individual or abstract discernments, at least two people come to build up a typical coding.

Neurolinguistic programming incorporates a wide range of procedures that license specialists to effectively reevaluate their observations. Also, specialists, experts, and chiefly patients profit by this diversity of remedies in light of the fact that each individual methodologies life in his own particular manner and ordinarily reacts better to a specific methodology. As indicated by specialists' contemplations, NLP methodologies are contrastingly deciphered and named. For example, a few advisors approach NLP as an upgrading strategy for our own qualities; different authorities take them for renovating or corrections systems.

It merits referencing that meta-programs, meta-reflect, hypnotherapy, self-hypnosis, or care are very mainstream procedures as they have helped numerous individuals recapture their inward harmony. In spite of the fact that the relationship of terms and ideas (Neuro, semantics, and programming) may appear to be modern, actually, it rearranges the manner in which we adapt to everyday difficulties. In addition, it prompts an essential end. Incredibly, we are no different yet entirely unexpected.

NLP represents Neuro-Linguistic Programming. Neuro alludes to your nervous system science; Linguistic alludes to language; programming alludes to how that neural language capacities. At the end of the day, learning NLP resembles learning the language of your own psyche!

We should make this easier with a model.

Have you at any point attempted to speak with somebody who didn't communicate in your language, and they couldn't get you? The exemplary case of this is the point at which somebody goes out to a café in a Foreign nation, and they think they requested steak; however, when the nourishment appears, it turns out they really requested liver stew.

This is the sort of relationship that the majority of us have with our own oblivious personality. We may think we are "requesting up" more cash, a glad, solid relationship, harmony with our relatives, and having the option to adhere to a sound eating regimen... yet except if that is the thing that appearing, at that point, something is presumably becoming mixed up in interpretation.

In NLP, we have an adage: the cognizant personality is the objective setter, and the oblivious personality is the objective getter. Your oblivious personality isn't out to get you–rather, it's out to get for you anything you desire throughout everyday life. Be that as it may, in the event that you don't have the foggiest idea how to convey what you need appropriately, it will continue bringing steaming bowls of liver stew out of the kitchen.

Actually, proceed at the present time and consider if there would one say one was a thing you could transform, one propensity you could break, what might it be?

• Would you resist the urge to panic during work introductions?

• Quit tarrying and investing such a great amount of energy on Facebook?

• Not eat up an entire pack of potato chips or tub of frozen yogurt in one sitting?

Whatever it is, understand that your oblivious personality just does that since it imagines, that is the thing that you need. ("Sir, here is your lingering alongside a side of tension. I've likewise advised the valet to raise your psychological weight according to your solicitation. Will you need something else?")

Neuro-Linguistic Programming resembles a client's manual for the cerebrum, and taking an NLP preparing resembles figuring out how to get conversant in the language of your psyche so that the supportive "server" that is your oblivious will at long last comprehend what you really truly desire.

NLP is simply the investigation of astounding correspondence both with yourself and with others. It was created by demonstrating astounding communicators and advisors who got results with their customers.

NLP Training

At the point when the NLP engineers started to share their insight, NLP Certification got accessible with different mentors. Thirty years after the NLP origin, cutting edge NLP preparation comes in all shapes and sizes, some brilliant, some great, a ton of normal, and some distinctly poor. At the NLP Academy, we are glad for our preparation record.

We are pleased with every one of the individuals who graduate with the NLP Academy and attempt to help their future advancement. With the arrival of the NLPedia Study Sets, we remain solitary as the main organization in the UK, offering veritable multi-tactile home learning bundles that help the quickened learning NLP accreditation courses.

Chapter 3: How to Analyze People

There are so many different methods to analyze others, and it can be hard to pick it all apart. Where did this practice come from? Why is it important to understand how to analyze others?

As it turns out, the art of analyzing others has existed since—well; we had the intelligence to do it. Human beings are, by nature, herd animals. We are highly in tune with others, and our lives are driven by societal expectations. It can be easy to get caught up in our instincts, though, and to forget that we need to tackle things logistically. This is where learning how to actively analyze others comes in.

Studies consistently show that we are attracted to confidence and leadership. We like to take the burdens of everyday life and put them on other people's shoulders. Part of this is allowing ourselves to be far too trusting in situations where we would benefit from awareness surrounding red flags. Unfortunately, people are not always genuine; they can be terrible—evil, even. This is a world where we need to be on high alert. While analyzing people will help you in many aspects, such as work and in leadership roles, it can also help keep you safe.

Being situationally aware is simply not in practice anymore. People are constantly unaware of their surroundings and putting themselves in harm's way as a result.

So, as you can see, there are many reasons to unravel the techniques of analyzation. Scanning people for warning signs or just for information about them puts you ahead of the pack. There is nothing more beneficial to your life, your relationships, and your protection. Spot narcissists before they have a chance to victimize you. Understand your boss's motives and learn how to nail down what they want from you without even hearing them say it.

Here are some jobs which actively employ analyzing others:

- Politicians
- Lawyers
- Criminal investigators
- Military officials
- Psych professionals
- Forensic experts

As you can see, it truly is a universal tool. Many different people have to analyze others daily in their day-to-day lives.

I hope that these are the skills you want to learn. They are invaluable, and it is my pleasure to help you improve your life, one impression at a time.

There are, of course, incredible benefits to consuming the knowledge I am offering to you today. First off, you will find that you can communicate your needs to other people far more effectively. Being able to tell how they are reacting and changing your approach accordingly is more than helpful. Communication is the most important skill that we can hone, quite frankly. It helps ease tension, earn the confidence of others, and put us in a positive light. Emotional intelligence goes hand in hand with communication as well.

This is another skill that will be furthered when paired with the power to analyze others. Your emotional intelligence greatly relies on your ability to understand others. The goal is always to meet people where they are: understanding what they need and being able to tell how they need to be handled. Whether you lead a team, need to help your children through their struggles, or are feeling the tension in your love life, I am here to help.

Strong relationships are the glue of society and, more importantly, of families. We need to know how to handle our spouses, children, and anybody else directly related to us. Strained relationships lead to strained relations, and none of us want to be caught up in a family feud. Learning how people tick and how to handle tough situations is the key. You will also learn how to watch for red flags with your children. Knowing how to read their body language and pick up on their verbal cues do wonders for seeing warning signs well in advance.

If you are a parent, this will be a key book in taking your parenting to the next level.

As for another skill, leadership, you will soon be at the front of the crowd. You will find that people not only listen to you but that they actively want to listen to you. Becoming a strong leader means being able to tell who a person is just by carefully observing them. True leaders understand the absolute power that body language holds. After all, it is the oldest form of communication of them all. Many leaders in the business world, as well as in other areas, actively take lessons and classes on analyzing others. This is a skill that can be applied in almost every situation you can think of. It builds your confidence, knowing that when you take the lead, others follow suit.

I am pretty sure you are beginning to get the idea of what analyzing others can do for you. The benefits are boundless, and there are new ones at every corner. You cannot imagine how much life will change!

I would like to get you started with a few rules. As you can imagine, there is a baseline to start when it comes to analyzing others. You can remember some steps to help you begin, which are not hard and fast but excellent for helping you to understand the process. Practice makes perfect, so make sure you pay close attention to this list.

These rules are as follows:

Understand What Their Baseline Is: Everybody is just a tad bit different from the rest. It is almost like how parents can tell their twins apart, but nobody else can. Learning how to analyze others means you can tell them apart on a much different level. Understand that you can only tell their "baseline" after knowing them for a while.

You can watch for signs that they are nervous. Perhaps ask probing questions you know will elicit the emotion you want to pin down. If they tend to become physically restless under duress, you know what sort of body language to watch for.

This is the first rule for many reasons. Most importantly, it reminds us that we need to see the whole person. Cold reading is great. We will go over it later in detail, but true analysis takes time and consideration.

Notice the Changes: Take into account the entire picture of the person. This builds off of the first rule. Understand that any gesture can mean something, but you need to put several clues together to really solve the mystery that is a person.

This will also build off of noticing what signs of nervousness you may be looking for. We are using nervousness for these examples, but it goes for any emotion. Anger, unease, discomfort–they are all negative emotions you can begin to pinpoint.

Watch For Warning Signs. When certain behaviors are brought into the light and therefore meaning in your eyes, you can start to piece it together. If you have noticed that they shift their eyes around when nervous, and their eyes tighten up when they are angry, you will know when you are treading on dangerous territory.

There are several different clusters of behaviors that can be seen across the board. As mentioned, humans are pack animals in nature. This means that we have learned how to communicate with each other, whether we like it or not. Certain tip-offs are pretty well-known. However, a lot more will be missed to the untrained eye. That is why you are reading this!

Compare Behavior Changes: The next rule in this line-up is to always make sure you watch how they behave with others as well. It is a popular belief that you do not watch the person who is speaking–you watch the reaction of the person you want to impress. Making sure you are taking note of your boss's body language while listening to co-workers, for example.

Notice the changes between them talking to you and them talking to others. This will help cue you into their true emotions about you as well as how they feel about others. Are their arms crossing when they talk to their friends? Is their body still turned towards you even while engaged in conversation elsewhere?

Watch Yourself. One of the most powerful things you can do is be aware of your body language. We do not just need to understand others but also ourselves. We influence others with our facial expressions without even knowing what it looks like. That is not what you want to be doing. To control a situation or a conversation, or even influence it, you need to practice expressions. The best way to do this is to do it in the mirror. Again, this will be gone over in-depth later on. I guess I just keep giving you small teasers!

Listen To Others Talk. Identify the strongest person in the room. You will notice them right away, most likely. Sometimes, however, it takes a little time. Look for open body language being used purposefully but elegantly. A big smile, a voice that commands attention and self-confidence, are all ways of saying, "I am the boss in this situation." They do not need the approval of others, and they often hold the most sway in the situation.

Same idea as watching the boss when others are talking. Even if somebody is technically the boss, that does not mean they are completely in control. A confident, strong person will make an impression and quickly become somebody whose opinion the "head honcho" deeply trusts. Knowing which strings to pull will push you further and further toward getting what you want out of a situation.

Watch Them Move. Looking at body language while they talk to you, especially sitting or standing still, is one thing. You also need to watch their general state of being while moving around. You can tell quite a bit about a person just by the way they walk and how they move. Confident people tend to stand tall, with their shoulders back and chest pushed a little out. They walk with purpose, as though they always have somewhere important to be. On the other hand, somebody who is unsure of themselves embodies the exact opposite traits. They try to make themselves look small, perhaps hunching over a little, keeping their head low.

Listen For Speech Patterns. Another rule is to listen closely to how they talk and what they are saying, both about the topic at hand and about themselves. How a person speaks tells you so much about them, both literally and figuratively! When you can identify how they speak when they are truthful and genuine, you can figure out when they are the opposite. There are several different ways to go about this. However, looking for "action words" is one of the best. A lot of ex-agents talk about how looking for these words, especially strong verbs; it helps you figure out how their brain works. These words do not just convey their thoughts, but they convey the patterns of their thoughts as well.

Key Into Their Personality. The last rule is to always put all of this information together. You cannot use one of these rules without following up with the others. These are the cardinal tenets off of which all analyzation of others is built. Once you put together their verbal communication, their body language, and understand them as a whole, you have won half the battle.

Chapter 4: Nonverbal -Verbal Communication

Language is incredible. As humans, we have an incredibly heightened ability to communicate with one another. This level of communication is a part of the reason that we have been able to advance so far in our evolution. The advancement of our communication results in advancement in our society. More importantly, we will define nonverbal and verbal behavior and also give two differences between the two and learn how to analyze the statements that other individuals make verbally. More specifically, we will learn how to analyze these verbal statements using nonverbal language. We will also go into the intricacies of analyzing the nonverbal behavior of those around us.

Defining Nonverbal Communication

Nonverbal behavior or communication is the subconscious or conscious relaying of ideas or emotions through physical motion or a series of well-known and understood gestures. Messages can be transferred non-verbally through a variety of signals and methods. The first of these defining signals are methods known as proxemics. Proxemics essentially means the distance between two individuals. The distance between two individuals or proxemics carries a lot of weight in terms of nonverbal communication. The second method of nonverbal communication is known as kinesics and is simply another word for body language. Kinesics or body language is the transmission of ideas through gestures and often unconscious motions of the body. Meanwhile, another defining method is known as haptics. Haptics is another word for the act of touching something. In the world of nonverbal behavior, the way that somebody touches something carries a lot of weight in communicating their emotions to another individual. A soft touch on the arm can mean a lot of things, which becomes very different in comparison to a firm grasp of one's hand. Not all touches are equal, and every touch—depending on its longevity, intensity, and location on the body—has many different meanings behind it. Another form of nonverbal communication is our appearance. People use their appearance to communicate their personality in a variety of ways. Most of this is a conscious decision made by the individual, but there are some factors almost entirely caused by our parents that aren't necessarily chosen by us but still say things about ourselves. Most likely, the biggest and most common type of nonverbal communication using our parents is simply judging whether or not somebody cares about their appearance. By just looking at another person, we can instantly tell whether or not they care about how they appear to those around them. This carries a huge amount of weight in the snap judgment that we make about people every single day. The final common form of nonverbal communication is the use of eye contact. Eye contact is extremely important in us as humans. Humans are very focused on an individual's eyes, as that is often one of the first things that a person looks at when they see a new face. Your eyes are often considered the windows to the soul, and this is true in the sense that they can reveal a lot of factors about yourselves. By looking into someone's eyes or measuring the amount of eye contact they give, we can understand a vast amount of information about their personality. Do they have strong eye contact? Do they avoid eye contact? Do they have really intense eye contact? The answers to all of these questions give us different definitions of a person's personality. As humans, we put a lot of weight on an individual's eye contact as a defining portion of their personality. This is why we must keep eye contact in mind when attempting to understand someone's nonverbal communication.

Defining Verbal Communication

Verbal communication seems quite obvious when spoken out loud. Verbal communication obviously does consist of any form of speech or language that is used to relay ideas or thoughts to another. Verbal communication includes much more than simply speaking to a person, the way that we string together ideas and thoughts with word shows a lot about their personality in the words that we choose in the cadence that we choose to put them together. There are multiple ways that we can express ourselves through verbal communication. The first and most obvious way that we can express ourselves through verbal communication is through speaking to those around us. By stringing together words and sentences, we create cohesive thoughts and ideas that express our feelings to those around us.

In addition to being able to accurately and positively express our emotions and feelings to those around us, the act of speaking is also quite easy to use to persuade or to alter our true meaning. It is much easier to lie to a person verbally than it is to lie to a person with our body language. Because of this, we often find people who lie very easily vocally to a person but whose body language cues do not match their words.

The second form of verbal communication, writing, may come as a surprise to some people reading this text. The act of writing, while not technically verbal, still comprises verbal communication because it uses common vocally spoken language simply in written form. The difficulty in this is that a person reading a text has a much harder time guessing and understanding the cadence of the person who wrote the text. Because of this, written ideas and emotions can be misconstrued due to the fact that people cannot quite tell the intonation of the author of the text through the words.

Another form of verbal communication is an underlying feeling within our words known as denotation or connotation. The connotation is considered as the feelings or emotions associated with the meanings of certain words or phrases. This is not to be confused with its antonym, denotation, which is the literal or primary meaning of a word, opposite to the emotions or series that the word suggests. In order to convey these important forms of verbal communication, a person has to use our neck form of verbal communication.

The next form of verbal communication that we will be discussing is tone and volume. An individual's tone, when talking to another person, can express a lot about that person's inner thoughts or feelings. The tone is a very difficult form of communication to pin down and explain to people. For some individuals, the tone is very easy to control and change in their language—while for others, it can be very difficult. You cannot describe the tone as based on the inflection that an individual puts on to certain words at certain times. The tone is very interesting because every person is able to understand the meaning behind other people's tones almost in perfect connection with one another, but it is very difficult to explain to others. In connection to this, a person's volume also holds a great deal of significance in their verbal communication. Ever since childhood, we have all learned about the difference between an inside voice and an outside voice. Do volume levels show a lot about our emotions? We can read a lot about how someone feels in a certain situation based on their volume at that time.

It is important always to remember that you have to use both verbal and nonverbal forms of communication together in parallel to understand the grand total outcome of a person's ideas and theories. A common misconception amongst individuals is that verbal communication and nonverbal communication are contradictory. This is not the case. Verbal and nonverbal communication must go side-by-side when communicating with those around us. It is the combination of these two complex forms of communication that make the translation of our ideas and theories the most effective. One cannot exist without the other—in most cases. It is often asserted by body language specialists that nonverbal communication can play one of five roles when trying to read another person. These five roles are known as substitution, reinforcement, contradiction, accentuation, and regulation.

Substitution - certain types of nonverbal communication are started as a substitution or placement for verbal communication. Examples of this are nodding your head for yes or shrugging your shoulders for "I don't know."

Reinforcement - nonverbal communication can often be used to reinforce a previously given statement. By reading an individual's body language and judging it consistently, you can almost entirely ascertain whether they are telling the truth or not.

Contradiction - this is the opposite of reinforcement. If a person's body language appears to be contradicting something that they are saying, then by the rule of contradiction, they are almost certainly lying—depending on their environment, of course.

Accentuation - body language often serves as a method of accentuating something that a person says vocally. Examples of this include smiling when someone says that they are happy or shivering when somebody says that they are cold. This can also be used to put a greater level of importance to a statement that somebody has given out. An example of this is creating the quotation mark symbol with your fingers while saying something sarcastically. By adding body language to the statement that you're making, you are reaffirming and showing importance in your statement.

Regulation - an individual's body can also serve to regulate that person's vocal language.

Chapter 5: Manipulation

Manipulation is the influence a person uses to try to alter the perceptions or behaviors of others. Often, it's done through underhanded, deceptive, or abusive techniques, but not always. In some people's opinions, when a manipulator advances their own interests using these techniques, without consideration for the needs of others, the methods are exploitative.

Negative Manipulation: This is when you intentionally withhold information from someone to get what you wanted, play up your own emotions in a false way to persuade someone, or otherwise threaten them indirectly for selfish reasons. Negative manipulation has harmed countless people in the world. Being under the negative manipulation of another person can make you feel like you're crazy or act in ways that you would normally never act.

This method of manipulation relies on hidden agendas, ulterior motives, and attempts to force others to give in to your will. Although the manipulator looks in control and strong on the surface, they often feel very insecure on the inside; otherwise, they wouldn't need to engage in such behaviors. The actions of these people (such as disregarding and exploiting the rights of other people) are a signal of a lack of health on a mental level. In fact, people who engage in these behaviors have a hard time finding and keeping positive relationships with others.

Positive (or Ethical) Manipulation: Also known as persuasion or influence, this is when you convince someone to come around to your ways of thinking or acting, but in a way that also benefits them. This has a positive, rather than harmful, effect. There are a few clear distinctions between negative and positive manipulation, and it's important to make sure you know the difference. Everyone uses positive manipulation and influence to further our own goals with other people, which is perfectly fine and normal. This method of manipulation acknowledges the boundaries and rights of others and uses honest and direct communication. This method of manipulation is a simple way to function efficiently and effectively in your environment and to benefit and make use of the social order that exists in our world. It recognizes that other people have basic integrity and a choice of whether or not to follow through with your persuasion attempts. In essence, this acknowledges that each person should be autonomous and acknowledges a baseline of human respect between you and others. We are all social creatures who need each other, in one way or another.

Manipulation in Leadership

With the term leadership, most people assume that it refers to a lucrative position where one has the ultimate decision-making powers over the people they lead. The term must be taken holistically. This means that it should include even the most trivial, often ignored leadership roles, for example, when one has as few as five followers or even less. A good example of this is when the parents are out of the house and leave one sibling, often the eldest, in charge of the others. For such a case, consider the sibling left in charge as a leader.

All leadership positions require some level of manipulation for efficiency. As a leader, you will need everyone under you to trust your leadership capabilities and must, therefore, present yourself in a certain manner. You must portray certain qualities that are associated with your leadership style. For instance, if you are a dictator, be dictatorial; if you are a leader for a revolution, be revolutionary; if you are a CEO or a manager of a company; be managerial; or if you are a class representative, act in your capacity. Irrespective of the capacity in which you serve as a leader, manipulation to some extent is inevitable.

Manipulation in Friendship

It is common to hear people saying that trust is a hard thing to come by and that it is earned the hard way. What is not often addressed along with this statement is how easily people betray the trust that they take so much time building. The most cunning people of this lot would betray a person's trust without the betrayed ever suspecting anything. They are merely reduced to puppets dancing to other people's tunes without the least bit of suspicion. It is in this area that manipulation in friendships reigns supreme. A common term for this manipulation is 'use'—where a person would accuse another of using them to advance their personal selfish agenda.

The key to success in any form of manipulation is stealth, patience, and a good plan. These qualities alone show that manipulation is a lot like an elaborate game of chess, where one player holds all the pieces and makes all the moves for the other oblivious player. It is obvious from this analogy that one player is set to lose from the beginning and may never even find out that they were played in the first place. The same keen mind that is required to beat a worthy chess opponent is the very same one that will be required to identify, let alone beat a scheming manipulator.

Manipulation in Marriages

That love is blind is a very common saying. It has its foundation from the very widely accepted book, the Bible. This saying alone has many implications regarding the topic of manipulation and how the same may have the perfect conditions to grow in relationships where there is love. First and foremost, it implies that even when the schemes of a manipulator fail or are discovered by the potential victim, they will most likely be viewed through the blind eye of love and be chalked down as a minor mistake. For this reason, under these conditions, it will be very difficult for a regular victim of unsolicited influence to notice regular trends of the same.

As such, they may never be able to react accordingly to correct the situations and may, therefore, wind up living as unknowing slaves forever at the mercy of their manipulators. At this point, it is necessary to discuss some of the specific tactics used by married couples to influence one another.

Chapter 6: Subliminal Manipulation Techniques

Subliminal messages are a very effective part of mind control and are a very crucial technique to learn if you want to effectively persuade anybody. Subliminal messages are so powerful that they actually exist all over the modern world, and most of us don't even acknowledge it. They can be found in marketing, movies, news, and far more. Finding out to utilize subliminal messages will help you effectively utilize mind control on individuals in the most masterful way. You will have the ability to persuade anybody into thinking and acting in the way that you desire for them to act, and you will have the ability to have any outcome you desire when you master this strategy. This is next-level mind control that lots of people take years to master, but you are going to learn to master it easily and efficiently with these actions.

Downsizing

This method is an incredible way to utilize subliminal messaging to get individuals to do what you desire them to do. Using this method will enable you to get individuals where you desire them to be easily. The method is virtually uncomplicated and is typically used in sales and other comparable scenarios. You can modify it to work for anything. Essentially, all you require to do is begin with a large request and scale it back as you are talking. For instance, let's state you want to get somebody to talk to you on the phone. You could start by asking to hang out and maybe go on a date together. As the conversation progresses, nevertheless, work your way backward and simply ask for a call. Because it is not as grand and intense as the original request, they are most likely to say yes. After all, a call seems to bear much less pressure than a request to go on a date, right? Once you have them on the phone, you can press for the date!

First Name Basis

People absolutely enjoy hearing their first names. It has a specific result on people that are not attained through practically any other name in any language. Utilizing someone's name is a sort of flattery that also confirms someone's presence. Individuals like knowing that they are recognized for the core of who they are, and they are far more likely to adhere to what you are asking if you are utilizing their given name regularly. You likewise wish to refer them to what you want them to be for you. Let's state you desire "John" to become your friend. You could say, "John, did you take pleasure in the video game last night?" and when he says, "Yeah, it was respectable!" you might say, "I agree, friend!" This associates them with being your pal and is most likely to encourage them to actually feel as though they are your pal as well. This brings particular perks, such as trust, that are required to effectively use brainwashing and mind control, too.

Flattery

Lots of people argue that flattery will get you nowhere, however this is incorrect. Flattery will get you everywhere if you use it. Individuals are attracted to those who are naturally captivating, and part of being captivating is using flattery. If you take the time to charm those you are speaking to, they are more likely to react in your favor because you make them feel good. Something that is essential to acknowledge with individuals, nevertheless, is the level of self-confidence they carry. Those who have high self-confidence will like to be flirted with heavily since you are validating their greater sense of self-confidence. Those who have low self-esteem, however, will end up being uncomfortable and daunted if you flatter them excessively. It triggers them to feel as though they are being "buttered up" and makes them experience a conflict considering that they cannot relate to what you are stating.

Paraphrasing

Individuals love to be confirmed, and paraphrasing is a great way to verify them. When you paraphrase somebody, they feel as though you are listening to them carefully and that you are confirming what they are saying. This makes them feel good and develops a fantastic sense of connection between the two of you. This is an excellent way to create that connection and use it as a chance to develop a trust between you and the person you are talking with while also discovering your way into their subconscious mind so that you can speak past their conscious mind and into their subconscious. This is how you will get optimal success with getting them to do what you want!

Nod A Lot

Nodding is gotten in touch with a favorable agreement between you and the person you are speaking to. Nodding frequently throughout the discussion, instills a very positive feeling into the person you are talking with and helps them feel as though you are truly listening to them. When they see you nodding and agreeing with lots of parts of the discussion, they are going to feel more likely to nod and also agree when it comes your turn to talk. This creates a total positive scenario where you can easily get them to agree with you, because the sense of "agreement" is high in the discussion in general.

Repetition

One of the best ways that you can survive with subliminal messages is repetition. If you do not use repeating, your message is going to fall on deaf ears. The more you duplicate specific words and phrases, the more the subconscious mind is going to hear it, and you are going to have success with getting someone to agree with you and do what you desire them to do. When you repeat something, it essentially "warms up" the mind to the concept and assists people begin to actually feel and believe it as reality.

Visual Subliminal Messages

Lots of people think that audio messages are the only way to get subliminal messages through, but this is simply not real. In this day and age, we have access to text-based interactions, and aesthetically seeing the recurring message can have a significant influence on someone's possibility of agreeing with you and making a favorable connection with you and the message you are sharing.

You can text your message to people without being excessively apparent, and you can likewise discover imaginative ways to share it on social media if you have them added. This will lead to them seeing the message beyond your conversations with them, which will even further warm their mind as much as the concept and have them agreeing with you in no time. Subliminal messages are a big part of brainwashing and mind control.

These messages are usually believed to have little to no weight behind them, however they are meant to load a punch and truly leave a lasting effect on your listener without them even understanding it. To them, you might be innocently passing along a message, whereas to you, you are deliberately instilling these details into someone else's mind with ulterior motives of some sort. Learning the methods of mind control is not always the most convenient and will not be an overnight process.

It is necessary that you are prepared to practice these techniques with time and that you want to allow yourself to broaden your skills with practice. Brainwashing and mind control is a really effective skill that you can discover, but you need to be exceptionally proficient at it if you are going to have the kind of effect you wish to have on people. You ought to refrain from attempting to utilize too many of the methods at once, since this will cause you to become overloaded and will diminish the quality of your attempts. It might even lead individuals to see right through you and lead to you having the opposite result of what you want to accomplish. Start at the very beginning and practice one or two strategies at a time.

Option Restriction

You wish to restrict choice without it being obvious that you are doing so. For example, instead of asking an individual the type of white wine they would like, ask "red or white?". The second question will restrict them to either white or red. You will eventually get to select the white wine based on the color that they picked. They will not realize that you basically persuaded them to permit you to pick which red wine the two of you are going to consume. Giving individuals choices that distract them from the one choice that you do not desire them to make.

Making use of Reverse Psychology

This is a method that is used by individuals to get what they want by asking or demanding what they do not want. Researchers use another term: self-anticonformity because your need goes against what you want. Another way that psychologists discuss reverse psychology is through the term reactance. It is describing the unpleasant feeling that individuals get when they feel that their freedom has been threatened. The typical way to react to that risk is to the opposite of what has been required of you. It's the going against authority element.

Examples of Reverse Psychology Reverse

Psychology prevails in various kinds of occupations because it can assist individuals get what they want, and it can be efficient, in addition to effective if performed right. For example, some methods in sales are based upon this very concept, such as the Door in the Face technique. We have all fallen victim to this. Let's say that you are in a used vehicle lot trying to buy a car or truck. The salesperson gives you this outlandish cost that you would never consider paying. You want to buy the car, however you do not wish to pay that much. You make a counteroffer for less. This is exactly what the salesperson desires.

You get the lowest rate, and the salesperson makes the sale, which was his goal in the first place - putting you in a vehicle. The strategy can also be used in marketing. Here is an example of a store that offers top quality merchandise. Most of the time, when we go shopping, we see ads and the name of the shop on the outside of the shop. We understand where we are going. Well, what if the high-end store has no signs or ads on the outside of the store? It just looks like a regular building. You would need to understand where the store was or have been there before to understand that they did offer clothes. All of us know that this indicates that the merchant is not attempting to offer to just anybody.

This enhances the mystery of the location, and it makes it a special place. What does the parent do? They use this strategy by getting the kid to wish to consume them. How do you they do that? Haven't you ever purchased some sugary foods that you didn't desire the kids to consume? You put them in the refrigerator and tell the kids that those come from you and not touch them? What happens? The kid finds a way to consume sugary foods due to the fact that they can't have them. They're yours. Why not try that method with the broccoli? See how quickly the kid jumps on those due to the fact that they can't have them. We constantly want what we can't have. Utilizing this tactic in relationships can be a bad thing if the person utilizing the technique is trying to get something at the cost of their partner.

Chapter 7: Favorite Victims of Manipulators

Just as predators have several traits they often all have, so to do their targets. The people that predators choose to target are typically chosen methodically, seeking out those who are least likely to rebel or try to fight back from any sort of manipulation. They can identify potential targets at a glance, needing little more than seconds to pass judgment on whether that person should be pursued with shocking accuracy. They can tell based on body language, clothing, situations, interactions, and more, who will be able to serve them best, and they frequently act upon it. Here are some of the most common traits people who find themselves victims of manipulators often have.

Lacking Confidence

Due to lacking confidence, an individual can be quite easy to steamroll. Looking for body language that marks someone as lacking in confidence is a surefire way for predators to identify an easy target. Those who lack confidence are not likely to put up any sort of fight, either if you attack physically or emotionally. In lacking confidence, the predator can be sure that the individual also lacks the ability to defend boundaries or him or herself.

When someone comes across as self-confident, he or she exudes an air of someone not as willing to put up with any sort of manipulation without a fight. Those with confidence will fight back when they feel wronged, violated, or hurt and would have no qualms walking away from a relationship because they trust their own judgment.

By seeking someone lacking confidence, a predator goes after the easiest possible target to get whatever is desired, whether it is physical affection, arm candy, money, a home, a sale, a vote, or even just the feeling of having dominated someone else. The predator is able to boost his or her own ego through completely taking over another person's life and making decisions for the person. T hey may want someone around that will always defer to them, allowing them a position of power, even if it is undeserved or unwarranted. They may want someone to make them feel better about themselves, and someone with low self-confidence is likely to do that.

Have Something Desirable

Sometimes, personality has nothing to do with being targets. Sometimes, predators go after someone because they have something the predator wants. Whether it is money, status, a relationship, or anything else, the predator may choose to go after that person in hopes of getting it by association. If the person is someone powerful or influential, the predator may weasel her way into a friendship with the sole intention of pulling from that person's influence in the future. By winning what the other person perceives as a friendship, the manipulator creates an arsenal of people with a wide range of skills, abilities, and prestige that can be used when the need arises. If she wants a new job, she may be able to get a friend to pull strings and get her one, for example.

If what she desires is money, she may worm her way into a friendship or relationship with someone that has a lot of money in an attempt to attract that kind of lifestyle. If her boyfriend is wealthy, he would likely have little issue spending money on her.

Caregiver-type

Some people are more prone to being caregivers than others. People who are compassionate can become easily manipulated because they seek to believe the best in others and seek to ensure that others' needs are met as thoroughly as possible. The caregiver-type person is likely to see the manipulator and all of his or her flaws but proceed with a relationship anyway, believing that all that is needed to remedy the situation is love and patience. Unfortunately, that resilience to make sure that the manipulator is cared for and nurtured back to mental health also makes the caregiver an easy victim as well.

Because the caregiver is willing to take all of that negative behavior as signs that the manipulator needs more help, he or she will often completely overlook the warning signs and endure the manipulation, feeling as though it will stop eventually. Unfortunately, no amount of love or patience is going to change who someone is, and they are likely to be disappointed as the manipulative behaviors continue to grow, eventually beginning to drain on even the caregiver, whose personality type is prone to patience and resilience.

Empathetic

Considering that most of the manipulators you will encounter either lack empathy or know how to turn off their empathy to steel themselves from other people's emotional states, it should come as no surprise that they are naturally drawn toward the empathetic. Empathy is the ability to sense and really understand how someone else is feeling. It is as if you have taken yourself and placed yourself in the other person's shoes, understanding exactly how they feel because you know how you would feel in their situation. This sense of putting yourself in someone else's shoes enables humans to ensure that those within their family or tribal unit are taken care of. It extends to other people as well, and those who are particularly empathetic find themselves identifying with other people. They may see the manipulator and decide that they see a person who is clearly in dire need of love and attention. They see the manipulator's flaws and want to try to fix them because they understand how lonely or down they would feel if they lacked confidence, lacked friends and family, or lacked whatever else it is that they believe the manipulator may be lacking. The empathetic individual, like the caregiver, will take more than his or her fair share of abuse, justifying it as the manipulator being in a bad situation and that any rational person who had suffered the same way would behave similarly. The empathetic target is also far more susceptible to mind games relating to emotions and guilt trips, and the empathetic nature of the individual is eventually used as a weapon against him or herself.

Dysfunctional Upbringing

People who have grown up in dysfunction have the disadvantage of never learning what normal, functional, and healthy relationships entail. They typically associate their own upbringing with what is normal and seek to replicate those sorts of relationships in adulthood.

If a child grew up around parents who fought and argued all the time, with the mother always giving up what she wanted while the father took endlessly, the newfound adult is going to attempt to replicate that dynamic in any adult relationship.

Likewise, someone who grew up in dysfunction is not likely to understand how to set normal or healthy boundaries or how to enforce those boundaries. They will be easily steamrolled, especially if boundaries being disrespected were a common theme growing up. This leaves the individual quite vulnerable, as he has no sense of normalcy and no sense of how to protect himself within a relationship. He does not understand that relationships are supposed to be symbiotic, and because of that, he is far more likely to deal with misbehaviors and abuse from a manipulator.

How to identify yourself as the Victim of Covert Manipulation

No one likes being manipulated. When manipulation occurs, you lose your power and your will. You must do what the other person wants. You often have no idea what the other person is really planning, and you have no say in the situation. This makes life very difficult, and it can cause you to do things that you don't want to do.

Now that you know the secrets to covert manipulation, you also know what to watch out for. You can reverse the techniques in this book to see when others are manipulating you. You can also flip these tactics on people and give them the manipulation that they are trying to run on you. There are various ways that you can protect yourself against manipulators.

Identify When You Are a Victim

Everyone has a gut instinct that rears up when they are used or misguided. Your gut instinct is very sound. You will know when you are a victim. The problem is, a lot of people ignore their instincts. You might ignore yours. You might think something like, "I'm just being paranoid" or "What could possibly go wrong if I hang out with this person?" You might think that the harm will be worth the benefits that you could get from knowing this person who gives you bad vibes.

Maybe everyone else likes this guy, so you think that you are just being weird, and you should like him too. Or maybe he is able to charm you and convince you that he is not so bad, and over time you start to get over your initial bad vibes.

But vibes are not something that you should ever ignore. The minute your gut warns you about someone, listen. Your first impression of someone is never wrong. If you get a bad first impression, don't give the person a second chance. You know more about someone by just glancing at them than you would think. The human brain is amazingly powerful; you only are conscious of roughly ten percent of your brain, so there is a lot going on under the surface that you are not consciously aware of. Your brain is capable of reading people and determining the future far more than you realize.

If you are just not in touch with your gut at all, or if you have doubts about someone, you might want to consider looking at some other signs. You can identify a manipulator based on his actions and language choices. You can also tell by how you feel around this person. There are various clues that point out who someone really is and what his intentions are.

What Makes You Vulnerable

You may wonder why manipulators are attracted to you, especially if you have had multiple encounters with manipulative types. You may also wonder what you should change about yourself to avoid running into a manipulator in the future.

One thing that makes you vulnerable is accepting manipulative treatment and emotional abuse. If you were emotionally abused or repressed as a child, this type of treatment may seem normal to you. You don't know anything else. You don't know how a healthy relationship is supposed to feel.

Another thing that may make you vulnerable is neediness or weakness. If you are in a vulnerable time in life, you might be more open to manipulators. Manipulators can see that you are in need, and they see it as an opportunity to offer you what you need in exchange for what they really want. They will use any opportunity to gain control over you, and when you are in a bad period of life, you basically hand them opportunities. You need to guard your heart and mind especially well when you are at a disadvantage. Be wary of extremely kind strangers or lifeguards. Not all heroes are good guys. Your heroes may help you, but they may have hidden intentions. Most people won't do something for free, so watch out.

You may also be a target for manipulation if you have low self-esteem. Events in your life or your childhood may have stripped away your self-esteem and confidence. You may be emotionally vulnerable. So you want people who build up your ego. Manipulators can spot this, and they will move in on you, working hard to please you and make you smile. They see a way into your mind through your bruised ego. Try to build your self-esteem by yourself and work on loving yourself.

Chapter 8: Dark Seduction

Seduction and sexual conquest are sometimes common features of dark psychology. This is an important topic to discuss because all of us have been or know someone who has been seduced by someone else who used these dark psychological principles.

The human sex drive can be a very powerful urge, and not being able to fulfill it can sometimes lead to unhappiness, worry, and stress in the person's life. On the other side of things, some of the most famous historical figures are known for their frequent and full fulfillment of sexual urges. For example, emperors and kings have often been afforded the finest women as their reward just because of their status.

One example that is very famous is the powerful seducer King Henry the 8th from England. His appetite for women was so strong that he decided to create a new religion in his country so that he could change his wife and marry any woman that he chose. He also exercised utter control over all the wives he had, and many of them were beheaded when they didn't satisfy his needs or help him meet his goals any longer.

This begs the question: Is all seduction a form of dark psychological seduction? Of course not! Yes, all seduction is going to involve the perusal of the other person. Those who don't have the skills of dark manipulation will do this in a clumsy manner. This is shown in some of the popular romantic comedies that come out, where the clumsy guy keeps making mistakes when they try to pursue the girl.

But a dark seducer is going to be someone who knows what they want, and they know how to get it. They will go after the other person in order to fulfill their own personal needs, and often they don't really care how the other person feels about it. They can be charming, and they are not going to be clumsy at all, and they always know the right thing to say and do.

Why Do People Choose Dark Psychological Seduction?

One question that people will have is: Why would someone want to choose this path for attraction? Is it not a better idea to go on some dates and court someone in an honest manner?

A dark seducer doesn't really want to get into a relationship, at least not into the boring stuff with it. They want to just get certain things out of the area of romance. They don't really care about the other person because they know they can use the techniques of dark psychology to find another partner later on if this one goes south later on. This allows them to approach life, and the relationship, with a non-needy and carefree mindset. If the seducer does decide to settle down with someone later on, they are going to be able to do it without feeling like they rushed or settled into the first relationship to get what they want.

So, how is a dark seducer have so much success and influence within the world of dating? It is because they understand the dark psychology principles, and they have the right skills in order to execute these principles.

One of the key advantages that the users of dark psychology will have over their rivals, especially in the world of dating, is that they understand the human mind, almost like a secret weapon. While others may feel like the human mind is impossible to understand, the dark seducer is able to read it like a book and get the information that they want from it.

Someone who works on the principles behind dark psychology in the dating world may find that it is really going to change their dating experiences when compared to their past efforts. They will have a feeling of confidence and control, rather than feeling doubtful, needy, and insecure.

Sure, it may seem kind of mean. The dark seducer is able to jump from one partner to another, using each one in the manner that matters most to the seducer. And there are people who are harmed in this process, especially the ones who are looking for more of a long-term relationship or those who are looking for more out of it.

But a dark seducer is only interested in what matters to them and nothing else. They can read the mind of their victim and be the exact person that the victim wants. But they only do this to get their foot in the door and get what they want. As soon as the victim isn't meeting the needs of the seducer, then the seducer will move on.

Where Does Dark Seduction Begin?

Now that we have an idea of the basics of dark seduction, it is time to move into some of the steps of how this seduction can work. Most dark seducers are going to have a guiding approach that is going to motivate their efforts. They will also have tactics that are going to come from their philosophy. Let's take a look at some of the different philosophies that are there that a dark seducer may choose to use.

One approach is the deployment of a process that is rigid and structured. These seducers feel that they have mapped out how the sequence of attraction should be in great detail, and they may have a process that seems like it is from a flowchart. They want their seduction process to be replicable and predictable. These systems not only work for the dark seducer but can work for others who understand these systems and learn how to implement them in the proper manner.

These seducers are going to use a series of stages in their process. They will try to get the target to go through a range of emotions. This range is designed by the seducer to fit their own needs. They will move them through emotions such as interest, attraction, and then excitement. These seducers will see the whole process as a series of checkpoints that they need to pass through to help them reach their goals.

The strength of this method is that it gives the dark seducer a feeling of certainty because they know the exact steps to take each time. They won't have any surprises that come up during the seduction, and it kind of becomes routine and habitual for the seducer. The biggest problem with this is that it doesn't take into account that sometimes people are going to be unpredictable and won't go along with the structured emotional program that the seducer planned out.

Another option is the natural approach. This approach is going to involve the dark seducer cultivating a genuine emotional state internal to the seducer and then expressing them freely to the one they are working to seduce. An example of this is when a person who uses this is likely to spend some time trying to understand their own emotions and then try to perfect these. They are then going to express these to others. The philosophy behind this one is that "I can't make others feel good until I can feel good."

You can also work with hypnotic and Neuro-Linguistic Programming (NLP) seduction. NLP is a combination of neurological processes, language, and behavior. This is kind of a subset of dark seduction. Unlike the structured seduction that we talked about before or even the natural version, NLP and hypnotic seduction are going to involve triggering specific emotional states in the victim and then linking these back to the seducer. Let's look at an example of this. The NLP approach to seduction is going to involve allowing a person to explore their own intense positive emotions. The seducer may even try to get more of those emotions out. Then, they will work to anchor these to the seducer. That way, when the victim sees the seducer, they will naturally feel intense physical pleasure, even though they may not know why that happens. Hypnotic seduction is another option to work with, but it can be a difficult one to work with on a regular basis. This is because few things are going to make someone suspicious about a seducer than the odd techniques that come with NLP. The other seduction types are going to seem somewhat normal to the victim, but hypnotic seduction doesn't seem this way. However, there are some who will respond to it. Dark seduction can allow the seducer the ability to get exactly what they want out of the relationship. It can sometimes be used by those who are not looking to take advantage of others, but who are open about what they are doing and just use the techniques to give them more confidence and avoid a boring relationship. But there are plenty of dark seducers who use it as a way to use the other person, with no care about how it is going to affect the other person at all. Either way, it is still important to be on the lookout for this kind of behavior so that you don't end up getting into a relationship that is bad for you or isn't what you are looking for from the other person.

Chapter 9: How to Defend Yourself from Manipulators

The best way to prevent you from becoming manipulated is to know the warning signs of what manipulators might look like in the first place. We all have things about us that can help lead others to get a sense of the person that we might truly be at our core, and manipulators are no exception. Unfortunately, there is no uniform that all manipulators will wear. Every single one is going to present themselves differently, and it's up to us to do our best to ensure that we aren't letting these people into our lives. Manipulators will usually come from a place of deep insecurity. Anyone who has control issues usually does so because they don't feel as though they have control over their own lives. Maybe they were in a situation in which they weren't able to change the outcome. Perhaps they were born into a life that they don't want, or they haven't advanced as far as they thought they would have. Perhaps they grew up under the control of someone else and are looking to take that freedom back. We won't always be able to know exactly why someone might be a manipulator, but we can at least understand what their basic intention is. Remember that hurt people hurt other people in some cases, so you don't have to shut manipulators out of your life right away. Confront them when they are trying to be controlling, and you might discover that you are actually able to help them work through some of their biggest issues. The first thing that you will notice about a manipulator is the way that they try to make you feel differently. We are all in control of our own emotions. You can influence how other people might be feeling, but you will never be able to outright control the emotions that they might be experiencing. Notice if someone seems as though they are trying to make you feel bad. A manipulator is going to be really good at pointing out your insecurities and making you feel guilty or silly for having these types of feelings.

If you say something that's less than intelligent, they will make sure that you feel ashamed because of this. They will laugh way harder at you than what someone would normally do, and they might ask you things such as "Why?" with a very passive-aggressive tone. For example, imagine that you are in a restaurant with some friends, and a cheesy pop song comes on. You might say something like, "I actually love this song!" Your friends might all laugh a bit, but for the most part, good friends wouldn't cut too deep in terms of how they might tease you for liking it. A manipulator, however, would definitely want to make you feel bad about this choice. They might say something such as "Oh my God, what's wrong with you?" or "You always like the worst songs." They will take this opportunity to make fun of your overall character, not just tease you in this singular moment.

Manipulators will dangle themselves as bait in front of you in order to be more fearful of withdrawing. They will want to instill you with the fear that if you don't make them a central part of your life, they will completely isolate you. This is when they might start to use the silent treatment as well. If you say anything to make them upset, they might completely withdraw and ignore all your efforts to reach out. They are trying to break you down and feel desperate, so rather than talking things out like a healthy person, they will instead try to make you feel guilty to the point that you're begging them to come back.

A manipulator is going to talk about themselves excessively. They might listen to you, but they will only pretend to do so in order to get you to try and listen to them. If you have an issue with them and present it like, "I feel like you really hurt my feelings the other day," then they will turn it back around on you. They will say something such as "OK, but what about that time you did this to me?" They will deflect and make sure that the point of the conversation comes back on their own hurt. If you are trying to open up and share something with them, such as "I've been especially anxious today," they will again make the problem about them once again by saying something such as, "Oh my gosh, I have been super anxious too." They will then make the conversation about themselves and ensure that everyone is listening to their side and disregarding everything else. They will be under the impression that no one else has problems as big as them. They will only care about resolving their own issues, but wouldn't offer you the same kind of help in return.

Manipulators aren't afraid to push boundaries. They will not be concerned if you ask them not to do something, and they will just go about their lives as they please in a way that suits them more than anyone else. They will also pay close attention to your emotions and the things that you say in order to use that against you. If you state that you are in a bad mood and later in the day try to bring the issue up with them, they will say something such as, "You're just in a bad mood, don't worry about it now." They will hang onto every last word that you say as if they were recording your conversation and use your own words against you whenever they are presented with this opportunity.

Look at obvious signs of manipulation as well. These might be more natural with people not realizing that they are doing it. It is the subtle and hidden manipulation that can be a bit scarier because it might have taken more planning on their part. Making statements such as "You should do this" with authority, is an obvious sign they're trying to control you. They might also obviously talk with a really loud tone and try to control the room just with the power of their voice.

Oppositely, they might keep their arms crossed and stay quiet in the corner of a room where everyone else is having fun. By doing this, they are making that situation about them. For example, think of a boyfriend and a girlfriend that are having an argument because the boyfriend wants to go to a party and the girlfriend wants to stay home. This part has been planned for a while, and that's what they had all originally wanted to do. The day of the party comes, and now the girlfriend doesn't want to go and is being very adamant about staying home.

He tells her that it's fine and that she doesn't have to go but that he is going to go at least. The girlfriend then decides that she is going to go to the party because she doesn't want him to go without her. At the party, however, she sits in the corner and has a terrible time. She doesn't even try to have fun, even though she easily could have just stayed home and done the same thing. This is a manipulative tactic that is seen too frequently. People who are clearly in bad moods will try to make everyone else have those same negative emotions rather than trying to bring themselves into a positive mindset. It isn't seen as manipulation because it's not like they're outright telling people to have a bad time or running around the party being mean.

They are still present, and by being in a group with people, there is a certain responsibility to be an active member. This doesn't mean being the life of the party, but it should involve at least an effort to be a little more positive in order to allow others to have fun and not have to worry about whether or not someone else is enjoying their time. None of us have to live like this, however! We are all in charge of our own emotions, and it is time that we start to bring that power back into our lives.

Chapter 10: Ways to Put an End to Your Manipulation

The best way to be certain that you won't be in the center of someone else's manipulation is to be highly aware of the things that you are promised and what you deserve as a human being. You should always practice increasing your emotional intelligence and look for ways that you can consistently improve your mental health. It will all start with ensuring that you are highly aware of the things that you are entitled to. Others might influence if you are feeling a certain way, but it will always be up to you to act on this emotion. The more you can remember your basic human rights, the easier it will be to be sure of yourself and able to stand up and against manipulation.

Always remember that unless you take respect away from someone else, you deserve to be respected. Just because of your skin color, gender, age, location, wealth, or anything else in your life, you do not deserve to be treated any differently. If you are meeting someone for the first time, then they should be giving you respect right away. If they don't, then this is their own issue that they need to work out themselves. If you are meeting someone for the first time and you are immediately rude or insulting to them, of course, they aren't necessarily going to treat you the same way. You deserve to be respected. You are entitled to be happy as well. Just because another person is miserable does not mean that you have to be unhappy as well. Everyone else is in control of their own emotions, and though you could joke and laugh and make someone happier, you still wouldn't be fully responsible for the way that they feel. We are all in charge of our own emotions. Next time someone makes you feel guilty for being happy, remind them that this is your fundamental right. Back to the example where the girlfriend was upset at the party, her partner has every right to still be happy and enjoy himself regardless of her negative mindset at the time.

You will always be entitled to your feelings, and as long as you are not hurting someone, you are allowed to express these feelings however you choose. If someone makes you feel guilty for being angry, stressed, or sad, then they are in the wrong. That is not OK to do. If you choose to handle that anger or stress by punching a wall, then, by all means, they are allowed to be mad. You have gone beyond the expression of emotions and turned it into aggression inflicted externally. Remember to separate emotion from action. If you tell someone that you are angry and they state that you are wrong or that you shouldn't have said that, then they are in the wrong.

This is common when it comes to gaslighting. Let's imagine another scenario, two best friends this time instead of a heteronormative couple. There are two girls, Ashley and Megan. Ashley is having a small party and decided to invite a maximum of four people so she could have an intimate night with her loved ones. One of these friends is Megan. Megan shows up to the party and brings about six other people that Ashley has never met. Being the passive girl she is, Ashley lets these people stay, and they have a somewhat decent night until one of Megan's friends gets too drunk and breaks one of Ashley's favorite plates. Ashley asks them to leave, and the night is over.

The next day, Ashley brings this up to Megan. She states something such as, "It made me really upset that you invited people without asking, and it ended up resulting in one of my things getting broken." A healthy response from Megan would be an apology, and she would understand where Ashley was coming from. Instead, Megan might be the type to consistently manipulate, and she ends up saying one of these things instead: "You're overreacting. It wasn't a big deal at all. You're taking this way too far."

This is called gaslighting. Megan is making Ashley feel as though she is crazy for even bringing this up in the first place. Megan is entitled to her own feelings as well, and maybe she does think that Ashley is overreacting. However, she should not be making her feel guilty about bringing this up. Both girls are entitled to their opinion, and the discussion shouldn't be about which one is right, they should be looking for a mutual understanding instead. Megan might also say something such as, "You're making me feel really guilty for even bringing this up." Ashley might have influenced some of that guilt in Megan, but it is not Megan's right to blame Ashley for her emotions.

Megan is in control of whether or not she feels guilty, and that is not something that she gets to blame Ashley for. That is also called gaslighting and wouldn't be done in a healthy relationship.

We have to remember that we also have the right to ensure that we are protecting ourselves. If this means cutting someone out of your life or at least taking a break from them, then we are entitled to this. If we decide that someone in our life is toxic, then it is not our responsibility to keep them around. They might be an individual that even needs us in a way, but you are only responsible for yourself and your happiness, so it is not selfish to take a break.

Remember that you will always have the right to say "no" whenever you want. Don't do anything that makes you feel uncomfortable, no matter how hard someone else might be trying to persuade you to do so. It is always going to be your right to use those two letters next to each other. If people start leaving you or aren't as involved in your life because you don't say "no" as often as you used to, then good riddance! It was clear that they were just using you because you might have been passive, so it's perfectly fine for you to move on.

When it comes to actually being in the moment of being manipulated, remember that there are still some things you can do to help you out of this situation. Always ask them further questions so that they explain themselves more. Make them really question what it is that they might be asking you. If they are being vague, always ask "why" more and more in order to get you to a place where you are able to fully understand what it is that they are asking. If you aren't sure whether or not you should do something, ask yourself if they would do the same. If the answer is "no," then that gives you a little insight into whether or not you should be doing what they are asking of you.

Everyone else should be respecting your boundaries. Remember the things that you are entitled to, and don't allow someone else to make you feel bad or guilty about being yourself. There will always be manipulators in your life, some more skilled than others. No matter what happens, you will always have the right to walk away and protect yourself. Anyone that truly loves you is going to be understanding and forgiving, and those who are just manipulating you will eventually go away after you cut them off.

Chapter 11: Hypnosis

Hypnosis or hypnotherapy is a state that is trance-like where a person's focus is heightened as well as their concentration. Hypnosis is done with the assistance of a therapist that uses verbal repetitions and mental pictures.

When a person is put under hypnosis, they normally feel relaxed, calm, and are open to suggestions.

Therapists have used hypnosis to help individuals gain control over behaviors that are undesirable. In dealing with anxiety and pain, hypnosis has also been found to be helpful. Although a person is relaxed and more open-minded to receive various suggestions, it is important to know that a person doesn't lose control over their behavior.

Why is Hypnosis Done?

Therapists say that hypnosis is an excellent way to cope with anxiety and stress. For instance, if someone is supposed to go for a medical procedure that they are anxious and stressed about, hypnosis can help calm them before the procedure. There are various conditions where hypnosis is used. These may include:

- **Pain control** – if a person is suffering from chronic pains from cancer, childbirth, joints, headaches, among others, hypnosis may help in bearing the pain.

- **Hot flashes** – when a woman is going through menopause, she will experience hot flashes that are uncomfortable most of the time.

Hypnosis has been known to help with the discomfort of hot flashes.

- **Behavior change** – some people may find themselves having behaviors that are undesirable. Such include bed-wetting, insomnia, eating disorders, among others. The use of hypnosis has been known to help in transforming these undesirable behaviors.

- **Side effects of cancer treatment** – during cancer treatment, patients go through chemotherapy and radiation treatment. These forms of treatment leave the patient with undesirable side effects. The use of hypnosis helps cancer patients deal with these effects and cope with the treatment.

- **Mental health conditions** – many people suffer from various mental health issues such as post-traumatic stress, anxiety, phobias, among many more. The uses of hypnosis help a person deal with these conditions and bring relief.

What Are the Risks of Hypnosis?

When hypnosis is done by a trained therapist or a medical practitioner, it is considered a safe addition and alternative treatment. However, in people with serious mental health issues, hypnosis may not be the best method to use.

There are various reactions to hypnosis. However, these reactions are rare, and they include:

- The person may feel dizzy after therapy Experience slight headaches

- After therapy, a person may feel drowsy. A person can be distressed or anxious

- In rare cases, hypnosis can create false memories

Preparing for Hypnosis

There is no need for special preparations before a hypnosis session. However,

it is recommended for a person to be comfortable and relaxed. It is also important for a person to be well-rested to avoid falling asleep during therapy.

Before you go for therapy, research, and ensure the therapist you have settled on is certified to perform hypnosis. Look for someone you trust that has undergone hypnosis and ask for references. You can also opt to interview the therapist before the session by finding out some of these:

• Does your therapist have psychology, social work, medicine training?

• Is your therapist licensed and certified to perform hypnosis? Where did the therapist get his training from?

• How much training does your therapist have in hypnotherapy, and where did they get the training from?

• Does your therapist belong to any professional organizations, and if so, which ones?

• How long has the therapist been in practice?

• How much the cost per session and are their sessions covered by insurance?

Once you have settled on a therapist, he or she will explain the expectations and the process. The therapist will also review your treatment goals with your help to ensure they have it right. The therapist will then embark on talking in a gentle, soothing voice as he describes pictures that create relaxation, well-being, and security.

When you are relaxed and in a state of reception, the therapist will begin to suggest ways you can achieve your goals. A therapist may also help you have a vivid mental picture of yourself accomplishing the goals. Once the session is over, you can bring yourself out of it or the therapist will help get out of your relaxation state.

During hypnosis, one does not lose control of their behavior. A person is always aware and remembers all that happened during the hypnosis session.

Hypnosis is used to help in coping with pain, anxiety, and stress and is used in cognitive behavioral therapy to change the behaviors and thoughts that are undesirable. However, hypnosis is not recommended for every person. Some people find it hard to get hypnotized, while for others it is easy, and they enjoy the benefits.

Three Stages of Hypnosis

Hypnosis is a process that involves deep body and mind relaxation. Before we get to the various hypnosis stages, it is important to first understand how hypnosis works or the process of hypnotherapy.

1. **Getting ready** – every hypnotherapy session with a qualified therapist must be carried out in a relaxed, safe, and calm environment where there are no interruptions of any kind. There is usually a preliminary discussion between the therapist and the person to be hypnotized. This is usually done to establish if the person has had prior hypnotism sessions and their experiences, as well as trying to establish the problem one needs working on. Most of the problems usually include a behavior or thoughts a person needs to balance or completely changed. For instance, a person may be struggling with bed-wetting; this behavior with the help of hypnosis is addressed and changed. A skilled therapist should gather as much information as possible during the preliminary talk. This is important so that he may work on the best technique for the particular person and problem. The pattern most therapists use during the session is loose. It follows:

- Preparing and screening a client

- Inducting a client to an altered consciousness state

- Deepening the trance state that opens suggestibility

- Posthypnotic suggestions. This is where advice is given regarding the problem the therapist worked on.

2. **Induction** – in a typical hypnotherapy session, the initial 15 minutes are for helping the client relax their mind and body. This stage is referred to as the induction stage. It involves helping a person to enter into a light state of trance by the use of relaxation techniques that work on the mind and body.

Gradually, the person is encouraged to relax their muscles and mind. This technique is aimed at ridding a person of any tension and releasing anxiety. The therapist focuses on instructing the client to slow and control their breathing. This is also to help relax and distract the conscious mind so that a person focuses on the subconscious mind. Because of many methods of induction, it is important for the therapist to understand their client and apply a method that works for them.

3. **Deepening a trance** – this stage is where the subconscious mind is made ready to be more receptive to suggestions or new behavior. Once the mind accepts new thought patterns, a change in behavior follows. To deepen the trance, some therapists may opt to continue reinforcing the induction method used. The method can be accompanied by visualization techniques that are very deep to increase the trance. A qualified therapist knows that it is important for a person to be deeply altered in consciousness before starting hypnotic suggestions.

Now that you know how hypnosis works, it is important to understand the three stages of hypnotism.

Stage 1 – Hypnoidal State

This is the stage of light induction. At this stage, the person is encouraged to relax and have an internal focus. This stage is light and is characterized by the fluttering of the eyes of the person.

Stage 2 – Cataleptic State

This is the stage where the therapist moves to deepen the trance state. To know if a person is in this state, their eyes move from one side to the other.

Stage 3 – Somnambulistic State

This is the deepest stage in a trance. This is evidenced by the rolling up and down of eyes. This is the stage where suggestions are given and received at a subconscious level, and the person in some cases may not remember hearing them.

Applications for Hypnosis

Hypnosis has been known to have existed for as long as records have been able to show. According to the American Society for Clinical Hypnosis (ASCH), the use of modern clinical hypnotherapy goes back to the late 1700s. Since 1958, the use of hypnotherapy as a form of reliable therapy and tremendously increased. Hypnotherapy has found use in the modern world in different ways.

Hypnosis is used in various ways, from mental health conditions to psychological and physical conditions. It is used on people suffering from chronic pain, depression, in sudden and acute illnesses, among others. Most health professionals nowadays recommend the use of hypnosis to treat their clients facing different conditions. Some of the uses of hypnosis include:

Treatment of Phobias and Fears

Irrational fear or phobia of anything can be treated through the use of hypnotism. Many people struggle with phobias on a daily basis, causing them not to function normally. Some of the fears that paralyze people are fear of spiders or arachnophobia, fear of enclosed spaces or claustrophobia, fear of heights, snakes, flying, or agoraphobia; the fear of leaving home.

A hypnotherapist will work with a patient while under hypnotism to try and identify the reasons for the fears and work on finding solutions to them.

Stopping Smoking

There are people that want to stop their habit of smoking, but it becomes very difficult. Most smokers attempt several times to quit smoking and find themselves falling back. Regardless of how committed a smoker is to cease smoking, it is not easy, and they may need help to do so. A hypnotherapist may be able to help them. In a relaxed environment, the therapist works on understanding the various stress factors in the life of the client that may be causing fall back to smoking every time they stop.

A therapist will go to the subconscious mind to find these reasons and make suggestions on how to stop. Once the subconscious mind has received the suggestions, it is then possible for the person to change their behavior by addressing the stress factors.

Weight Loss

Many people struggle with weight loss and often feel they have lost the battle with food. With a qualified hypnotherapist, a person can learn more about their relationship with food. They also learn why they have no control over food and how to overcome their cravings. Through hypnosis, a therapist can suggest ways to overcome the destructive behavior and have a healthy relationship with food.

Boosting Confidence

There are many people that suffer from low self-esteem issues. To gain their confidence back, such people may require assistance. Most people lose confidence because they can seem to embrace their good qualities. A therapist can help such a person find their confidence by tapping on their best qualities that are subconsciously hidden.

Anesthesiology During Surgery

There are cases where a surgeon may hire a hypnotherapist to supplement medical anesthesia. In some extremely rare cases, hypnotherapy has been used solely as an anesthetic during a surgical procedure. Some procedures that surgeons have used hypnotherapy include the removal of the gallbladder, cesarean, hysterectomy, and amputation. There are patients that have sensitiveness and allergies to chemicals used in anesthesia. However, they can still benefit from health-improving and life-saving procedures through the use of hypnotherapy.

Hypnosis has been credited with improving the lives of many people. For cognitive-behavioral therapy, hypnotism has been known to help many patients transform their thoughts and, in effect, changing their outward behaviors for the better.

Chapter 12: Brainwashing

Brainwashing is a tactic that we often hear. We are told that television commercials bombard us with what to buy, and we are exposed to people's rants on television, radio, the newspaper, online, and social media. These rants tell us what we should look like, what we should be eating, reading, voting for, wearing, etc. We are all subjected to the art of brainwashing on a daily basis, and the amount of brainwashing continues to grow.

Before the creation of social media, we were still exposed to social media. However, they would only market to their target audience. If they weren't meant for you, they would be ignored until the next commercial or show came back on the air. For example, you wouldn't have paid much attention to a Polly Pocket or Barbie commercial unless you were a ten-year-old girl or someone who might buy the product for their child.

But things are not like that anymore. Advertising has moved past gender roles, and with the inception of social media, advertisements are now personally geared for us. These websites take information that we provide them. For instance, Facebook uses our likes, comments, status updates, etc. to find the perfect things to advertise to us. They are utilizing brainwashing techniques in the 21st century.

Today, we are bombarded with mind control techniques daily. There are many different types and levels of mind control. We will go over an overview of the types, and we'll talk about some examples of them. There are three basic levels of mind control. Each level corresponds with a different type of psychology. So far no technology can control what you choose to believe. So we will talk about the methods to defend it, and we will also look at some of the implications that it have on civilizations. Mind control skills are used for wrong for the obvious reason, whether it's politically or scientifically speaking. Simply by existing in a society, we are constantly subject to manipulation or indoctrination.

The first-level appeals to consciousness. The second level corresponds to unconsciousness, and the last level appeals to biological. Now in terms of psychology, the first one consciousness has to do cognitive psychology. Cognitive means being aware of what's going on. The second one is unconsciousness, which corresponds with behavioral psychology and while the last one is biological psychology, which talks about psychiatry. This is where you can try to control the mind using physical things like drugs and electrical shock. Every mind control technique fits into its own methods. Some of the mind-control technique will fit into one of these levels, while some mind techniques will fit in between two of them. But every mind control technique fits inside the sun part of the chart. Now let us talk about the different levels of my control and what fits in between.

The Conscious Level

The first level is the Conscious level. This level is the level that deals with information. It does not talk about punishment or physical pain. It appeals to your reason. The basic forms of this are education and ideological indoctrination.

A good example of this is when you get your driver's license. You take to decide to take fighting classes, and you learn the rules of the road, and the intention is to make you behave a certain way when you are driving. Now, most people don't have a problem with this because if you don't behave a certain way when you drive, then you will have a problem.

So ideological indoctrination is the worldview and your philosophy, and what you're educated in, in your worldview. So this includes your political choice, your education, your religious education, and even your science education. Now this means how do you view the World and by what you were dictated by. Now, at this level, you have to mention the fact, which means information. Now because propaganda has been abused in the past, people normally have a negative view of it.

Now the basic idea is that somebody wants you to view the world in a certain way, so they are educating you to do so. Propaganda is just information control. Now information control isn't that bad. For instance, have you ever seen a billboard that says that 50000 people die when driving and drinking? Now that is propaganda, and it is not bad. Hitler used propaganda to educate Germany into the idea that all Germany problem was because of the Jews. Now that is bad propaganda.

The Unconscious or Behavioral Psychology

Now let's look at the next level of mind control, which is unconscious or behavioral psychology. This does not appeal to the Conscious mind. It is an attempt to control somebody without his or her conscious decision being involved. The biggest school of psychology is behavioral psychology that comes from Pablo psychology. A great example of that is the story of the man who rings the bell for the dog to salivate that we talked about above. So this deals with stimulus-response. Stimulus means when something happens – in the man and the dog case, it's ringing the bell. Response - in the man and the dog case, is the dog's salivating. Now, this does not appear to be a conscious mind. The dog did not decide to salivate; they just did it automatically. Now, unlike the Conscious level, this level often includes physical pain, punishment, and torment. For instance, you can implant a commanding chip in somebody so that when they hear the command, which is the stimulus, they will go and do something, which is the response. It is a stimulus-response. The person that is programmed to do that thing doesn't decide to do it because it is an automatic response, and in fact, he doesn't even know that he is being programmed because that thing is in the subconscious. It is at this point that we have hypnosis, and the reason why it's so is that hypnosis is implanted commands into the subconscious. For instance, there is the operator that says: when I say bubble gum bark like a dog. So the stimulus is the bubblegum, whereas the response is the barking like a dog. Or the operator says: when I snap my fingers, you should act like a stripper. So he snaps his fingers, which is the stimulus, and acting like a stripper is the response. Creating a stimulus-response mechanism is called conditioning. Part of the conditioning is programming somebody to associate pain or pleasure with something. Now another part of this level is called punishment. Punishment is an attempt to make somebody associate pain with undesirable behavior.

Now let's go with: if you have a kid and the kid flicks the switch off. Now on the Conscious level, you could sit your child down and explain to the child why it is wrong, and hopefully, your child would make the decision not to do it again. Now on the unconscious level, you can beat the hell out of the child until the child tends to associate pain with switching the switch off and hope and hope that doesn't do it again.

Now behaviorism is an attempt to control somebody's behavior, like the way you train a dog using rewards and punishments. Now the cognitive approach is the best, and this is the level where we have brainwashing or interrogation. And you will do this using physical pain to control someone. Now another note about brainwashing is that it has the word washing, which means to wipe something away and to wash it away. The word brainwashing comes from a technique that was used in China, which is called political re-education. The idea is that when you want to wash something away, you put something else in its place.

In the MK-ultra program, the psychiatrist called it de-patterning. Now when you take somebody from their religion and use mind control techniques, you will be able to wipe out their religious beliefs and put another belief in his place. This is called programming. So under brainwashing, we have political re-education, we have the patterning, and we also have religious education or de-programming.

Biological Psychology

Now the last level is Biology, which equates to biological psychology or psychiatrist. Now at this level, you are attempting to control someone's behavior through physical interventions. Physical interventions include brain surgery, drugs, electrical shock, or implanting something into the brain. Now for the child that flipped the switch off, the cognitive approach will be sitting the child down and explain to him why is wrong now. The behavioral approach will be to spank him, and the biological approach will be to give him a psychotic drug. Or a remote control robot. Now those are the basic levels. Many different types of mind control techniques that fit into these levels, but we will not be going deep into them.

Now in between the Conscious and unconscious levels, there are different levels to control somebody's behavior, and we are constantly subjected to this daily. One of these techniques is public relations, and it is aimed to make you feel a certain way about something. Now, this is not to just make you feel good about something. It can make bad about a competitor, a group, or a person. And it is called Black public relations. Now another mind control technique is marketing and advertisement. Another mind control technique that falls between the Conscious and unconscious level of mind control is pandering, and the word pandering means to fulfill a moral desire, a prostitute pandering to a sexual desire, a drug dealer pandering to an addiction.

So what this means is that you're controlling someone by giving them what they want. Now under pandering, future control by destruction is included, and that includes television, pornography, and video games. And another mind-control technique on the biological level is addiction. Manipulative people keep their victims to them by making them addicted to drugs. And beyond that, there is a reason why caffeine has been added to soft drinks, and there is a reason why energy has been added to fast food, and there is a reason why sugar is added to almost everything in the grocery store, it's because it is a type of mind control.

Now the last technique, which is at the very bottom and is when you give up on trying to controlling the person's mind, and you restrain them. An example is a straightjacket, institutionalization, imprisonment, and heavy tranquilizer. Now, if everything fails and you can't control the person's mind, there is still something left, and that thing is to shoot the person. So that is basically what dark psychology brainwashing is all about.

Chapter 13: Famous Dark Psychology Case studies

The way we use words in writing, especially if we are touting ourselves as an authority such as an established newspaper or news organization, has a big impact on how such information is received on a wide scale, there are ways to twist the expression of news in a way that automatically instills certain opinions about the news piece and the individuals involved. This is clear when you browse around on news sites, which are quite clearly leaning in one political direction versus another. If you compare two sites with opposite political inclinations, you will see major differences, including aspects like which stories to run, how the people in a news story are portrayed, the quotes that are chosen for the piece, and even the photos which are used for the news story. A flattering photo may be used on a site that is supporting that particular candidate, and a not-so-flattering photo might be used to portray his or her opposition. These things hit us on a superficial level, and we automatically are given opinions, especially when we don't have a solid opinion of this person in the first place. It is easier to sway the public's opinion on something that is not widely known than it is to try and change people's minds about something. Just like American President Trump likes to convey to people that the media shouldn't be trusted. He does this because he knows that if the public were on the side of the news media and felt they could trust it, they would have to contend with some of the more unsavory aspects of his character and background. It is much more favorable for him if the public simply had an uneasy feeling when it came to the media altogether. And this is where the popularization of "fake news" came into play.

A man or woman in a new romantic situation might use electronic communication to string potential partners along, even when they are barely interested or are already seeing other people. You might have seen online memes or jokes about how young players might have two, three, or even four different phones for the purposes of juggling all of his potential girlfriends and hookups. Many people find this kind of lifestyle thrilling, but it can be dangerous territory, especially when you mismanage things, and fires start all around you as you piss people off.

However, if you have a single target who has some level of emotional attachment to you, it is certainly possible to shape the way this person perceives you through text messages with very specific language. The more you know about a person emotionally, the more you can accurately assume how your words are going to be interpreted when you send them. Let's look at an example. Theresa just met a man at a bar named Clark. Clark is funny, charming, and held her attention for hours without ever looking at another woman. She is fairly interested in where this is going, and so she gives Clark her phone number.

Let's say Clark has just nailed one of his signature strategies for picking up new women. He has a few that he visits in a rotation, and he is interested in adding Theresa to the list. After their initial meeting, Clark feels pretty confident that Theresa is going to keep up communications with him, and he uses this knowledge to his advantage and to help him manage his schedule between women. For example, it is possible to convey false emotion in text messages in a way that you could never do in person. This is, again, because you don't have the physical feedback and signals through text messages that you normally would get in person. Clark sends a message saying, "Hey, I'm so sorry, but I can't see you tonight. I got to work. Can I see you tomorrow night? I really miss you." Then perhaps he inserts some kind of cute emoji to drive home his point. Clark may really be spending his evening with another woman, but Theresa is interested in Clark enough that she is willing to believe reasonable information that tells her he can't make a previously planned date, but he is excited to see her as soon as possible afterward. Doing this a number of times would likely cause Theresa to wonder about his true motivations, but at this early stage, people are more willing to be flexible because they are holding on to that initial excitement that was started when they first met and felt some sparks of excitement.

Clark, if he starts to get tired of Theresa and only wants to see her once a week instead of two or three times, might start to introduce some kind of emotional angle to his text messages. He is experiencing depression or anxiety issues due to some family thing, or he is fighting with his boss and must put in some extra hours at work to keep from losing his job. One of these routes is going to be more effective than the other, depending on the target's personality and emotional state. Clark must also be aware of how Theresa is going to react. She might get worried and offer to talk with him even more often to help him through his emotional battles, and she may get offended and back off, serving his purpose all the better.

Chapter 14: Profiling a Sociopath

Sociopathy and psychopathy are two different kinds of antisocial personality disorders. But there are many people, including professionals like psychologists and those that are involved in crime investigation, that is having a misconception on how to use them technically. For quite a long time, leading experts had numerous debates and studies about the differences between sociopathy and psychopathy.

Sociopaths and psychopaths have differences, and they also have something in common. The commonalities that they share according to the American Psychiatric Association are:

- Sociopaths and psychopaths violate laws and ethics.

- They don't care about the rights of the people around them.

- They do not feel guilt or remorse for their crimes and misconduct.

- They have a high inclination for violence and aggressive actions.

Now that we have their commonalities let's enumerate their unique traits that define their differences. Sociopaths are nervous individuals, and they are easily disturbed. They are very impulsive that might lead to emotional breakdown and anger. They commonly have low educational attainment compared to psychopaths, and they live on the outer reaches of society. When it comes to their career, they sometimes incapable of having a permanent job or even residency. Though sociopaths do not care about society and its rules, they can still establish an attachment to other people or groups. Deep and meaningful involvement with others is rare and limited to a selected few. Others deemed sociopaths to have a troubled spirit and pessimistic perception in life. For professionals and nonprofessionals, sociopaths are much easier to identify than psychopaths because they are not that organized when performing their crimes, and evidence can be obtained easily by forensic officers. Sociopathy can be acquired through relevant experiences like trauma and abuse. Therefore, it is a product of what has been nurtured by the environment.

While psychopaths strongly project that they don't possess any conscience and incapable of sustaining emotional attachments. They are more aggressive, and they are like predators that always look for prey. They see individuals, as well as animals as toys created for their amusement and that would quench their thirst for violence. Even though they are not empathic, they do have a very pleasing personality, and due to vanity, their charm can disarm the people around them. They can gain people's trust and make it an opportunity to manipulate them. Psychopaths were born to be natural actors, and they have the power to fake emotions even though they don't feel them. They may appear as normal individuals for regular people. Psychopaths are educated, and they can stay as long as they can in a specific job or career.

It was mentioned earlier that psychopaths don't actually establish a meaningful and deep relationship with others. Some already mastered the art of manipulation and imitation that they have their own families and friends to cover their destructive tendencies. Even their relations do not actually have the slightest hint of who they really are unless evidence about them will be presented. Psychopaths are very well-organized and detailed when planning for their crimes, and they usually have backup plans when the original plan fails.

Psychopaths are very tricky that makes them cool, relax, and picky. According to forensic experts, psychopaths have a cold-blooded nature, which makes them effective villains of society. They are difficult to identify compared to sociopaths. Psychopathy, according to many psychologists, is a product of genetics and is already natural to the person who has it. Psychopathy is due to the physiological deficiency that leads to the underdevelopment of a brain's part that is responsible for impulse and emotional controls.

It is considered that compared to sociopathy, psychopathy is rarer and is the deadliest among the antisocial personality disorders.

Personality Traits

According to statistics, about 3 to 5% of the human population are sociopaths. Therefore, you could have, or you may encounter one in a lifetime. By giving you a thorough description of the red flags that you need to have an eye on, you will spot functional sociopaths and be aware of their cunning schemes.

- **Sociopaths are intelligent.** Though psychopaths are more organized and detailed when working on their crimes, sociopaths do also have high IQ, which also allows them to plan and organize their actions that would be vital to control and exploit their victims.

- **Sociopaths are less empathic.** Compared to psychopaths, sociopaths can still establish empathy but not as high as those who are normal and healthy individuals. They are less empathic, which means that they are struggling to understand and feel what other people are dealing with emotionally. Sociopaths do not understand the emotional implications of their actions, especially when they hurt others.

- **Sociopaths are narcissistic.** Sociopaths see themselves as privileged individuals, and they have a strong affection for their whole being, and they used to romanticize the sad reality of their lives. They tend to be narcissistic because of low self-esteem and make-up facts.

- **Sociopaths are very charming.** Since sociopaths can imitate other people and obscure their real feelings and comments about others, they can be really charming because they can adapt easily.

- **Sociopaths keep their secrets.** Typical loners because of this antisocial personality disorder, sociopaths are at their best in keeping the intimate details about them, and they do not see the significance of sharing it with others. Sociopaths will tell very little information about them once they selected their victims and use a piece of them to gain control over their victims.

- **Sociopaths engage in casual intercourse.** Lacking guilt and having difficulties in establishing emotional attachments, sociopaths can be easily involved in multiple affairs that include casual sex.

- **Sociopaths are sensitive to criticism.** Being a narcissist and even though they are less empathic, sociopaths want social approval, and they don't take criticisms lightly. They get angry easily when they are put into question or directly criticize.

- **Sociopaths are impulsive.** Time is very precious for sociopaths, and they don't want to miss their opportunity to play on their prey. They use to do the things that they know are necessary to achieve their goals.

- **Sociopaths are good at lying.** Sociopaths will lie to get what they want, to protect their image, and hide their crimes no matter who suffers.

- **Sociopaths need to be stimulated.** To be always prepared and to possess the necessary energy to do their tricks, sociopaths must be physically involved in activities. Being actively engaged prevents them from getting bored.

- **Sociopaths have vices.** It is typical for sociopaths to get their victims in any place, or they can find them in any activities. Most of their victims do not have a strong personality. Thus, sociopaths tend to be domineering than them. So, their victims usually have vices like substance abuse, alcohol, gambling, sex, and the like. Therefore, sociopaths have to morph and acquire the same vices to exploit and manipulate more people.

- **Sociopaths may engage in criminal activities.** Sociopaths have a high tendency to be inclined in illegal and criminal activities like rape, murder, theft, fraud, obstruction of justice, and other forms of cruelty.

Now that you have the list of sociopathic traits, which are the common red flags that you need to observe, you may now assess the people that you have in mind that fit into our list.

Behavioral Indications

Sociopaths are very creative when it comes to their tactics to effectively get the trust of their victims. They tend to start with the very simple approaches that everybody else is doing that have become a routine. Sociopaths have their daily routines and habits that will help you to identify them. The most common behavioral indications of sociopaths are listed below.

1. **Sociopaths are very vain.** Sociopaths are also narcissists, and they are very concerned about how they look physically. To be always in shape and to be presentable at most times, they have a very intense grooming ritual. They dressed to impress and to be good-looking and attractive, they can attract more victims that they would manipulate and exploit.

2. **Sociopaths don't want to mingle with others sometimes.** Though sociopaths can empathize with other people a little bit compared to their psychopathic counterparts, they usually want to be alone just to focus more on themselves. Being alone can also give them ample time to plan how to manipulate or exploit their victims.

3. **Sociopaths love to watch movies.** A lot of people are fond of watching movies as a recreational activity. Watching movies is a form of relaxation, and it delivers viewers to other dimensions. Sociopaths also love watching movies as well. According to clinical psychologists, sociopaths are very obsessed with seeing movies because they might be trying to get pointers about normal human behavior and mimic them afterward. Most sociopaths enjoy movies with darker themes that typically display murder, violence, and cruelty.

4. **Sociopaths are self-centered individuals.** Sociopaths are arrogant, and they think that they are genuine enough to be a company of other people who they see as their inferior. Their personal goals motivate sociopaths who are trying to blend in society and getting closer to other people.

5. **Sociopaths have risky behaviors.** Having a lot of thrills and adventures in life keeps sociopaths away from boredom, and they will do anything, even breaking the law or exploiting others just to stay active. Sociopaths are very impulsive and irresponsible. To maintain such a level of activity, they have a high tendency to have excessive alcohol consumption, substance abuse, unsafe sexual intercourse, gambling, and criminal activities.

6. **Sociopaths are very controlling.** Once sociopaths earned the approval and the trust of other people, they will become friends with them and can be even closer. By being so, this is where sociopaths will begin to manipulate their victims and will do things to control them, especially when there are things that didn't please sociopaths. They may employ emotional blackmail or any other strategies to control their victims and turn the table in their favor again.

Root-Cause Analysis

There are so many wonders in our universe that until today are unexplainable. While some had been studied and as the passages of time elapsed, we will discover that what humankind learned about such things is just partial. Just like in psychology, there are things that we don't know yet about the brain. Same as with the concept of how anti-social personality disorders plagued some individuals like those who are sociopaths.

Sociopaths are very much misunderstood and generally branded as vile and corrupted souls who can destroy life. When we try to understand sociopaths, since we are already aware that they have a little empathy towards others, they don't necessarily have a bad intention for other people.

Their desire to do destructive actions to individuals, especially those who are very close to them, is due to their lack of deeper understanding of intense human emotions like empathy and suffering.

Becoming a sociopath is not genetically transmitted. Sociopathy can be acquired, and our painful experiences in life might affect the way we think and trigger the sociopath in us. Sociopaths became who they are because most of them went through traumatic experiences, sexual abuse, exploitation, or they had struggled in life. They might be regular individuals before, and their abominable pasts changed them, and learned how to play tricks in their environment and use every resource they have to compensate for the injustice they believed they suffered.

Sociopaths are like a coin that has two different faces. They can be good when a large crowd is gathered, and they can be consumed by negatives thoughts when they are alone or when they are with their friends and intimate relations. They can show positivity and even display empathy at your first meeting. But gradually, as you have established trust and affection, sociopaths are there to unleash their dark side and play their dirty tricks and use them in the most advantageous time and places.

Chapter 15: Subconscious Mind Suggestions

Some say that the most successful people in the world are that way as they have mastered the strategy of using their mind to draw their desires toward them.

Imagine having the ability to attract what you want most, without having to do anything about it, and that it quickly concerns you.

Imagine being able to manifest your goals and desires by the sheer discipline of your train of ideas.

Actions are based upon ideas, and everything starts with thoughts, which is something most people do not understand.

Before we handle the techniques that actually make use of the power of our mind, it will be wise to first ask, what is the subconscious mind?

The subconscious is known to be a part of the mind that, though not completely aware, affects an individual's actions or emotions. Some consider the subconscious mind as being associated with the spirit or soul of an individual. It is said that it is empowered with the capability to create your reality through the messages it gets from your actions and beliefs.

If this is actually true, then the most intelligent transfer to make will be to take a great look at your subconscious mind and think of what you really want or prefer. This is the personification of what is easier said than done. The intricacies of one's life and the large number of experiences of both negative and positive nature will not quickly enable one to completely take control of what is fed to the subconscious mind.

It is only in recent years that the discovery of the creative power of the subconscious has been exposed. Ever since many e-books, learning, and audio cd's taking on different subconscious mind power techniques have been made and sold.

A typically disregarded technique to get usage of the subconscious mind's power is to know the subconscious mind and befriend it. By and large, this area of the mind is considered to be one of the most enigmatic parts of human anatomy.

Most consider the subconscious as the direct connection to the source who is the supreme developer of the vast universe, a higher power that wills to exist, a being that is more unlimited and flawless than the cosmos itself, and the someone who meant everything for what is good. To accomplish effective results with subconscious mind power techniques, then self-questioning is the key.

Nevertheless, that in itself has ended up being uncommon and unheard of in societies that celebrate their physical self and being as the ultimate source. What results in most failures is the failure to understand that the natural good intent of the source, or the creator, that is fundamental for the subconscious mind, has been derailed or at times weakened by our mindful, thinking minds.

The external world's modernization and the dictatorship of what is popular, present, good, and moral take control of one's consciousness, with the subconscious mind relegated to taking the back seat and delight in the flight.

This ultimately brings right before you what you purposely think, say, and do, unless you stop and choose to change it for what is right and positive.

Subconscious mind power techniques are absolutely worth a try, but only if you're willing to engage in complete goodness, through and through. Your subconscious mind is crucial to you attaining every objective and dream you've ever preferred.

Here are some of the most well-known mind power techniques:

1. **Affirmations**: Positive declarations repeated to your subconscious mind to form wanted outcomes.

2. **Dream interpretation**: Assigning meaning to dreams in an effort to better comprehend messages from the subconscious mind.

3. **Hypnotic recommendation**: An idea made to the subconscious mind while a person is in a deeply relaxed and responsive state.

4. **Journaling**: A tool used to support other mind power techniques by strengthening efforts to connect the mindful and the subconscious mind.

5. **Meditation**: A state of deep relaxation that brings a sense of calm and prepares an individual for subconscious exploration.

6. **Visualization**: To better get ready for a similar event or activity, in reality, this mind power technique includes experiencing an occasion or activity in your mind as preparation.

Letting Loose the Power of the Subconscious Mind

The power of the subconscious mind is something that has lots of people talking. It appears that all over you look you run across something that discusses releasing the full power of the subconscious mind. With the start of a brand-new year, the topic is even more well-known as everyone is out to better themselves. Letting loose the full power of the subconscious mind will put you on the course to completely ending up being a much better person, no matter if you are attempting to become more effective at work or just want to be a happier person.

Your subconscious is the section of your mind that stores a variety of things that you might have forgotten about. Emotional reactions, as well as our beliefs and memories, are stored in the subconscious mind. This storage area, so to speak, greatly influences our lives; our conduct is directly connected to our values and morals. In order to change how we react to certain situations, we should change our values and morals, and also our inner beliefs. Releasing the full power of the subconscious mind is the only way to achieve this.

Just one thing that you are going to see when it concerns unleashing the full power of the subconscious mind is repeating. No matter what mind exercises or strategies that you use to reach your subconscious repetition is crucial.

The reason behind this is that to completely unleash the power of the subconscious mind you should communicate with your mind, you need to tell your subconscious mind what you actually believe in and what you want. With how deep-rooted your initial ideas and beliefs are, it can take months to change your subconscious, so time and repetition are the only ways to accomplish that change.

A better example of how repeating works on your mind is being told that you are dumb over and over again; the more youthful this started, the worst it usually is. By people constantly telling you that you are stupid or made silly choices, your subconscious is picking up those theories and applies them to your current life without you even recognizing it.

In addition, no matter how hard you may try, you are going to not succeed at anything new because your subconscious tells you that you cannot really do it because of how silly you are. In order to change that thought procedure, you must tell yourself over and over again that you are wise and can do anything you set your mind to in order for your brain to adopt a new idea.

Meditation, hypnosis, and subliminal messages are the three most popular approaches used to reach the subconscious mind, and all three of these methods count on repetition to unleash the full power of the subconscious mind. No specific technique is considered superior to another, so you can use whatever technique you prefer, or you can use a combination of techniques to get you on the path to a much better life.

1. **Meditation is most commonly used in spiritual settings and also a way to unwind.** Using meditation to reach the subconscious mind is necessary because of well meditation relaxes you and also quiets your mind. It is much easier to focus and listen to your subconscious mind when you aren't listening to your mindful mind. The mindful mind tends to disrupt the mind just because of how loud the ideas are, they are typically overpowering. Unwinding and quieting your conscious mind allows any thoughts or memories from your subconscious mind to come through, and the quieter your mindful mind is, the louder these ideas can be!

2. **Hypnosis is another powerful tool in letting loose the full power of the subconscious mind, no matter what you may think.** Many individuals find hypnotism to be a joke; they think that it does not work, partly just because of all the buzz surrounding this method. However, hypnosis is a valuable tool that can be used to change your inmost feelings. Hypnosis resembles meditation in the fact that both allow you to unwind, but hypnosis goes further than meditation, it is another state completely. Hypnosis wakes up your mind and allows it to get in touch with your mindful mind, enabling any change in personality or habits to happen. For example, cigarette smokers who undergo hypnosis lose the urge to quit smoking within a few sessions.

3. **Subliminal strategies, which include subliminal messages, are another well-known way to release the power of the mind.** The best part about subliminal techniques is that we often don't even realize they're being used. The reason this work so well is that these techniques are tailored to reach the subconscious mind straight, the conscious mind doesn't even recognize they exist. The most common place to find these techniques is in audio or video recordings.

Chapter 16: Using Dark Psychology to Manipulate a Man

Now we are talking about making a guy crazy, we are not talking about making the guy not to have a sense of self. We are not talking about destruction; we are just talking about making the guy emotionally weak for you to the point where he reacts when he hears from you. Up to the point, whereby he can't be normal around you, and that is the meaning of what it is to be attractive when you make a guy weak for you. He gives everything to you, and he's willing to do almost everything for you. Now, these things are manipulative, but they work.

Lust

The first one is lust. It is not just about lust, but it's about how to manipulate a player and how to crush a fuckboy. We'll talk about some bad psychological events that you can use to your advantage because it is time to turn the tables around on people that you have been manipulating you. Oh, most men are very simple, and they're very one-dimensional. Guys are very easy to understand, so if you learn how to read the signs. You will be twisting the theories and your facts to suit you.

You're not reading the writing on the wall and knowing that he doesn't like you or he's a cheater, or he's not going to leave his wife or girlfriend, but instead, you choose to see what you want to see. Instead, choose to believe that he's proper treating some incredible complex emotional scum on you, whereas you are just your own enemy.

You are the architect of your own misfortune. So it's time for you to get out in front of this. We are talking about the Tactics of men, but these tactics can also be applied to women.

Play Seduction War Strategy

Let's talk about war strategy. War is meant to keep your enemy off balance and to be unpredictable, and seduction is war. Robert Greene talks about the world of Seduction, and he says that the person that you are trying to seduce is a victim, and that is the way you should think of the men that you want to potentially seduce. That you should not think of them as a potential boyfriend or a guy who wants to fall in love with you. If you are trying to make a guy who doesn't like you to fall in love with you, then you are digging your own grave because you're going to lose big, because the person who cares the least is the person who wins. And that is the foundation of human interaction. If you care the least, you carry the power. If you look at yourself in a situation looking for a job where you are fresh out of it college, and you need the job, and you're tired of driving and leaving your dad's basement. Then your boss doesn't care because thousands of you are looking for the same position in the company.

So he's not going to negotiate for shit, because he doesn't need to make deals, but you care a lot. But it doesn't really care a lot, so he has the power. So it's the same thing in seduction. When you're trying to manipulate somebody, you need to divorce yourself from your feelings as much as possible, that is why if you're trying to manipulate someone, then that person should be someone fresh. You shouldn't lie to yourself where your heart stands because Robert Greene also said in his book that you shouldn't just know yourself, you should also know your enemy. You should know exactly where your enemy's position is and exactly the machinery that they are using because if you don't, you won't be able to predict the outcome of anything.

So if you feel really strong about somebody, you need to abort the person because it is going to go bad. It isn't saying that you can't get revenge about somebody, but you need to let the emotion dust and settle down. Otherwise, you're going to make no neutral decisions. So you have to pull back and look at it mutually and make a flowchart. You need to be able to evaluate things mutually and not allow your emotions to get caught up because when you are emotional, you are easily manipulated, but now you are trying to be the manipulator.

Use Your Shadow Self

So here's what you should do you should try to do is to use your shadow self. Shadow self is the dark and the unseen side of everybody that the society doesn't validate or that we are too shy to express. For instance, if your guy tells that you that he wants to work in fashion, you can press on that weakness because it is his weakness, and it is his emotional underbelly. So when you use that thing that he exposes to you against him. When an animal goes hunting for meat, they don't target the tough part. They target the soft part, so that is the same thing you want to do. When you want to manipulate him, you should play into that.

You can also ask him to help you pick out your outfit or let you guys go into the house show or the fashion exhibit, so you should ask his opinion and make him feel valued in that category and make him feel like an expert. Build up his ego, and then you remove it. All this has to happen when you don't like him very much so that you will have him by the throat. So you have to be neutral and don't allow him to sense your weakness and then keep on pressing him. You have to know your own army, you have to know what is your shadow self.

You have to know what is not acceptable in your family, in your group of friends, in your hometown, or in your society. What are the things that people have rather overlooked in you? So you have to identify your shadow-self, and that is going to make you more bullet-proofed in terms of being manipulated because when somebody says something bad about you, you can say thank you. After all, you're not surprised, since it is not a hidden side of you.

Shift Your Shadow Self

Your shadow self can shift. So how do you do this for a fuckboy? Fuckboys are on up the whole bottle, and they are so hard to break. If you can get close enough to them to sense their weaknesses, you'll be able to overcome them. But first, you have to start with their family, you have to provide what his family did not provide for him, and you have to replicate the craziness in his family. But do it right.

Because normally, as human beings, we are not drawn to people who make us happy, but we are drawn to people who feel familiar. There have to be some elements of familiarity because if you grew up in a happy family, then he is familiar with happy things.

If you grow up in a toxic family, then it is not. That is why you see people in co-dependent relationships, whereby they are mutually abusive to each other, but both of them have refused to break up because it is familiar to them. If he didn't have stability with his family, then you should you can give it to him. For instance, if he is all by himself with his family and you decide to take care of him, he will be surprised, and he will become in the palm of your hand. He will do anything that you want him to do. Because as human beings, we move towards people who remind us of our most difficult parents because we are trying subconsciously to do the relationship over, fix it, and do it right. You also need to be very careful about your end game.

You shouldn't be too fixated on whether he likes you or not. So if you're trying to like get a guy to fall in love with you, then you will lose. You have to define what success looks like to you. If you want to get back to the relationship, you have to understand what the endpoint is. If not, you will just be going and going, and you will exhaust all your troops, and you will have a huge catastrophic loss of life. So you have to know what's the point is before you even know if you reach it. If your goal is to make your guy love you, then it is dangerous because you are emotionally caught up in it.

If you love him and he doesn't love you, then you're not in the position of power because he who cares the least wins. Now aside from the shadow self, you need to be able to engage in something called trauma bonding. It is very important to keep your enemy off and to keep your target and your own victim off so that they won't be able to predict your behaviors. If you're incredibly moody, you'll be very good at this. Be careful about what you are establishing. If you can establish a parent-child dynamic in your relationship, and then you become co-dependent, and that is not fun. Because you are just in the cycle of mutual manipulation, and it is really toxic.

To define what success, revenge, and destruction looks like to you and then work backward at it, and then when you reach that point you can capture the castle and retreat. Now revenge won't always feel as good as you think it will. It will feel good when it comes in terms of rivals and work, but with love, it is like a losing game, because you are emerging energy in attention that is no longer feeling you. You don't know what your last stand plan is, and that is not what you should be spending your time on.

Become Inconsolable

And if you guys are not talking, you become inconsolable, and when you guys are talking, you start seeing through time, and you'll become so happy and so addicted. And it goes on and on. It's like a psycho on drug use. So what you should learn is that you should give and you should take it. You should give him, and then you should take it away. One thing for you to do is be fun and engaging. Listen and then lie at the same time, and it will make a guy feel like a man.

You should know how to use charm and sweetness on him. So you should be wonderful when you're on a date, and you should be different when you're on a date. You shouldn't write back right away for him. You shouldn't reply back to him with emoji, but you should text him something at the last minute. You want him to get addicted to real life and not addicted to texting or to Snapchat because that is what builds a relationship. Don't DM you for 2 days straight. So you should give him and then withdraw and then try to create that trauma bond. So if you want to manipulate somebody, which is what you want to do.

So to recap, you want to hold on to somebody's shadow self and then replicate familiar patterns. But with the healthy spinner needs, and with this comes the resolution that they are looking for on a deep psychological level, and then you want to throw the bond, and you want to give him and then take it away. You want to overwhelm him with sensations of Flattery and that he's so smart.

Chapter 17: Power Techniques on Reading People

One of the most important skills you can learn knows how to read people. The best part is, just like any other skill, it can be learned and developed. You do not need to go to any particular school or have some form of training to hone your people-reading skills.

The art of reading people is a natural skill that people are born with. In all forms of social interaction, we are continually reading people and situations to make conclusions.

From reading the body language to decoding subtle signals of the eye, emotional intelligence, and learning to manage people, reading people is a pretty broad field.

It does take practice, commitment, and insight to be good at reading people. Besides, the ability to apply your people-reading skills to the world at large helps you get better at reading people.

The Importance of Reading People

The world is made of people. Life is better enjoyed when you have people to relate with. However, your survival in the world also depends on your ability to decide when not to cooperate with some people, and that is why your ability to read people is important.

There are times you are unconsciously cooperating with others. The fact that you walk gently to your place of work without causing a scene or doing anything to warrant unnecessary attention is an act of cooperation with the rest of the society on some levels. You don't just wake up one day and decide to go on a killing spree. You are connected to the Internet and the rest of the world alike. All these things require some form of human cooperation.

For this to take place, people unconsciously have to come to a reasonable form of agreement and acceptable behavior on some level. All in all, cooperating with people is pretty important, and your decision whether to cooperate or not comes down to your ability to read people.

The best salesman knows how to coax you because they are good at analyzing people. They can get you into buying what they have to offer, even if you do not need what they are offering. The better you are at reading other people's motives, the better you can deal with such a person.

The Natural Ability to Read People

As established above, the ability to read people is inherent in everyone. In all your day-to-day interaction with people, the following takes place:

You consciously judge them. In other words, you assess the way they dress, the way they look, and their overall appearance. You try to understand their motives and behaviors.

You consciously read them. In other words, you judge their body language and thinking about their appearance. This happens to anyone you are interacting with. You consciously examine a couple of things about them.

You give an appropriate response based on your assessment. This is after the first two steps above and just in the first minute of interaction.

Throughout the conversation or interaction, you evaluate the person consciously. This is the basic in which all forms of human interaction take place.

To explain the above, let us assume you are on a bus on your way to work, and a young guy walks up to you and says hello with a smile. Instantly, your brain starts analyzing him. You judge his overall body language and his looks. You give a general assessment of him to know whether he is a potential threat.

Even if the analysis and assessment are not conscious, your subconscious is busy doing it. Let us assume you reply with a "Hi" in a warm, friendly tone. This is a reciprocal behavior based on your assessment and reading of him.

Should you continue with the conversation, it will flow based on your words, behavior, and manners. Throughout the interaction, consciously and subconsciously, you still keep forming inferences.

Take, for instance, you want to have a meal. You enter a restaurant to buy a plate of food. Subconsciously, you must have scanned the environment and the people in it to decide whether it's safe before you sit down and eat. Even while eating, your subconscious is still busy assessing the environment for potential threats.

All in all, reading people is something we all do. It is an inherent ability that people possess. This skill was well developed by our ancestors, who constantly faced danger and had just a few seconds to pass someone off as a friend or foe.

The Art of Reading People

All the examples above point to the fact that we all read others, even though many people have this skill more developed than others. There are tips on reading people that you might not be able to figure out on your own. Some skills will prove really helpful in your job, your relationships, and all other aspects of life.

With time and experience, reading people becomes an easy job. You get to see beyond the mask people put forth. This will help you get to understand their behaviors, intentions, and beliefs.

Shall we get started on the art of reading people?

Understand the Basic Need of People

You need the knowledge of Maslow's hierarchy of needs for you to learn to read people. Maslow's hierarchy of needs is a simple model with a whole lot of practical information about human psychology. One of the essential things to keep in mind is that the motives and behaviors of people depend mainly on their basic needs and desires. Maslow's hierarchy of needs teaches that these needs and desires come from a ground up approach.

Maslow's hierarchy of needs starts from the bottom in which the person prioritizes meeting their psychology needs before any other thing. Hence, someone hungry might go to any extent to make sure the need is met. This is because every fiber of the person—the physiological processes in the body and the emotion—will scream against the person to compensate for the need.

People will try to act to fulfill their most pressing need, depending on how pressing the need is, the level on the chart, and the personality trait. This explains why a hungry man will either walk to a restaurant and pay for a plate of food or rob a store to get something to eat. The choice depends on that person's desperation, personality, and circumstance.

Based on Maslow's hierarchy of needs, physiological needs come first, followed by safety needs. This explains why emotions like anxiety, panic, and fear will rise if a person does not feel safe and secure.

Third on the list is love and security. This is true because many people will naturally want to seek love after they have their basic needs (safety and psychological) handled.

Finally, on the top of the pyramid, we have self-actualization and esteem needs. It is with this that a person's life has meaning. Here, people act to satisfy their ego. These needs are not critical to survival, although they help give life meaning.

Significance of Maslow's Hierarchy of Needs

All human behaviors can be interpreted in the light of this classification. You see this evident when people act emotionally or drastically. Hence, in a bid to read people, be sure to know the very need they are acting on and try to respond.

If you threaten someone's ego (self-esteem needs), do not be surprised if that person attacks you verbally, perhaps you have said something that made them feel terrible about their belonging in the world. The extent of their reaction, however, is a matter of their emotional state, self-esteem, and how likely they see you as a target.

You will see someone attack you when you threaten their sense of security. You might have passed a bad comment about a person concerning their job, and that person might interpret this as a threat to the security that comes from their job, thus attacking you fiercely.

As another instance, a man who is going for a visa interview and is running late will be furious at anyone that causing traffic. This person is trying to seek greener pastures in another country, which is his security, but he is faced with a credible obstacle in the form of traffic. The fear of missing out on the opportunity to migrate to another country fuels his anger, causing him to lash out at what is causing the traffic.

Know About Emotional Intelligence

The ability to understand others stems from the ability to understand oneself first. This calls for the development of your emotional intelligence. Emotional intelligence is a combination of a couple of skills, such as the following:

- how to manage your own emotions

- how to utilize your emotions to help fulfill your goal

- understanding other people's emotions

- ability to respond to other people's emotions accordingly

In developing your emotional intelligence, you have to understand that you are a rational being that has limitations. In other words, feelings will always come before thoughts.

Maslow's hierarchy of needs reflected this order very well. Security and physiology needs are at the bottom because this is how the brain evolved. We have self-actualization at the top since it is something we aim for when all the other needs are met. Emotions are critical to survival and reproduction. Here are some examples:

- Anger helps protect our ego and scare off threats.

- Fear is there to keep us alive, even if it means holding a man back.

- With love, we reproduce, protect, and provide for our offspring and loved ones.

- Anxiety and worry prepare us for perceived threats, real or imaginary, short-term, or long-term.

- Happiness rewards us for good behaviors and decisions.

This is how the human brain develops. It is more important to reproduce and survive than to reason. I bet you now understand why some people stay in an abusive relationship despite all physical and emotional threats. Emotions are powerful and easily seen. In a very emotional situation, usually, we suspend our thoughts and all rational thinking.

A student who failed the semestral exam, for instance, is going to be downcast. For days, even weeks, they are not going to think about any other thing except the failure. They will be upset about the situation, and a host of other emotions will follow.

Now here is the problem: There are times when emotions seem to be less noticeable. There are times when people do not feel emotional, yet their emotions still guide them without realizing it.

This explains why many novice investors do not realize that just a shred of optimism does affect their investment decision. All in all, emotions are strong and known to dictate one's actions. Thus, to control someone, all you have to do is manipulate their emotions.

This is one button terrific marketers know how to press. Great marketers know that people will hardly make a rational decision when buying; instead, they buy on emotions.

They have learned the act of playing and appealing to people's emotions for them to make a purchase.

In reading people, it is vital to understand that other people get emotional as you do, and some, more than you do. People's daily activities, decisions, etc. are all influenced by their emotions. The knowledge of someone's emotions and the implication it has is essential. Here are some instances:

- You do not want to ask someone that is upset for any favor.

- You can capitalize on someone's fear to make a sale.

- You might want to comfort someone sad.

- You will want to have sex with someone horny.

Chapter 18: Confidence and How It Is Displayed

Confidence is a very powerful emotion in today's society. An individual who appears very confident is able to go very far places. By appearing confident, a person can attract suitable mates as well as be given promotions based on their perceived leadership skills. Because of this, confidence is very commonly displayed in different ways. However, confidence is also faked a lot of times in order to get ahead in life. We will go through the common ways that confidence is displayed through body language. In addition, we will also go through how you can spot a lack of confidence in an individual.

Displaying Confidence

Posture

Posture is very important in the appearance of confidence. An individual's posture can say a lot about their perceived level of confidence. Confident posture is defined by legs that are lined up with the individual's shoulders and feet approximately four to six inches apart. Weight is typically distributed equally on both legs, and shoulders are pushed back slightly. A straight back is also very typical of someone with extreme confidence. Individuals with this sort of posture are considered assertive and tend to project confidence. This is because an individual with this posture is seen as being able to "stand tall" regardless of their height and are also perceived as being very open to those that are talking to them, as they are unafraid of any attacks or criticism.

Hands

Hands are very important in trying to appear confident. It is important to remember when trying to display confidence through your hands to keep them calm and still. Rapidly moving one's hands is a sign of nervousness or anxiety.

Eye Contact

Having the ability to maintain long and strong eye contact with another is a very good sign that an individual is feeling confident. This is because showing eye contact with another person is a very vulnerable feeling and position. This is because our eyes can show a lot about how we actually feel in a situation. By maintaining good eye contact, we are showing to the other person that we are unafraid of what they may see within our eyes. This is a sign of extreme confidence, as it shows that you are self-assured in your feelings and believes that you are unafraid of how a person will interpret what they see in your eyes.

Mirroring Body Language

Mirroring the body language of those around us elicits a sort of understanding and seeks acceptance from those around us. This raises our confidence level as we humans strive to be liked by those around us. Because those around us will subconsciously begin to like us more by mirroring their body language, they will also be confident because of their positive view of us.

Fidgeting

It is very important to remember not to fidget when you are trying to display levels of confidence. Fidgeting in any form—no matter what part of your body is doing the movement—shows signs of nervousness and anxiety. In addition to this, it can simply annoy those around us. People are often irritated by constant rhythmic tapping or brushing noises. This is something to keep in mind if you are an individual who likes to bounce their leg or tap their foot at simple moments.

Ways to Spot a Lack of Confidence in a Person

A very common sign of lack of confidence in an individual is if they are constantly touching their phone while in social situations or while alone. If an individual finds them unable to sit still during a social situation in which they don't know very many people, this may be a sign that they lack confidence.

Checking their phone is a sign that they feel uncomfortable in a social situation and are unable to connect with those around them.

Another sign of a lack of confidence in an individual is a quick backing down during a disagreement to avoid arguing with another person. An individual with an extreme lack of confidence will not want to cause problems with a person that they disagree with. Because of this, they often negotiate their views in order to avoid conflict. This shows that a person lacks confidence because they are not assured in their own opinions and would rather back down than express themselves honestly.

Another common sign of a lack of confidence in an individual is their inability to leave their homes without any sort of makeup or hairstyling. This is a very obvious sign of a lack of confidence because it shows that an individual doesn't feel that they are worth being looked at unless they have something on their bodies or face to make them look more beautiful. Putting makeup on or doing their hair gives a false sense of self-esteem to an individual, which people with low self-esteem or confidence rely on very heavily.

An individual with low confidence will also tend to take constructive criticism far too personally. If a person gives this individual constructive criticism about something, they will take it way too seriously and will end up feeling very strong negative emotions. This is a huge sign of low confidence and low self-esteem because this individual is not emotionally balanced enough to handle constructive criticism from those around them.

Individuals who have low confidence or self-esteem will also find themselves afraid to contribute their opinion in a conversation. They will often second-guess themselves before they say anything instead of diving into an interesting conversation. They may find themselves stuttering or putting themselves down. This is because these individuals don't know how well their opinions will be received and are afraid of other people taking their opinions negatively. This is a sign of low confidence or self-esteem because these individuals care very deeply about how the people they make contact with see them.

An individual who has difficulty with confidence also fined themselves extremely indecisive with very simple and basic decisions. They may change their minds very often after coming to a decision. This is a sign of low self-confidence because this individual cannot trust their own opinions or decisions. This is especially a sign of low self-confidence when this applies to very simple tasks or simple decisions.

Individuals with low self-confidence will also have extreme difficulty handling genuine compliments from those around them. They tend not to think that they are worthy of such good compliment, and they usually put them down or not accept them.

Individuals struggling with low self-confidence will also tend to give up very soon with things that they are trying to do or achieve. They may have goals and dreams that they want to accomplish but will give up before they even really begin. This is a sign of low self-confidence because they do not believe that they have the ability to accomplish these goals and dreams before they even start. Individuals that struggle with low self-confidence will also tend to compare themselves with those around them. They tend to have very strong attention to the people that are doing better than them and will point out all of the ways that they are not doing as well as those around them. This is a strong sign of low self-confidence because it says that the person in question does not view themselves as very successful or doing very well in their life.

Slouching is a very common display of low self-confidence in an individual. Why so? It is because lowering the center of a person's body is a sign that a person is not willing to hold up the weight of their upper body themselves. It sends off a signal that that individual is not proud of himself/herself. Because of these things, this is a big sign of low self-confidence.

In order to detect low self-confidence in an individual, all you have to do is look out for some of these common signs of low self-esteem and self-confidence. You can also detect low self-confidence or low self-esteem within yourself by looking out for these common signs. If you find that you or someone you know has low self-esteem or confidence, you can begin to work on them by saying very positive statements about yourself on a regular basis.

Chapter 19: Spot the Lie

Most people think that they are naturally good at detecting lies. Those people are wrong.

Studies show that the average person has only about a fifty percent chance of accurately detecting a lie. So, despite popular belief, people are not exceptionally good at detecting lies without very specific training in doing so. Paradoxically, however, people are generally quite good at telling lies, although they generally feel uncomfortable doing so. This means that with a working knowledge of and sufficient practice in observing the signs of discomfort commonly present in a liar, people can achieve a lie-detecting success rate of approximately eighty percent, despite our genetic predisposition towards the contrary.

For our purposes, a lie is defined as any statement made either physically or verbally or any omission intentionally made in order to dispossess another of knowledge of the truth.

There are four types of liars. They are: the Hobbyist, the Regular, the Habitual, and the Expert.

The Hobbyist will only lie occasionally in order to avoid embarrassment, uncomfortable situations, or admitting that they were wrong. The hobbyist has not developed a particular comfort with lying, so he will be the easiest of the four to spot through body language, voice, and appearance.

The Regular lies more frequently than the Hobbyist and has therefore developed a greater degree of comfort with the practice. Because the Hobbyist is comfortable with lying, their body language, voice, and appearance will not as readily reveal that lies are being told. To catch a Regular in the act, your best bet is to focus on logical inconsistencies and contradictions in the words they use.

The Habitual liar lies so much that often times they do not even realize that they are lying. A Habitual liar will seldom, if ever, give any behavioral or vocal clues that a lie is being told. However, because the Habitual liar lies so much, there are usually a lot of lies for this person to keep track of. Like catching a Regular, the best way to catch a Habitual liar is by pointing out logical inconsistencies and contradictions in their statements.

The Expert is the liar that lies with a purpose and is almost impossible to identify. This person will tell lies that have been thoroughly thought through and will not contain any logical inconsistencies or contradictions. This person will also not indicate that they are lying through body language, voice, or appearance. In order to tell if an Expert is lying, you will need to verify this person's story or statements with an independent third party that is capable of doing so. For example, if a realtor tells you that the foundation of a house is in pristine condition, and you have reason to believe you are dealing with an Expert liar, get your own housing inspector to take a look at the foundation and tell you what the actual situation is.

The first step in trying to determine whether someone is lying to you is to identify if that person has a motive to lie, then to ask yourself what that motive might be. If you determine that a person has the motivation to lie, then you can begin looking for both verbal and nonverbal cues that will tell you if the person with whom you are speaking to is in fact being deceitful.

It is important to note also that most people believe it is easier for them to spot a lie coming from someone that is close to them, such as a friend, child, or partner, than it would be if the lie were coming from a complete stranger.

In order to be successful in detecting lies, then you will need to be objective when assessing each person. "Objective assessment" here means approaching the person in question with an open mind as to their guilt or innocence, while at the same time analyzing both their verbal and nonverbal mannerisms for indications of deception.

Detecting a Lie: The Process

When analyzing whether someone is lying, it is important to employ a simple and specific formula in order to increase the accuracy of that analysis and to prevent inaccurate conclusions. The formula is:

- Is there a motive?
- Establish a baseline.
- Ask incriminating questions.
- Check for signs of deceit.
- Double check.

1. Is There a Motive?

The first question to ask yourself when assessing whether a lie is being told is, "Does this person have a reason to tell a lie?"

Most people, even liars, like to think of themselves as fairly honest people. However, studies have shown that sixty percent of people lie approximately once in every ten minutes of conversation.

At first glance, this statistic paints a pretty bleak picture of human nature. The bleakness of that picture is tempered when we take into account the fact that not all lies are negative and destructive. For the purposes of our discussion, lies can be of one of two camps. Lies can either be ego-centric or altruistic.

Ego-centric lies are, as the name suggests, lies that are told with the express intention of assisting the liar in one way or another, whereas altruistic lies are lies that are more often told for the benefit of someone that is not the liar themselves.

Altruistic lies are the "little white lies" that we are all familiar with, the motivation behind them being to protect or benefit some other person in one way or another. These lies are generally told with pure intentions under circumstances in which, if the truth were to be uncovered, it would not be very detrimental for the recipient of the false information. These lies are generally encouraged by society and demanded by etiquette and therefore are not generally the type of lie people tend to discourage. Examples of situations in which one might use an altruistic lie are those in which the person asking the question is not necessarily interested in the truth, such as: "Does this dress make me look fat?", "Isn't my baby the cutest?", "How did you like my cooking?" "Do I look like I have gained weight?" "Do you like my new suit?" etc. When these questions are asked, the person asking is not necessarily looking for the truth but for affirmation. Altruistic lies are also employed automatically to general questions such as "How are things?", "How's your family been?" "How have you been doing?" etc. The general response to these questions is "fine," despite the fact that your entire family may be ill, you may have been laid off a month ago, and your car may have just gotten totaled. Regardless of what the honest answers to these questions are, most people will respond "fine" as an acknowledgment of the courtesy given by the asker, since the person asking is really only extending a courtesy and not looking for a completely honest answer. There are, after all, only so many hours in a day!

As you can see, while altruistic lies are most certainly lies insofar as they are told with the intention of depriving someone of the truth, it is difficult to shake a finger at those who tell these sorts of lies. In fact, there is a generally held societal expectation that certain altruistic lies will be told fairly regularly. To see why, think about what would happen to your social life and charisma if you were to be one-hundred percent honest to everyone with whom you interacted for one week. Odds are you would not have as many people to interact with the week after that. Ego-centric lies are the lies that most people want to watch out for. These are the lies that are told for the protection or benefit of the liar. Studies have shown that approximately half of all lies told are of this type. People will generally tell ego-centric lies for one of four reasons, either to:

- Prevent embarrassment;

- Make a positive impression;

- Gain some sort of advantage; or

- Evade some kind of punishment

Preventing embarrassment is probably the least harmful motivation for telling an ego-centric lie, and lies told to prevent the liar from being embarrassed are generally not detrimental to those being deceived.

Telling an ego-centric lie in order to make a positive impression is usually a result of the liar's insecurities that make the liar feel as though they need to exaggerate certain aspects of themselves. We all have been known to add some spice to our stories or accomplishments for the sake of keeping things interesting. There are some, however, who feel the need to conjure complete fabrications with the intention of impressing other people. Internet dating is one medium in which people will frequently lie in order to create a favorable impression, fabricating personal aspects of themselves such as yearly income, the type of car one drives, familial accomplishments, one's position in a company, nature, and extent of involvement in community associations, or the presence and extent of interests in a particular topic. The list goes on and on.

Lying to gain some sort of advantage is an extreme form of making a positive impression and can be just as extreme in the harm it can cause. When someone lies to gain an advantage, which is a lie, you will probably want to spot. Examples of this type of lie include inventing circumstances to induce someone to give you financial assistance, spreading false rumors about another in order to make yourself look better, making false claims on a resume or job application, etc.

When lying to evade punishment, a person's attempts to lie will be directly proportionate to the potential consequences of being found out. If the consequences are great, the lie will be equally intricate and forceful.

Studies have shown that ninety percent of lies are told with both verbal and nonverbal cues that can be detected by someone who knows what to look for. So, if you determine that someone has a motive to lie to you, you can then stop speculating and start looking for actual indicators that a lie is being told.

2. Establish a Baseline

When trying to determine whether someone is telling a lie, you will first need to establish a baseline for that person's behavior.

Everyone is a distinct individual with their own distinct peculiarities. Consequently, while speaking in generalizations does help in analyzing a person, they can only operate as guidelines, since each individual will react to situations differently. How, then, does one go about determining what a person's behavioral baseline is?

In order to establish a baseline of behavior for a particular individual, you will need to carefully note that person's responses, both verbal and nonverbal, to a set of questions to which you already have an answer or to which you know the person will provide an honest answer. These will constitute your "Control Questions." While the person is answering your Control Questions, watch for and remember their verbal and nonverbal behavior, as you will be comparing the person's responses to these "Control Questions" with their responses to your incriminating questions.

3. Ask Incriminating Questions

Once you have gotten a flavor of the person's individual mannerisms, it is then time to ask your incriminating questions. Obviously, in order to spot a lie, you need to provide an opportunity for the lie to be told. You can provide this opportunity by asking questions that will give the person the choice of whether to answer honestly or dishonestly. It is important to remember here that a person's cognitive response will try and employ measures to counteract their nervous response, so you do not want to give them the opportunity to fortify their defenses. Depriving the person of the opportunity to shore up their defenses is best done by introducing your incriminating questions subtly and as a normal part of the conversation.

4. Check for sign of deceit

-Eyes- The liar usually doesn't like to keep his eyes in touch with yours, he knows that it is dangerous: "Eyes are the mirror of the soul." He thinks who lies. So he'll look over here and over there, on the ground or on the top. But be careful, it's not always like that, sometimes liars who know the secrets of body language do the opposite. I mean, they'll look you in the eye, like to see if their lie is working or to look more credible.

-Non verbal communication - Liars are sometimes agitated, blink their eyes quickly and more often, smile less (to look more credible), have small changes in the tone of voice or only talk slower than usual

Some liers can shake a part of their body, for example, beat a foot on the ground all the time. Sometimes liars start to touch their face or their mouth, ears or nose or play with keys or other items that hold in their hand. You just remember: body language does not lie!

-Liers love to add useless details- Those who lie think enriching their story will make it more credible.

-The micro expressions of liars- A micro expression is a very short expression of body language, often lasts about a quarter of a second. Micro expression is always a revealing of hidden emotion. It can be half a smile that lasts just for a second or a second anxious look.

In other words, when someone acts like he's happy, but he's actually very angry about something, his real emotion will be revealed in a subconscious flash of anger on his face. No matter what emotion is, it can be anger, fear, jealousy, or happiness. What's interesting is that emotion seems to be looking for a moment of rash on the person's face in an instant, this is a micro-expression.

5. Double check

In case you didn't spot the lie or the liar just didn't shows you any sign of deceit, you can ask to the liar to repeat the story; remember: liars hate to repeat their lies. And so you can check again if they will have some more "trips" in their body language to detect.

Chapter 20: Understanding Psychopaths

Psychopaths have three parts of the dark triad; they are easily at the top of the list for whom to look out for, especially if you yourself are not one. However, the first interesting thing to note is that while all psychopaths are narcissistic, narcissists are not necessarily going to be psychopathic. Knowing this may be one of the weaknesses that may allow you to spot a psychopath if you find yourself crossing paths with one.

Psychopathy is identified as Antisocial Personality Disorder (APD). It has a lot of characteristics that, similar to narcissism, tend to be misconstrued by the public. This is often due to ignorance or misinformation, like that of the psychotic serial killer one sees in Hollywood movies. While this image isn't entirely untrue, largely due to the fact that these people are the most likely within the dark triad to become abusers and serial killers, many psychopaths are actually very good at blending into society. In fact, psychopaths are often well educated and intelligent.

Regardless of how well they blend into society, there is a way to help unearth the truth about them. Firstly, they will often have the same grandiose sense of self mixed in with compulsive lying and highly manipulative behavior that shows no regard for morality or the wellbeing of others. For one thing, research shows that they tend to be born the way they are. This means that your average psychopath educated or not will probably show a history of bad behavior from an early age. They may even have a criminal record.

Examples of Psychopaths from the History

Brain scans carried out on psychopaths show that the parts of the brain that are activated when most people feel stress, guilt, or empathy remain inactive when they are given stimuli that are meant to trigger these kinds of feelings (MedCircle, 2018). Their very autonomic system (which is largely responsible for reflective responses like the fight or flight and the immune system, etc.) are wired differently from most peoples. Depending on the kind of psychopath, you will find that they often excel and be found in higher concentrations in occupations such as lawyers, stockbrokers, assassins, salespeople, surgeons, and (quite surprisingly) chefs.

How Do They Operate?

High functioning - while people think that the term psychopathy is monolithic, it actually has two subcategories that are important to understand if one is to know what to look out for, the first of these being the high functioning psychopath.

These people are just more controlled and calculating. They are far less likely to become serial killers and rather channel that energy into something else, like their careers. In fact, these kinds of psychopaths are far more likely to be seen occupying high power jobs like CEOs of companies.

Don't think this makes them anything like the rest of society. These people are still vicious predators who will eliminate anyone in their way with a ruthlessness most people are not capable of. They aren't afraid to go as far as commit murder or ruin a business at the cost of countless people losing their livelihoods. They are incapable of remorse or shame and will not lose any sleep over their actions.

Low functioning - these are more the types we see in the slasher movies in theaters. The low functioning psychopath usually has a much more difficult time managing their instincts and emotions, so they are far more likely to become serial killers. However, they just don't operate the way most people would imagine.

They are more likely to draw their victims in with charm or glibness. This is when they prepare to ruin their target's life. They are still calculating but don't have the ability to redirect those instincts the way their high functioning counterparts do.

They still tend to be very good at concealing their true selves under a veil of normalcy. They are great liars, so leading a double life is not difficult for them. They are typically also well educated, so hiding their actions is no great feat since psychopaths generally seem to be intelligent people. So, don't count on them giving themselves away so easily.

What Can We Learn from Them?

Now as dangerous as the psychopath might be, regardless of their specific brand of crazy, they are not to be ignored. They have a lot to teach, especially for those who are looking for upward mobility in life. These skilled predators among us are good to study for multiple reasons, the most obvious one probably being one's own safety.

While they only make up about 1% of any given population, you will find that it still makes a lot of people when you consider how many people there are on planet earth. This means that there is a very good chance that everyone will meet at least one psychopath in their life. So, it probably for the best that you know how to identify them and act accordingly for your own best interest and for that of those close to you.

One of the best things we can learn from psychopaths is their ability to detach their emotions from any action. While this cannot be mastered to the same degree by most people, it can be adopted to a certain extent. Finding detachment from the things and people around us can be a great end in itself. One does not need to become cold to everything, and everyone they know and love. It is good enough that one simply learns to embrace solitude so that they can focus more on their own self-interest.

Chapter 21: Mind Control Tactics

With a basic understanding of what mind control entails, you are then ready to move on to the tactics involved in mind control. These are particularly dangerous, especially in conjunction with the steps to priming the target for mind control. This is best done when an individual has already had their own sense of self-esteem eroded down enough for them to be relatively malleable. When this is done, they are far more susceptible to the rest of the priming and the techniques that will be used. Remember, this is absolutely an unethical practice. There is very little way to spin this to be positive in any way. This is always detrimental to the target involved and absolutely can cause irreparable damage if done. Nevertheless, we shall delve into the steps involved in gaining control of someone else's mind, as well as the methods typically utilized.

Steps to Mind Control

Develop Trust

The first step to set up control over someone else's mind is to develop trust. You cannot mind control someone else without first developing the trust necessary for the rest of the steps to follow without detection. You can utilize mirroring and other body languages in conjunction with love bombing or other manipulation tactics to create an artificial relationship. Regardless of how you do it, you must make sure the person you seek to control trusts you.

Destroy the Old Personality

Once you have established the relationship sufficiently, it is time to move on to the next step. Here, you need to essentially destroy the individual's old personality. This is absolutely essential since without this, you cannot create the pseudo-personality that is meant to be loaded up with your own thoughts and beliefs rather than those of the individual you have targeted.

To destroy the old personality, you must convince them that their old personality is flawed in some way. This is why someone with low self-esteem is so much easier to overtake than someone who is confident. When you are able to convince someone that they are inherently broken, flawed, or weak, they are more likely to enter a stage of questioning and doubt in their own identity.

Debilitation

With the individual busy questioning who they are and what they want in life, you are then able to move on to the debilitation stage. While not strictly necessary, especially if the person you are attempting to manipulate was already particularly malleable as an individual, when you debilitate your target, you make them far more susceptible to your own manipulation and thoughts and feelings you wish to install. This can be done through several methods—sleep deprivation, abuse, poor diets, drugs, or even physical or sexual assault. Anything to weaken the person as a whole and enable them to be more easily controlled goes here.

Personality Insertion

Through many of the mind control tactics that will be listed below, you will be able to understand exactly how you can insert the personality of what you want into the other person. Thought control, such as limiting choices and repetition and reinforcement, could slowly impose your own thoughts and beliefs into the other person, slowly becoming internalized until the other person believes them as well or thinks he or she believes them.

Testing Your Control

That's it! With those steps, the other person should be within your control. The particular methodology you will use within each step depends on your particular target. You will need to ensure that the methods you choose to use match up with who you want to control and how you want them to behave. You can now test your control through methods such as testing to see emotional reactions or watching to make sure that you have thoroughly conditioned the person to go through with whatever it is you want.

Methods of Mind Control

Now that you have a general idea of the steps to mind control, you can begin to understand the actual methods used, take a close look at each of these methods of mind control.

Repetition and Reinforcement

Repetition and reinforcement utilize the idea that if you say something to someone enough, they will begin to internalize it, this is what many people use to utilize affirmations, and it absolutely works in the negative as well. Through this method, you can convince other people to behave in ways you never thought possible, simply by inserting your own thoughts into their minds and making them think they were their own. This is perfect for inserting a pseudo-personality to replace the personality of the individual you are controlling.

Limiting Choices Available

Limiting choices available is another way to insert thoughts—you can sway the direction someone is thinking by making them think that they must choose between an artificially created false dichotomy and limited selection.

Think of how you can give a child the illusion of a choice by providing them with a few choices that you approve of rather than letting them make the decision themselves, such as asking whether the child wants carrots or broccoli with dinner instead of asking if the child wants veggies for dinner. You can do this with adults as well—by implying that there are only a few choices that are acceptable to you, the other person's thoughts are limited just enough to be acceptable to you, no matter which choice is made.

Sleep Deprivation

When you need to break someone down, sleep deprivation is one of the easiest ways to do so. Through sleep deprivation, with as little as 21 hours being necessary before signs of impairment become apparent, you are able to make someone far more susceptible to manipulation.

If you can keep someone awake long enough, you will be able to subsequently control them simply because they are already exhausted and ready to pass out. They are not going to have the mental fortitude to defend them.

Chapter 22: Dark Psychology Steps

Do you know that when you first start to crack open yours and others' mentality, it will be easier to pick up on little cues as you go along? Remember that it will always be a practice. At first, you might think that you can make easy assumptions and that you have it all figured out. There will always be layers to all of the truths you are uncovering. You might have realized that someone was manipulating you but look deeper. Why were they doing so? How did this affect you? What can you do to recover?

There are still some steps here that you can understand to better avoid being manipulated and, if you choose to, use for your own purposes. That is not advised, but then again, we can't manipulate you into not being a manipulator. We can remind you that doing these things will never give you what you want. They might seem to at first, but you are filling a hole with all the wrong things. Eventually, you are going to need more power and more control. You will be addicted to the ability to manipulate others, and the simple things won't get you "high" anymore. You'll have to keep looking further and further for more ways that you can gain power over other people, and this is only going to hurt you the most in the end. You should never take advantage of someone else, but in harmless settings, such as getting something small you want or maybe closing a business deal, you can use these tactics. Perhaps you want to ask your parents for some money, so you do the persuasion preparation method. Maybe you are trying to get others to buy your company's flood insurance, so you use the fear and relief method. As long as you aren't maliciously trying to take from others, you can be assured that your persuasion is positive.

Victimization

There are true victims in the world. Though we all have choices we can make, those that are abusive can take this ability away from their victims. They will replace their victims' own thoughts with thoughts of their own, making the abused feel trapped and helpless. To be a victim isn't a bad thing at all. Not everyone will be able to help themselves from falling into the web of lies and deceit that many abusers create to trap their victims.

This method is especially useful for those manipulators who will see the good in other people. They will be able to see that desire to care for others and use that to their advantage. You can tell if someone is actually a victim or if they are playing the part by how they respond to compassion or care that might be directed toward them. If they are a real victim, they will be appreciative and receptive to the care. They will use it as a way to help themselves feel better, and they will have a strong desire to work through their issues. Those who use victimization will take care of everything they can. They won't want to change and will instead do their best to make others feel as bad as possible about hurting them. This method isn't going to work out in the long-run. People eventually grow tired of those that constantly put themselves in the middle of the drama. They will start to easily see through the wall of victimization that has been created and understand the intrinsic manipulation that has existed.

Fear and Relief

Fear and relief is the method of making someone scared, and then being the one to provide the solution. It is like pushing someone off a cliff and then being the one to reach your hand out and save them just before it is too late. The idea of the manipulation here is to help show that you are a vessel for comfort. The part of you that created the fear in the first place is often overlooked and not always realized initially. This is common in long-term relationship abuse situations. Think of a parent who always terrifies the child about the outside world. They might tell scary stories of all that could happen if the child were to ever leave home. Perhaps they are giving the child wild ideas about the outside world. But the parent will still act as the savior, making sure that the child always stays close by. They will use bad situations to validate their reasoning as well. A child might feel trapped by their parents, one day deciding to sneak out at night. They might end up getting into trouble, and when that is revealed to the controlling parent, they might say something like, "See, I told you something bad would happen!"

This is a tactic that is often used by advertisers as well. It is less harmful in this scenario and would be the method that you might use should you be selling something that would help to alleviate a person's fear. For example, a plumbing company might share a scary fact about frozen pipes during the winter season, helping to sell more high-quality pipes and replacement services. You might not have initially been thinking about frozen pipes, but now you are, so you want to buy their service. It's not totally vindictive, as it could be a real problem that can be prevented. If you feel as though someone is trying to manipulate you with this method, make sure that you are first aware of the threat that they're trying to make you believe. Are they inflating the issue? Is it really something that you need to spend time being afraid of? Are you in the middle of manipulation, or are you actually enlightened now by this new, fearful information?

The thing is that the abuser will never be the aggressor. They want to show compassion. They won't be evil and scary in this situation because they are trying to show the abused that fear is an outside source. They desire to be the ultimate point of comfort, so they won't show their aggressive side, as that would then make them too scary to be dependable.

If used in a gentle way, this method will not be so damaging. You should just focus on showing them the ways that you can help offer solutions for the true threat that already exists. Don't use fear alone to make them buy something. Use awareness to help enlighten them as to why it would be beneficial for them to invest in your product.

Sometimes, there is good news and bad news in a situation. It is important that you state the bad news first and then the good news. This can be your way of using the fear and relief method.

Think of the way that a doctor would tell patients about certain health conditions and frame it in a way that will actually get the patient to do what they need to do in order to improve their health.

For example, let's say that a patient is at risk for heart disease because they don't exercise and eat really unhealthily. The bad news is that they are a high-risk patient. The good news is that this can be reversed with a healthy diet and exercise. There are a few ways that this can be framed in order for the doctor to have a positive influence and actually get what he wants from this scenario. Here are the two alternative methods:

- "Unfortunately, we've discovered that you are a high risk for heart failure and other cardiovascular conditions. These kinds of conditions can be very risky, and with your age and health status, they won't be so easily reversed. You can seriously reduce your risk and prevent these from happening if you start on the DASH diet and exercise at least three times a week."

- "It looks like you're going to have to start eating healthier and exercising. If you don't, you make your chances of having heart failure higher than they already are."

The first one is going to work out better for the patient and will likely have a higher chance of actually influencing them in the right direction. The first one lays out a fear. It paints a really serious situation that could scare the patient. However, then the solution is offered, and the patient's fear is reduced, making them more likely to continue with whatever will make them feel better.

The second one kind of paints both as "bad news." It discusses first what the patient has to do and then follows with even more bad news. They are likely going to leave the appointment feeling bad about themselves and hopeless, whereas the first has a higher chance of inspiring positive influence into that patient.

Likability and Flirtation

If you want people to trust you, then it is important that you are likable. This is so much easier said than done! Many of us have been trying since before junior high to try and get people to like us. However, don't fear! Now that we are older and more emotionally aware, it's going to be a lot simpler to really see the ways that we can get others on our side.

This is a harmless method for you to use! If you are truly charming, then others will be able to like you more. If you are a likable person, that will involve you being kind, funny, smart, and compassionate.

None of these are bad, so of all the methods in the book, this is the best one for you to use with others. The biggest thing you will have to be sure of is that you aren't losing yourself or your happiness in the process.

If you are bad at being charming and people can see through your flirting, then only you will be the one suffering in the end. You might be able to charm some people, but there will still be the experts that can cut right through the façade.

Start first by making sure that your emotional reactions are under control. If you are someone who reacts angrily to news or can't handle the slightest change in a schedule, then it might be a little more challenging for others to get along with you.

Be very aware of the way that your face might appear to others. We're not talking about having an ugly or pretty face, of course. Keep your eyebrows relaxed with a slight smile. If you show happiness and positivity on your face, more people will be likely to respond.

Use open body language and engage with them in conversation. Don't just talk about yourself. Be giving and caring. Go out of your way to do things for them, no matter how small.

Have an overall positive attitude and always look on the bright side. Don't force this positivity on others, of course. If someone is in a bad mood, don't tell them to "suck it up, things can be worse!" That's true, but that's not going to help them. Instead, say something like, "I'm sorry you're going through that. Things will get better, and I'm here to help if you need me."

Don't be afraid to show your passionate and enthusiastic side. Some individuals get scared of showing their vulnerability because that means they might look weak to others. Don't let this stop you from sharing the love that you have and that others deserve.

Get creative with the compliments you give. Don't just pick up on one-liners from others that you hear. If you really want to be charming, it's time for you to get creative and come up with some substantial ways of impressing other people.

Chapter 23: Conversational Skills Techniques

Do you wish that you could ever have a conversation with a person that you have never met before, and they automatically like you?

Take a moment to think about people in your life who seem to always bring the best out of you whenever you have a conversation with them. You feel comfortable talking with them, and you could continue talking with them forever. They could be somebody that you have known your whole life or somebody you have just met, but the conversation flows naturally and smoothly.

If you wish you could have this natural ability, don't worry. There are ways to give you this ability. You can be in control of a conversation and gain the interest of others. Now, while I may use the word control, I don't mean that you are the one constantly talking and "controlling" everything. I simply mean that you know how to work a conversation so that it continues flowing naturally. The most important factors in a good conversation are active listening, show curiosity, and keeping the sarcasm to a minimum.

But to give you a good start, here are a few conversation tips:

1. Make the conversation about the other person.

Have you ever had the misfortune of sitting through a conversation with somebody who went on and on about something that you didn't have the slightest interest in? You likely felt wiped out by the end of the conversation, and it probably felt like they were talking to themselves. They are oblivious to the idea that you might not be interested in what they like.

The best conversations tend to be the ones that show an interest in the listener, their interest, and their world. Most people like to talk about themselves. Take the time to ask them an open-ended question about something that you may have noticed. If you make sure that you give them positive feedback or a sincere compliment, you will have made a great start. Conversationalists are sincerely interested in other people, take the time to notice things, and use that information to fuel and start their conversations.

2. Take the conversation deeper.

Think about the people in your life that you are most willing to open yourself up to and share things with them. What about them makes you comfortable disclosing personal things that you wouldn't typically tell others?

More than likely, they always make eye contact, and they make you feel as if you are getting their full attention. Pay attention to expressions that they make. Notice how they are completely with you, not only in what they say but in their facial expressions. They look happy when you share something that you are excited or happy about. They will look solemn when you share something that is sad. You are able to feel that they are completely into everything you are saying.

If trying to emulate what they do seems unnatural, continue to practice this, and push yourself until you have learned how to. You will start to notice that other people will react differently when talking with you.

3. Ask them good questions.

You can get other people to share more by showing them that you are interested by asking them questions. This will help the conversation to move deeper. Some good questions are asking them how they feel or think about something that they have been talking about.

4. Take into consideration the time and space.

Don't bring a conversation beyond pleasantries unless you know that you have time to listen to the person. Places that are loud with a lot of other people aren't the best to get into a good conversation. To have a good conversation, you need a slow and relaxed environment without a bunch of pressure and distractions. Coffee shops are good for conversations. Sports bars aren't.

Show Curiosity

Having a real conversation means that you have created a space for understanding. Real conversations give you a place for learning, and it helps to promote the deepening and nurturing of relationships. The most important of all is that real conversations feed our souls in ways that many other things can't. So, improving your ability to grow, maintain, and create real conversations is a skill that needs to be practiced, whether you are coming from it as a friend, spouse, child, colleague, or parent. One habit that can help you to nurture a real conversation in any area of your life is curiosity. Curiosity tends to be associated with children or highly creative adults. But curiosity is an important and fundamental quality that is needed for anybody interested in lifelong learning. There are four areas in conversations that curiosity helps with.

1. When curious, we ask questions.

Alright, who are the most curious humans on Earth? Kids. What is that they do ad nauseam? Ask questions. What is it that will keep interactions with others from developing into a conversation? No questions.

When you have a conversation and you say something, and they say something but no questions are asked, you might experience an exchange, but it doesn't go much deeper than that, does it? If you really want to stimulate the conversation, don't just create points and opinions, instead create questions about things that you would like to learn. If you ever start feeling like you are talking too much, shift the conversation, and ask them a question.

2. When curious, we listen for the answers.

Asking questions may be important, but having a barrage of questions thrown at you can feel like an inquisition. What takes us from an inquisition to a conversation is that after you ask a question, shut up, and listen. If you really want to learn the answer, you will listen to their response because you want to know. The main reason why real conversations are able to improve relationships is that they require a person to actively listen.

3. When curious, we are interested.

Curiosity is what drives interest. Think about classes you did well in school and those you didn't. What was the difference? My guess is you found some interesting and others, not so much. Being interested makes you want to learn more.

This happens with conversations as well. When you are actually interested in the conversation, asking questions and listening for their answers get easier.

4. When curious, we want to learn.

When you are ready to learn, you put yourself in a place to engage in conversation for the purpose of learning, not just feeling like you have to get through it.

With these four things; questions, listening, interest, and a desire to learn, you can create a conversation and get all of the benefits from it.

Active Listening

Listening is one of the most important things you can do. How well you are able to listen can impact your life in many areas. Since we listen so much, you would think that we are amazing at it. Actually, most people aren't, and research suggests that most people only remember around 25 to 50 percent of everything that we hear. This means that when you have a conversation with your significant other for about ten minutes, they are paying attention to less than half of what is being said.

If you flip this around, it also means that when you are being given directions, you don't hear the full message. You hope that the most important parts are held within that 25-50 percent, but what happens if they weren't?

Clearly, listening is something that everybody needs to improve. When you become a better listener, you will also see improvement in your productivity, your influence, and your negotiation. What's more, you will be able to avoid conflict and other misunderstandings.

The only way to improve your listening abilities is to practice active listening. This means that you are making a conscious effort to hear the words that are being said as well as the complete message that they are communicating. To do this, you have to carefully pay attention to the speaker.

You can't become distracted by whatever else may be happening around you or by thinking about what you are going to say next. You also got to make sure you stay engaged so that you don't end up losing focus. To improve your listening skills, you have to let the other person know that you are actually listening to what is being said.

To fully understand the importance, think about a time where you have had a conversation and ever wondered if the person was listening to what you were telling them. You wonder if they understand your message or if it is even worth continue to talk. You feel as if you are talking to a brick wall. Acknowledging what a person is saying can be as easy as nodding your head or simply saying, "uh huh." This doesn't mean that you are agreeing with what they are saying; you are just letting them know that you are hearing them. Body language and other nonverbal cues let them know that you are listening and can help you to pay attention. In order to become an active listener, there are five techniques that you should try.

1. Pay Attention

Make sure that you are giving the speaker your full attention and acknowledge what they are trying to tell you. Understand that nonverbal language also speaks volumes. To show attention:

• Make eye contact

• Push aside distracting thoughts

• Don't mentally think about what you are going to say

• Avoid letting the environment distract you

• "Listen" to their nonverbal cues

2. Show Them You Are Listening

You can also use your own body language and gestures to let them know that you are engaged in the conversation.

- Nod occasionally

- Smile and use other positive facial expressions

- Keep your posture interested and open

- Encourage them to continue by making small comments

3. Provide Feedback

Our beliefs, judgments, assumptions, and filters can distort the things that we hear. Being the listener, you are there to understand what they are saying. This can sometimes require you to reflect on what they are saying and ask a few questions.

- To reflect, begin your statement with, "What I'm hearing is..." or "Sounds like you are saying..."

- Ask them clarifying questions to make sure you understand things

- Summarize what they are saying from time to time

4. Defer Judgment

Interrupting isn't helpful and just wastes time. It also frustrates the speaker, and it prevents you from understanding the message. Let them finish their entire point before you ask them any questions.

5. Sarcasm

Sarcasm, by definition, is "the use of irony to mock or convey contempt."

There are people in everybody's life who love to use little sarcastic and passive-aggressive modes of communication.

They think their sarcasm is well-meaning, but based on research, sarcasm is simply thinly veiled meanness.

Sarcasm is basically a way to cover up hate or contempt. It is a quick way to ruin a conversation as well. But why do people use sarcasm?

Insecurity

When a person uses a sarcastic tone, they are trying to hide insecurity about something. Some use sarcasm or teasing to avoid confrontation because they are afraid to actually ask for what they want.

Social Awkwardness

When people aren't that great at reading people around them, or they aren't sure how to carry on a conversation will sometimes use sarcasm to try and sound affectionate or playful. This is simply another version of insecurity, but this is common to hear at parties or other types of events. They will use it to try to lighten the mood; unfortunately, it will often have the opposite effect.

Chapter 24: Psychological Warfare

Everyone out there is trying to make a name for them. Sadly, success comes at a great cost. And this is exactly why many people are ready to take short cuts in order to accomplish their goals. People with the Dark Triad traits are remorseless when it comes to exploiting various avenues that will lead them into glory. They look at other human beings as vessels to be exploited so as to hasten their success.

One of the major methods that people use to advance their causes is psychological warfare. It is the practice of manipulating others at the mind level so that they can do your bidding. The following are some of the techniques involved in psychological warfare:

The Spread of Misinformation

In most instances, when you are up against someone else and are both battling for the prize, misinformation comes into play. This is whereby each person tries to discredit the other person. Thus, they are ready to speak falsities and engage in inappropriate behaviors so that they can mislead everyone else. By making people misinformed, you make them reach erroneous assumptions, which turn everything upside down. Machiavellians, Psychopaths, and Narcissists are particularly good at misinforming others, as it helps them own the narrative and gain power over everybody else. In the long run, misinformation leads people to make wrong decisions and causes suffering. But then people with the Dark Triad traits wouldn't care about the negative effects of their actions.

Deception

In the case of misinformation, a person ensures that they throw in some amount of truth, at least to make the story believable. But when it comes to deception, it is a matter of outright lies, without regard for people's ability to think critically. One of the careers with the most deceptive people is politics. When a politician takes the stage to address the crowd, they might go about spitting lies, knowing that is what people want to hear all along. A lie can only lead you down the path of frustration and bitterness. People with the Dark Triad traits are pathological liars. This means they lie even when they have no reason to. They like deceiving people so that they can remain in control and achieve their heart desires. This habit of telling lies causes them to step on many toes and pit many people against them. Although deception might make a person keep power to themselves, in the long run, it turns everyone against you.

Guilt-tripping

Another method that people use to get their way is the practice of guilt-tripping others. They want others to feel guilty because of the state that they are trapped in. Narcissists are especially fond of guilt-tripping people in order to get their way. If they want something, and it appears that the other party is not open to that, the narcissist might start reminding the other person of various things that are supposed to make them guilty. They know that by making someone guilty they can be able to get their way. The irony is that people with the Dark Triad traits hardly ever fall to attempts of guilt-tripping, yet they are so good at performing it.

Humiliation

One of the experiences that most humans avoid is humiliation. It can affect your self-esteem and trigger insecurities. Yet Narcissists, Psychopaths, and Machiavellians use it as one of their favorite tools in order to get their way. They understand that the average well-adjusted person is not fond of pressure, and thus humiliating them would make them yield pretty much quickly. By humiliating a person, you put them in a state of shame, and people hate to be in this position. They understand that once they humiliate a person, they will confuse them and cause that person to do their bidding.

Being Unreasonable

Another thing that people with the Dark Triad traits are good at is being unreasonable. You will find them expressing demands or wishes that are out of touch with reality.

They might be unreasonable so as to create attention for themselves or so as to sow discord, considering that they like seeing people in a state of disharmony. Having unreasonable demands not only makes a person appear to have a small thinking capacity, but it forces people to have a negative outlook on them. But when someone is in a position of authority, and they have unreasonable demands, it brings about bitterness and resentment.

Empty Rhetoric

This is the practice of saying things just for the sake. Someone might say various things so as to aggravate a situation. They know too well that they are saying off things, but they can't help it. In fact, that's the plan. Some people are so corrupted that their only aim is to sow discord.

Fake Sincerity

Another form of psychological manipulation is by presenting themselves as sincere when they are not. For instance, when a narcissist comes up to you needing something, they will appear to be very sincere, when in actual fact they are not. They are good actors and can put on various masks in order to project the image that they want to. Sadly, most people are untrained when it comes to spotting fakes, and this is what makes them susceptible to the various schemes orchestrated by people with the Dark Triad traits. The reason why people with the Dark Triad traits get away with fake sincerity is not always because others are so dumb, but because they have perfected their act, and they put in enough half-truths to confound people.

Fear Mongering

Fear is the one thing that compels people to take immediate action. If someone is in a position of authority, and they want to accomplish a certain milestone, they may very well peddle fear, threatening dire consequences against anyone who doesn't toe the line. The people who are under such a fear-monger have no option but to give in to their demands. Most oppressive people ensure that they hold power over their subjects by threatening harm upon anyone who dares defy their orders.

Gaslighting

Another common psychological warfare tactic is gaslighting. This is the practice of making it seem like someone has totally lost it. It usually happens in relationships. When one party wants to mislead the other, they might start to gaslight them, poking holes in their beliefs and actions, trying to make them see where they are wrong. The bad guy has usually done their research and can articulate various areas in which the other person allegedly needs fixing. Since most people are in desperate need of approval, they find themselves falling prey to such cheap shots.

Chapter 25: Psychology and Self-Improvement

You probably already know that psychological principles are widely applied for self-improvement purposes. If you are like most people, there are definitely several areas in your life that you would like to improve. Maybe you want to be more organized, to give up junk food, to take up an exercise regimen, to improve your performance at work or at school, or to just live a more fulfilled life. The changes that you need to make in your life are going to be difficult and challenging, and you may need to rewire your brain in order to find the willpower or the motivation to take action to make those changes. That is where positive psychology comes in. Psychologists these days do not just focus on issues that are clinically significant—these days, psychological principles can be applied anywhere and to anyone in order to realize specific self-improvement goals.

The first step towards self-improvement is self-awareness. If you want to be more self-aware, you have to take stock of your sensations, your thoughts, your emotions, and your behavioral patterns. The reason we find it hard to start new positive habits is that we have certain emotions, thoughts, and behaviors that we have become accustomed to, so our brains will tend to resort to those old habits and resist attempts to develop new ones.

When we take stock of our current psychological state, we will be in a better position to figure out what areas need change and why we are reluctant to embrace new habits.

You can take stock of your psychological state by keeping a journal for at least a couple of weeks and then consciously reviewing all your tendencies and convictions to see which ones are inhibiting your ability to make progress in your life. Your goal, in this case, is to understand the things that limit you and to identify the psychological chains that bind you and stop you from achieving your self-improvement goals.

Ways to Improve Your Mindset

To achieve self-improvement, you first need to improve your mindset. Psychologists define the term mindset as a belief or a system of beliefs that orient the way a person approaches certain situations. Your mindset determines the way you perceive certain events and the way you select and execute a certain course of action in order to achieve a very specific goal. A positive mindset can help you see opportunities that are hidden, while a negative mindset can trap you in a cycle of self-defeating thoughts and behaviors and stop you from making any real progress.

As much as possible, you should avoid having a fixed mindset. The reason we have gone into so much detail in this book to explain the principles of psychology and the working mechanisms of the brain is to make it possible for you to understand that the human mind isn't a fixed thing and that it can be trained to think in certain ways, resulting in certain behavioral modifications. People who do not understand the basics of psychology tend to assume that their abilities are innate, and therefore their failure in certain areas of life cannot be prevented or reversed. A lot of people think that they are just "not good at math" or that they just "can't do public speaking." You have seen in this book how the brain learns and how it processes thoughts, memories, and emotions, so you understand that you are fully capable of changing your brain has thought patterns by using repetition and reinforcement as a learning technique. You know that the brain is not a rigid thing, so you understand that you are fully capable of changing your mindset if you work hard on it.

Do not be preoccupied with perfection. To have a positive mindset, you have to be less concerned with doing things perfectly and more concerned with making progress and making gradual improvements. If you are preoccupied with doing something perfectly and eliminating all errors, you are more likely to be stuck where you are and to be afraid of taking steps to change your situation out of the fear of committing errors.

Let's say you want to start exercising in order to improve your health and fitness. Your priority should be to get started as soon as possible and to make improvements as you go. You should not wait for the perfect conditions to get started. If you wait to find the perfect gym, the perfect outfit, the perfect instructor, or the perfect time, you may never get around to doing any exercise. The point is that perfection is an illusion, and looking for perfect conditions is just another way to procrastinate.

To improve your mindset, you need to learn patience. In most things that we undertake, it may take some time before we begin to see real results. If you have a well thought out plan and you have put it into action a few times, but you have not yet seen the results you have been hoping for, it does not mean you should give up immediately. Many people who go on self-improvement journeys expect to see instant results. If you are trying to pick up a positive habit, say, for example, you are trying to have a healthier morning routine, you have to understand that you are essentially overwriting years or even decades of old habits in your brain, so it may take some time before the new habit feels more natural to you.

How to Be More Optimistic in Your Outlook

To learn optimism, you have to acknowledge your pessimism. You have to consciously go through your pessimistic ideas and analyze them, then challenge all the negative assumptions that you are making. When you identify your negative assumption, you may be able to see the error in the pessimistic conclusions that you are drawing. Even when we are pessimistic, we do not want to be called pessimists, but for this to work, assume that every negative thought you have comes from a place of pessimism and not from an objective assessment of the situation.

In conflict resolutions, the two parties are often told to start by saying something positive about each other. You can apply the same trick to become more optimistic. For every situation that you find yourself in, try to have one positive thought about that situation, no matter how negative it may be. Even if the positive thought does not ring true at the time, try to have it anyway. Let us say you get out of the house in the morning, and you realize someone stole your car. There may be no apparent upside to that situation, but you should try to dig deep and find one, even if it is a weak one. For instance, you can decide to think of it as an opportunity to get a new car (even if it is going to cost you). The point of this kind of exercise is not to turn you into a "blind optimist." It is to stop you from being habitually negative.

You can form the habit of searching for positive aspects in all kinds of negative situations, and you can even turn it into a little game that you play in your mind. Did your date go horribly wrong? Well, at least you had the chance to dine in a fancy restaurant. Were you fired from your job? Well, it is a chance to search for a new and perhaps even better job that fulfills you. Were you dumbed? Well, it's a chance to find someone whom you are more compatible with.

You can also think of someone you may know who always has a positive outlook and try to imagine what they would have thought if they were in your situation. It can be anyone real (e.g., a friend or relative you admire, a historical figure, a famous person, a religious or spiritual figure, etc.) or even fictional (e.g., a character in your favorite movie, television series, book, comic book, etc.). For example, if you have to give a presentation to a group of people and your fear of public speaking creeps up, you can ask yourself, "What would Abraham Lincoln think or do in this case?" Honest Abe was pathologically shy, but he overcame his fear to deliver one of the greatest and most consequential speeches in history. If he could do that, then you could get yourself to keep it together for the duration of a PowerPoint presentation.

Finally, to become more optimistic, you must learn to practice optimism as often as you can. You have to overhaul your entire outlook in life, and you will not be able to accomplish that if you are ineffective in your approach. You must take every chance that you can to practice optimism and to sharpen your positive mindset. Your brain may be an "old dog," but from what you have learned in this book, it is fully capable of learning new tricks, as long as you keep reinforcing those lessons.

Chapter 26: The Dark Side of Marketing Psychology

Everybody likes to think that they are not affected by advertisements. But except, you have not seen a single advertisement in your life, your daily choices are normally influenced by all the adverts that you have ever seen. Every decision you make is being influenced by those advertisements. An advertisement changes your opinion about a product. You may see some advertisement where you think why anyone would decide to buy this product if they see this. But the purpose of advertisements is not just to have the consumer pick up the phone and buy the product, but not to inform the consumer about the product and its features.

The reason why companies like McDonald's Advertises is because they want to be their customer's opinion and that correspond their brand image into their consumer's mind. There are too many psychological methods that marketers use nowadays for advertising. Overall we know that businesses are made to make money. There is nothing really wrong with that, but to maximize profit, most businesses try to use tactics that are based on psychological principles.

The Mere Exposure

The first method is called the Mere exposure method. This addresses the bear a bone advert that makes you scratch your head and wonder why the company will spend thousands of dollars on them, but you have to realize that people are more comfortable in groups. If one line is longer than the other, people will go to the long line because they must be a reason why people choose one line over the other. They think that one line is better than the other or that the other line is more correct than the other line. It is a very comfortable decision for people. By exposing the consumer to the brand, most humans will start thinking that they know it, and so when the consumer goes to the store to buy the products, they will reach for the product. Sometimes, the product might be a couple of dollars more than the store brand, but what they will buy it because they know that the brand detergent works well. It won't be such a good brand if it doesn't work so well.

A great example of this is with painkillers and other over-the-counter drugs. In the pharmacy, generic brand drugs are the same products with the name brand and with the exact same composition of ingredients, but if they have a different composition of ingredients, they will not be allowed to be called the same drug. But people will still buy the one with a higher price because it is easier to choose what everyone chooses.

The consumer tends to be anxious to buy the cheaper generic brand. Now, does it mean that you should always buy generic drugs? Not necessary. In research, some patients were given two drugs. At first, they were told that it is a more expensive popular brand while the other one is a less expensive, non-branded drug. And when the patient took the more expensive drug, they got more results than when they took the cheaper drugs where in reality, both of them were the same solution. Their expectations were higher for the same brand drugs.

So the patients felt better. The other psychological method that marketers use is the classical conditioning method. This method came from a Russian physiologist in the 1890s. His dog was salivating whenever he enters a room even if he didn't carry food because the dog had an expectation that he will receive food whenever the man came into the room. After all, whenever he had food, he walked into the room. The man wanted to change that, so he started ringing a bell whenever he gave food to his dogs, and after some time, the dogs salivated whenever they heard the sound of a bell. Because the dogs have started associating the sound of a bell with the food, they were trained to have the expectation of food. Now, this same principle works with humans. Companies try to create certain feelings or images associated with their products. If the advertisement shows a certain image in conjunction with the product, soon enough, the consumer will subconsciously relate the images to the product. And it always works, no matter how much you try to block out the advertisement, as long as you see them, you will subconsciously relate it to them. Car brands are one of the biggest people that use this technique. Most times the advertisement doesn't have anything to do with the car or somebody driving the car. So, instead, they will show people pulling up to a red carpet event, or they will show some adventurous looking couple driving on some dirt road. So they know that their customers are not looking for buying a car, but they're buying a lifestyle. They're buying into the image of somebody that goes into the black-tie event or spends their weekend is being adventurous. The car brand matters at that point to them because it is the image that the customers are buying into.

Labeling Things

The first and the silliest example is labeling things as a conclusive or limited edition. This is a very effective tool for businesses because a scarcity of any item immediately increases demand and perceived value. This is why companies make companies wait months for their products that they paid $1000 for it. And Airlines and hotels do this too. Have you ever been to a hotel, and they said that they have only one room left at a certain price, but when you use your cognitive browser, it shows that there is no limit at all? By telling you that there is a limited supply that is running out, it will make you think that if you wait for longer, you won't be able to get on that flight or stay in that hotel, and that fear of missing out makes you feel pressured to be impulsive, so you decide to buy before you are ready. So almost all companies also let us talk about our amusement park, keep us there and make us eat their food. Apart from the fact that they don't allow you to bring in your own food so that you are forced to buy overpriced food, they also do strange things to make you think about eating even when you are not that hungry. For instance, Disneyland tries to put in specific smells throughout their park so that it will make you want to eat. This works because when you are becoming hungry, your body will intensify its senses of smell by activating the receptors in the brain. And it does this to make it easier for you to find food. Now, if you think about it, this makes perfect sense if we are still living in caves, whereby we were still hunting and gathering food. Our sense of smell helps us to find the food that our body needs more quickly. But Disneyland uses this knowledge to their advantage and tend to pumps in a smell of waffle cone being made or hot dogs being fried to give you the time to think about the food that you want and decide if you're going to eat it.

They also try to spray scents around the food canteen to give it an authentic feel. But the amusement park doesn't stop there. They also don't intentionally have shaded spot for you to sit and rest unless you make a way into a food court and then the thing that they lay around the park make it so hot in the summer that is why people move into the air conditioner food canteen to hopefully by a fruit. Disneyland has its AC cranked up so high in one of their shops, and it is the only shop that sells sweatshirts because without the psychological manipulation, who will ever think of buying a sweatshirt on a sunny time?

The Foot in the Door Technique

The next way that businesses use these psychological techniques to their advantage is the foot-in-the-door technique. This technique was created after a study done by a freshman in 1966, which shows that if you say yes to something small, you will probably say yes to something big. For instance, if somebody asks you that, "can I borrow a couple of books, and then you are much more likely to say yes to something larger." As long as what they are asking are similar in nature, you will struggle to say no to it. So the acts have to be similar. For instance, the person cannot just ask to borrow some books and then ask you to do his assignment for him. Now, this technique works because of cognitive dissonance, which makes you believe that you don't want to be contradictory to what you are doing. It's just like you have any evidence that clashes with the way you believed yourself to be. So this technique also works in a reverse way, meaning that if you say no to a big task at first, then you are much more likely to say yes to a smaller task. For instance, if a salesperson asked you to buy a line of beauty product and after you say no, the person then asks you to buy a $10 lip gloss, you're much more likely to say yes to the $10 lip gloss, and this is called the door in the face technique. It is a technique that was researched in 1975 by Dr. Robertson Irene. He claimed that this technique works because of the principle of reciprocity, meaning that if you say no to a much larger task first, you will feel that you owe the person something, and therefore, you will say yes to smaller tasks.

Chapter 27: Body Language and Dark Psychology

When we hear of dark psychology, then we think of personalities such as narcissists, sociopaths, psychopaths, and Machiavellians. Sometimes we wish that we can deny them the oxygen of nonverbal communication to minimize their charming ways. Unfortunately, they flourish in dark psychology, and they understand the power of nonverbal gestures very well. They know how to use them to manipulate others to their advantage. They take advantage of the power of body language to minimize their target, manipulate their emotion, thought, and behavior to achieve the ends they seek. Some of the nonverbal cues that they capitalize on are:

- The clothes they wear and how they wear them

- Body gestures such as posture and positioning

- A facial expression such as hypnotic gazing

- Maintaining eye conduct or avoiding it

- Voice, where they raise the tone of their voice intentionally

- Proximity where they manipulate the distance between them and their target

Hypnotic Staring and Gazing

Eye conduct is one of nonverbal skill, which is very important in communication. It inspires confidence and shows that you are attentive as the other person speaks. Maintaining eye contact has always been preached as an excellent way to make others feel like they are really being noticed. But manipulative people know how to take this vital skill a step further. They set their eyes on you with an intense and focused gaze. Such hypnotic gazing is usually done intentionally for the purpose of testing boundaries. The manipulator often does or says something weird after or before the hypnotic gaze. They then stare at you to test and monitor your response. In an attempt to lie to you, they may stare at you without blinking much. When someone lies, they usually break eye contact and look down or to the sides. But sometimes they go an extra mile to give a steady and cold gaze to intimidate and control you.

Body Touch and Space Invasion

Manipulative people playfully touch you in an attempt to break the rules and boundaries. They usually do this in a very subtle and charming way. They may reach for your shoulder, peck your cheeks, or touch your hand intimately to see whether you will permit it, especially on your first date. They carry you off the ground when you hug, intending to pass a particular message, and test whether you accept it depending on your reaction. They will also invade and violate your personal space to create false intimacy. They do this by leaning too close. Even if you step back, they step forward into your bubble to re-adjust. In this process, they also touch your shoulder or arm repeatedly to try to create rapport.

Constant Mirroring of Your Body Language

This is a famous manipulation technique that dark personalities use to influence their target. At the start, they are trying to mirror you so that they can control you. Later you find yourself reflecting them. This creates trust between you and them and helps to establish a connection that they use to exploit you. The technique is usually straightforward and a basic one, because it only involves copying the behavior of a person. The manipulator takes a close look at your body languages, such as gestures, facial expressions, and the tone of your voice. If you are standing with your hands crossed, they do the same. If you are speaking quietly without showing any emotions, they do the same. They do it as carefully as possible to make sure that you are talking in the same way. They also make sure that you won't realize or become suspicious of their behavior when they are mimicking you so that you do not become suspicious.

After some time, you will start feeling connected to them. You begin to behave like them, and that is the time that they realize you are ripe for their purpose.

Nice Dress and Haircut

Dark personalities understand well the power of the first impression. They are physical appearance if therefore the first thing that they bank on. They know the best hairstyle that makes them look good. Your entire outfit will be affected by how your hair looks. One of the things that a person you want to influence will notice is your haircut. When you ignore your hairstyle, you won't look good, and they will know it. Be realistic with your hairstyle and if a particular haircut doesn't make you look good, let it go and look for a better one. Don't rock around with a haircut that looks terrible on you.

Dress well, without going crazy on fashion if you know you can't sustain it. To impress others, you must be well dressed to create a first good impression. If your dress cannot capture the attention of your target, then they will not pay much attention to you. Those who manipulate others know this, and they spice their looks with flashy clothes and makeup.

Raising Their Voice and Displaying Negative Emotions

This is a sign of aggressive manipulation. They raise their voice when you are discussing something, while in the real sense, they are not emotional. They assume that by projecting their voice high enough to show negative emotions, you will give in to their demand and do or give what they want. They accompany their loud voice with strong body language like an excited gesture or raising from their sit to stand on their feet.

Self-Comfort Touches and Pointing

Lying comes with discomfort and stress. The liar then begins to make a gesture aimed at achieving some level of self-comfort. These are gestures such as hair-stroking, playing with wedding rings, rocking, and twiddling. Although we all use gestures often, they increase dramatically for someone who begins to fib. This is when they start to feel that their lie will not go through, and you have discovered their hidden motives. In an attempt to get away out, they may begin to use their hand to point to other things happening around to divert your attention from the matter. If you stick to the topic, they will feel embarrassed and never try to lie to you again.

Micro-Gestures

These are little gestures or facial expressions that flash across one's face quickly. They are hard to see, but experts tend to use filmed footage, which they slow down to analyze the body language and hence can recognize them in the middle of the lie when the person is performing it. In real life, these may not be spotted, but you can look for other facial expressions that occur after the liar is done speaking. Either the eyes roll, or the mouth skews as the liar is attempting a quick give-away.

Projected Body Posture

This is when someone stands towering over you. This may happen in the case where the narcissist is physically stronger than you and has a tall and colossal figure. He may lean forward to mask you and inspire fear to diffuse your confidence. He will bring his face closer to yours and look you straight in the face in an attempt to control and manipulate you. He may also stand straight next to you or in front of you, projecting his chest forward to fill up more space and try to minimize you. He may yell at you at the same time to make you yield to his demands and give in to what he is saying or give what he wants.

Avoiding Eye Conduct and Silence

When they are lying to you, and they know that you have realized it, people with dark traits tend to avoid eye conduct. They may begin to look down or blink their eyes quickly or even close their eyes in close succession. Looking to the sides is also another technique used by sycophants to prevent you from getting cues that they are lying to you. They may also remain silent for a while to avoid answering your questions if you have cornered them.

Another time when narcissists avoid eye conduct is when they have silent aggression towards you. If it is in the office, they will get in and avoid looking at your desk to prevent eye conduct with you. They may also greet everyone else in the office and fail to exchange greetings with you. If they exchange greetings, they do so look over your shoulder or looking down to avoid eye conduct. This may be the case when you failed to yield to their demands or when you have confronted them about their manipulative tendencies, which you feel tired of. They may use this silent aggression to see whether you will change your mind and live up to what they want. This may also happen in a relationship.

Fake Smile

A fake smile doesn't reflect the real feeling and emotions. Unlike a genuine smile that involves most of your face, such as the mouth and the eyes, a fake smile only involves the mouth. A smile that doesn't extend to the eyes is fake and may show that you are not reading from the same page with the deceiver. It means that they are telling you something else while their real motives are hidden. A deceiver will often use a fake smile to appear more genuine while trying to convince you to believe in them. By carefully monitoring their smile, you can find out whether it is a real one or a fake one. If you notice a fake smile, be careful, and steer clear of what they are telling you because the chances are high that such a person is not genuine.

Rate and Tone of Speech

Since they aim to control and manipulate you, a person with dark traits will speak quickly and adopt an audible tone so that they can present so many details to you without giving you time to think. They know that when they allow you time to digest the content, you may detect the exaggeration and the half-truths in the message. Sputtering without giving you time to respond makes you get overwhelmed with details. They also know that a tone that is audible enough will make them sound confident and truthful. The aim of all this is to overwhelm you with so much detail before they lay their claim to you. By this time, they know that you are already tired with very little energy to resist. The manipulator then drops the bombshell, and if you are not careful, you may find yourself falling head over heel for the trap. When you confront such a person, and you see their voice beginning to fade and their speech getting intermitted by moments of silence to figure out what to say, then you realize that theirs was a calculated move to achieve a selfish goal at your expense.

Conclusion

We live in a world where almost everyone we interact with has some form of agenda that they'll like us to buy into. While some of these agendas are open and good, others are very secret and do not serve our best interests. However, the real threat is not the hidden agenda, but the subtle ways in which unsuspecting individuals are influenced into executing these agendas.

From sales to politics and right down to our family members, several manipulation tactics have been deployed to get us to act in ways that are against our better judgments. In more ways than one, we have been tricked, used, and dumped.

Nevertheless, the reign of manipulative people in our personal and professional lives is over! With the methods outlined in this book, I dare say you can live a happy and fulfilled life without the fear of being a victim of mind control. Most of us are going to assume that we would never be comfortable causing some harm to those around us. We worry that we are going to be cast out from society or that something else would happen to us. Often, just the worry about feeling remorse and guilty in the process is going to be enough to keep most people away from using dark psychology and some of the other techniques.

We may not be able to completely rid ourselves of the negative influence people have on our minds, emotions, and behaviors, but we definitely can gain a good level of control over what others try to craftily influence us to think, feel, say, and do. The goal of this book is, among other things, to help you gain that level of control and protect your mind from devious schemes. The result is a healthy relationship both at the personal and professional level, where interactions are open, honest, and devoid of mind control games.

Mind control keeps people in abusive relationships, holds people down in a job they should have left long ago, and forces them to remain as puppets for others. Being compassionate and patient with the people we interact with is indeed vital for sustaining our relationships. But over-compassion and too much patience are among the factors that make us doubt our intuition when it screams at us to be wary of the manipulative behaviors of others. The need to be accepted seems to overshadow the voice of our intuition.

If there is a message, I would like to reiterate it is that your reaction to people's behavior is the most important factor in your interactions. In other words, when you react emotionally to a manipulator, they have achieved a part of their aim, if not all. When you are emotionally detached, rational, calm, and assertive while handling manipulative behaviors, you make the manipulator very uncomfortable and beat them at their own game.

Give yourself adequate time to let the lessons and messages in this manuscript sink in. You may not be able to break free from a controlling and manipulative partner or work colleague in one day. But the more you assert yourself and stand your ground without being defensive, the more your self-confidence will improve. Whatever damage has been done to your self-esteem will gradually be healed, and you will soon begin to enjoy the kind of relationships you always dreamed of.

PART 2

MANIPULATION TECHNIQUES

Introduction

Everybody has goals that they are bent on achieving and needs to be met, but the difference between these people and manipulators is that the latter wants to use underhanded methods and strategies to meet their needs. Manipulation is a way to covertly influence someone with indirect, deceptive, or abusive tactics in a bid to control and extort for personal gain at the expense of the person being manipulated. Manipulation may seem kind, or even friendly or gentle, as if the person is really interested in helping you and making your life more colorful, however all these are facade put up to achieve an ulterior motive. Manipulation also entails the use of veiled hostility, abusive methods, force, and threats, especially when the objective is to acquire power. The fearful thing about manipulation is that most times you are not conscious of being intimidated and manipulated.

Experiencing manipulation can be a very sad experience, you don't know what is going on but constantly feeling empty or sad. You might even have a feeling of guilt, and yet the manipulator will appear useless, using words that are pleasant, ingratiating flattering, reasonable, that plays on your guilt or sympathy, so you put away your goals and dreams to please or satisfy your partner, people that have trouble keeping up conversations, being direct and assertive and may use manipulation to get their way. This also makes it easy for them to get manipulated by narcissists, borderline personalities, sociopaths, and other codependents, including addicts.

Sometimes, manipulation is a bit more difficult to spot—it can be finding ways to use insecurities against the victim without them being spotted. No matter what, however, what holds true is that manipulation is designed to override everyone's inherent right to free will. This is not something to be proud of or to accept—if you are on the receiving end of manipulation, you should be trying to protect that free will as much as you can. If you are the manipulator, you may need to reconsider your motives and tactics.

Controlling people is typically considered quite underhanded and cruel, and it should not be occurring on the regular, or at all if it can be avoided. It can be valuable to understand the art of manipulation in order to understand how the mind works or how manipulators will attack, but ultimately, the use of true manipulation is not recommended.

People tend to believe that manipulation is effective for different reasons. They have different ideas about what makes manipulation effective. In particular, there are three criteria involving the manipulator that must be met in order to ensure that manipulation is successful. Ultimately, it is the manipulator that is primarily responsible for the manipulation and determining whether it will work, though there are certain personality traits that tend to be particularly vulnerable to the attempts to manipulate. Self-Promotion is used by most manipulators; they make themselves look good in the eyes of others. They make sure that other people don't have anything against them. They make their prey their friend. They don't give you any chance to doubt their words or actions. They make sure that they know your every move. After you are now comfortable with them, they now pounce on you and make you do what they want. It is very difficult to know that you are being manipulated by someone who has shown you his good side.

Chapter 28: Manipulation

It is human nature to manipulate people for their benefits, and in one way or another, we have all manipulated someone for some reason only known to us. Manipulation is done for many reasons. A good example will be someone in an office setting who feels fatigued and does not want to ask permission from their bosses. After going home, the person sends a message to their employer for sick leave the following day. This person is not at all sick but has used sickness to manipulate the employer into giving them a day off work. Manipulation of this kind is not at all entirely bad, and therefore it is good to identify between good and bad manipulation. When faced with an unpleasant situation or an emergency that you feel you don't need to attend to, you might find yourself manipulating someone else into attending to the situation on your behalf. This is not at all entirely bad. This is part of our nature, and changing this would be a bit hard for all of us. However, when manipulation becomes psychological, things tend to get a little bit darker. This is because it entails playing with somebody's thoughts and emotions with well-calculated tactics, like being abusive to the person or deceiving the person. In a case where there is psychological manipulation, the victim is not given any option, but has to comply with the manipulator and do whatever they want. Here the victim does not have a say; they are left with no choice but to do what is being requested of them.

There Is Always a Reason for Manipulation

People who engage in psychological manipulation have a reason as to why they do so. There are many things that would lead someone to engage in this hideous act, for example, for material gain, revenge, self-pleasure, and so on.

Manipulators always feel they need to be in control of everything and be on top of everyone. They feel no one can beat them to their own game. A manipulator in an intimate relationship always ensures that they are the ones that have the last say on everything. They always have a way of getting their partners to do what they want. Some manipulators love manipulating other people for fun. They don't have anything to do, and they use other people to have fun and pass the time. Others love to see people do their work for them. They love manipulating other people and forcing them to do their work as they rest or engage in other matters they deem more important. Some manipulators are just jealous, and they love to see people getting hurt for their self-pleasure. They drive people into doing awful things so that they would feel psychologically satisfied.

Lying Is Part of the Manipulation

This has to be the best tactic that manipulators use. They come up with huge stories that might not even be true to trick others into believing them. Some people have mastered the art of lying, and it is very hard to notice when they are telling the truth or when they are lying. A self-centered person, for example, might use the art of lying to manipulate someone into a relationship for their gain. They will show love to their partner and always be at their feet when they need them. After achieving what they want and the partner is truly into the relationship, they now show their true colors, and with the awareness of the partner or not, they push into doing what brought them into the relationship in the first place. The manipulator might have wanted their partner's wealth and might trick the partner into signing up legal property documents as a show of love to them. After the signing is done, the manipulator will now change; this is where the partner realizes that he or she was manipulated into giving out their wealth without their knowledge.

Manipulators Practice Humiliation

Manipulators do not like being questioned for their mistakes. Therefore, most of them use the art of humiliation or embarrassment to put you off and make you look bad. They are not to be trusted with your secrets, as they can easily spill them out to the world at the slightest provocation. A good example would be a school setting where a teacher is abusing another teacher, and how the abuser would turn the tables to make the other teacher look bad, leaving them not guilty before the eyes of the other teachers. The victim feels very humiliated and embarrassed because, in the end, it is told that he or she was to blame for what happened. With the manipulator's art of humiliation, nobody will listen to the other teacher's side of the story, and they will all conclude that this teacher was the one in the wrong.

The Art of Evasion

Most manipulators, when confronted about their character or behavior - often tend to change the topic or try to avoid the topic. They don't like being questioned, and hence, they give out answers that do not have any meaning. This is because they do not want their true colors to be known. They want to keep the spotlight off of them. They would redirect your focus to something else so that you can stop questioning them. This is because they feel insecure when they are under attack, and therefore, they use the art of evasion as a way of manipulating and controlling you into focusing on something else.

Rationalization

Manipulators tend to use excuses for an act committed to make it look good or not intended. They tend to make their behavior match up with their stories. Rationalization tends to make the act look good or plausible. They are then able to get away with what they did, whether it was intentional or not. They make an excuse seem logical.

Manipulators tend to use this art of manipulation to subject their victims to psychological manipulation. This is mostly used by women to manipulate men into doing what they want. A lot of women are now learning this art to get favors done for them. However, if this art goes wrong, and they are caught, they tend to react in anger to gain favor and benefit from the situation.

Chapter 29: Psychological Manipulation

Today, the greatest battles are not fought on battlefields but in our minds and hearts!

And one of the biggest and strongest reasons for an inner battle is psychological manipulation. The biggest problem with psychological manipulation is not only the fact that we are often not prepared to deal with it, but also the way we respond to it. And then, our greatest enemy, beyond the manipulator/oppressor, will become ourselves! One of the main characteristics of psychological manipulation is that the manipulator (who can be a father, a mother, a brother or sister, a romantic partner, or a friend) exercises great control and power over us. And in that instant, our life becomes a real hell, and we live in tremendous anguish. However, it is crucial to know that we are not, and should not be, impotent in this situation and that there are various ways of combating these techniques of psychological manipulation. The first step is to achieve consciousness, that is, to become aware of these techniques. Take a closer look and learn more objectively how your handlers "work" so you can protect yourself in the future. There are several Manipulation Techniques. See some of them below:

Psychological Manipulation Technique 1: Emotional Blackmail

Emotional blackmail is one of the oldest and most used manipulation techniques employed by human beings. But how does this work exactly?

Many people succumb to this trick because they feel they have no choice. At this point, phrases such as "If you really cared about me, you would do this for me" are very common and make the manipulated person feel "forced" to make decisions that they do not really want. The target will make them anyway just to please the person who manipulates.

To avoid this manipulation technique you will have to develop a strong sense of your own self, and this involves knowing who you are, what your responsibilities are towards others, and who your true friends are. Usually, manipulative and blackmailing people tend to stay away from people with strong and solid personalities. Always remember: you always have a choice, and it is you who decides what you do with your life and how you want to react to the world.

Psychological Manipulation Technique 2: Focus on Negative Aspects

Some people like to put a "brake" on another's ideas and brilliant projects by emphasizing everything that could go wrong with them. These people often push him to doubt his projects and all the good things they would bring if they were put into practice. And at these times, the manipulators offer an endless list of questions that will only serve to create and raise doubts in their target's mind and heart.

For example, if you are telling someone that you are thinking of traveling somewhere for a month to relax or go on vacation, and if for some reason that person does not feel comfortable with the idea, they will probably react to your news by talking about the immense travel hazards and the endless number of negative things that can be expected at the airport, etc.

At such times, if there is no apparent reason for such a reaction from the other person. If you are comfortable with your decision, bearing in mind that it will not harm you or others, choose not to listen to them and follow through with what you have decided.

Do not be overly swayed by this negative thinking pattern because if we think about something a lot, we attract it. That is, if you put it in your head that something bad will happen and focus on it excessively, it is very likely to happen because the thought has life and is a great magnet.

Psychological Manipulation Technique 3: Teenage Rebellion

Unfortunately, sometimes the manipulative person adopts a childlike attitude as a response to his decision or something you have said to him.

For example, you want to leave your home and live independently. At first, it may even seem like everyone is happy and comfortable with your decision. But with the passage of time, as soon as you start looking for the perfect apartment, things start happening one after another. Some kind of personal crisis occurs in the family, your mother or father suddenly (re) starts smoking, etc. These are adult people, but they adopt the behavior of a teenager and rebel against the idea.

The easiest way to deal with this is to make them see that their efforts in trying to make you give up are worthless and that you will go ahead with your decision.

At first, it can be very difficult and hard for you, especially if you have been exposed to this type of psychological manipulation for a long time. But as time goes by, it will become much easier, and you will see that even the people who manipulate you will come to respect you much more.

Psychological manipulation can be done throughout life, but always remember that you have the power to break this vicious cycle, and above all, remember that only one person can change your life: You!

Love and life together can be sources of well-being, pleasure, and support or a dead end in which you feel suffocated and as if you are in the dark. The worst is that in many cases, these can be combined in a single day. Both feelings and problems begin when the relationship shifts rapidly, and you find yourself immersed in a constant storm of feelings. This mainly happens to those who do not know how to escape such situations.

Many people are immersed in insane and toxic relationships in which they suffer psychological abuse of various kinds. They receive continuous damage to their integrity and their honor and levels of disrespect that when seen or heard from outside seem crazy, but to the person who is now accustomed to suffering does not even produce a minimal reaction in their daily lives.

Love is not an excuse to hide the emotional pain that another person can cause us, and it is our responsibility to ourselves to learn how to defend our rights and enforce them. Beyond your own insecurity, the parental patterns that you picked up in your childhood, and all the mechanisms of self-deception that you are capable of activating so as not to see reality, at the bottom of your being, you know how to differentiate what is right and what hurts you. That said, sometimes we need someone to tell us in a neutral and unbiased way that we have the right not to put up with what we know we do not deserve. Present a list of the main techniques of manipulation in unhealthy couples.

Manipulation to maintain social control: This technique usually begins in a very subtle way. The couple criticizes friends, family, work colleagues, and anyone in your social circle until they can completely annul the other's social network in such a way that the only source of effort and social support is the couple. This is manifested through jealousy: "If you really love me, you would prefer me over your friends," etc. Emotional blackmail: This mechanism is famous for being used between pairs of individuals. It is also widely used by almost everyone, and you likely know it very well. It is about using phrases to handle guilt and repentance as a tactic to get something or as an impediment so that the other does not do something or does not abandon the manipulator. The manipulative person usually uses phrases like: "If you do that, it means you don't love me," "I do not want you to suffer, I would never do that to you," "I want the best for you, even if you let me destroy my life," "If you let me die," etc.

Chapter 30: Manipulation and Emotions

Did you know that it can be hard for anyone to realize that he is being emotionally manipulated? Some people are so deep in the web that they would even refuse to believe or entertain the possibility that they are being manipulated by their partner.

In order to understand this, however, you have to become familiar with the concept of emotional manipulation.

What is Emotional Manipulation?

There are times when people will try to influence you or convince you of something you may not have thought of before, but this does not necessarily mean you are already being manipulated. Influence over someone only suggests a negative connotation when the influence on another is used to force him into doing something or allowing something he normally wouldn't. When a person's basic human rights become secondary, this becomes harmful.

A healthy relationship often has respect, trust, and mutual regard as its foundation. However, when one of the people within the relationship is playing or 'messing around' with their partner's emotions, it becomes a potentially abusive and harmful relationship to the one being subjected to the manipulation. Toying with someone's emotion for one's own gains can be considered a deep violation of trust.

What Constitutes Emotional Manipulation?

Every person on earth, in one way or another, has a self-centered side, a side that wants to get its way all the time, have people do what it wants them to, and have their opinions valued above all else. However, emotionally mature and healthy individuals often recognize the negative effects of this side of them and would control or adjust their behavior in order to accommodate everyone in their lives, becoming flexible in their desires and needs and allowing others to influence them, too.

Manipulative people, on the other hand, want none of this. They are geared towards having a one-sided relationship where only one person has control, often using psychological tricks in order to make their victim question themselves and lose control and resolve in their own desires and limits. They will use deception, trickery, and ruthless exploitation in order to have their way.

Everyone with strong passionate beliefs about things, whether it be about politics, religion, lifestyles, or even the little things, like how to use certain household appliances or how to exercise properly, will all try to influence others into considering and even adopting the beliefs they themselves have. What is important here is that the rights and boundaries of others are not violated or disregarded. Someone who wants to influence you into going to the same Church they are will not lie to you, threaten you, blackmail, or coerce you into going. They will tell you the positive things about the Church and invite you; they will also respect you if you didn't want to go or if you're busy. When it comes to manipulation, on the other hand, the manipulator will be willing to do almost anything, even cruel or hateful things just to get you to do what they want. It's not often that they consider themselves to be manipulators; that's just how they think, how they've learned to react to the world according to their personal and family backgrounds.

What you have to recognize is how you feel. If you feel violated or forced to do or say things you don't want to do, then it may be time to reassess the relationship you're in.

Spotting the Spider

Although emotionally manipulative people can come in every shape and size, there are certain tendencies that potentially abusive and manipulative people have. It is important to know how these people think and why they act the way they do and spot a potentially abusive and manipulative partner before you fall too deeply or get hurt.

1. What Makes Up an Emotional Manipulator?

Although there are many specific ways for people to become manipulative, manipulators have three general characteristics to successfully manipulate their victims.

- **They are often very deceptive** - They often get into a relationship with ulterior motives, lying and flattering their way into their victim's confidence, saying and doing everything necessary to gain their victim's trust and loyalty. They are very good at hiding who they really are and how they actually feel, hiding any negative feelings and behavior they have as they reel in their victims. They can be very charming indeed as they find their way into your confidence, telling you everything you will want to hear.

- **They are not beyond using secrets, insecurities, and confidences shared by their partner and using them to their advantage.** They will be willing to use the knowledge gained through their deception to find which buttons to push in order to control their partner and using those to their advantage to gain control of the relationship and the other person.

- **They are often remorseless in the things they do, no matter the harm they may end up causing the person they love the most.** They have a certain level of narcissism that makes them oblivious that they are already causing others pain or emotional turmoil. They will be able to justify how they treat others and will even find a way to blame their victims for their manipulative behavior. They also use guilt and threats to coerce their victims.

- **They often do not accept no for an answer.** They will find a way to make you say yes, whether it is by whining, begging, playing the victim, making you feel guilty or outright coercion. They are often very assertive and will take control of situations where they perceive that the other person is weaker.

Another useful thing to know is that these manipulations are often done through covert means, such as by the manipulator being passive-aggressive, such as withholding affection and being negatively inclined towards their partner, and through relational aggression, such as humiliating their partner or ruining any friendships their partner may already have with others, wanting to have all of their victims' attention.

2. What Makes a Person Vulnerable to Emotional Manipulation?

Just as in the case of the manipulators, those who are susceptible to being emotionally manipulated also have some things in common that make them easy prey for those who want to abuse and manipulate them.

• **The victims will often be eager to please others**. They have a natural desire to earn the love and acceptance of others and will often go out of their way just to make someone else happy. This trait makes them vulnerable to manipulation as they are receptive to how others react, and the manipulator will be able to send subtle messages through a few choice words and body language in order to control or influence how they think.

• **They are often rather submissive and are generally emotionally dependent**. This meekness and dependency can be easily used by the manipulative person, filling in a space in the victim's life that the manipulator is also ready to fill, without considering how the victim may feel.

• **The ones susceptible to manipulation often have low self-esteem/self-confidence**. They are often doubtful of their own feelings and do not really have a sense of who they are. This makes them malleable to the desires and demands of the manipulator. A lack of assertiveness can also be beneficial to manipulators.

• **They are also often naïve and impressionable, often easy prey to false promises and grand gestures**. Being naïve and impressionable, the victim will be more susceptible to believing whatever the manipulator says and is easily swayed when the manipulator lays on the charmed.

• **They often romanticize the relationship, believing that they can fix or help their abusive and manipulative partner**. They will find the difficulties as romantic challenges against true love, and they dream of the day they can change and fix their partner.

Unfortunately, such hopes are often dashed by the fact that their partner needs professional and trained help from people who know how to handle these cases, as manipulative people often have personality disorders such as narcissistic, borderline, and antisocial personality disorders.

The Games They Play

The emotionally manipulative often have their ways to take control of their victims, using the knowledge they have acquired about their victims in order to control them. They have some well-known and infamous ways to get under their victim's skin:

1. Love Bombing

Although the name sounds affectionate, love bombing is anything but. Love bombing is when the manipulator will try to take control through grandiose expressions of love and excessive flattery. They will say anything from 'You and I are meant to be together forever' to 'You are the kindest most attractive person I have ever seen,' making the victim believe that the manipulator's sun and stars are at the victim's feet. Although these are words that can be said in a genuinely healthy relationship, hearing these words from someone you just met should be considered a red flag.

The love bomber will shower their victims with compliments and pretend that they are vulnerable when it comes to the love of their victim. They will use love as bait, feigning concern, and passion in order to sink their teeth into their victims. Through a show of false vulnerability and dependency, their victims, especially if they have natural tendencies of being giving and nurturing, will fall into the trap of falsehoods and pretensions. This type of emotional and psychological manipulation was first used by certain cults in their recruitment strategies, "bombing" their chosen recruits with friendship, unity, and love, concealing, of course, their selfish agendas.

2. Gaslighting

This is another method emotionally abusive and manipulative people can use against their partners. Gaslighting refers to the mental abuse that a victim is subjected to wherein the abuser makes the victim second guess his own thoughts and actions by twisting the truth, omitting facts, and making the victim doubt his own memory and sanity. The term was derived from a stage play from 1938 of the same name, as well as its succeeding film adaptations.

When someone is trying to manipulate you by using gaslighting, he is essentially trying to make you lose faith in your own mind. This is done by twisting truth or words, making you believe that you were wrong or that you had forgotten the truth. They will say things like, "You're delusional, that didn't happen," or "You must have forgotten, you have such a bad memory," or other words to that effect, words that will make you doubt yourself and your perceptions, making you easier to convince and manipulate to their own ends.

3. Emotional Blackmail

As the name suggests, the manipulative one will try to control your actions by threatening you or his own self. He will often make you feel guilty and blame you for his actions, saying you forced him to do it. He may not even do it overtly or threaten you squarely; he may say things like, "I don't know what I'd do without you. Promise me you won't ever leave me!" or "You make me act so crazy, I lose control when it's you." In the former, he is forcing you into a promise that you may not be able to keep, giving him leverage in his manipulation and guilt-tripping, while in the latter, he is making you feel responsible for his actions, absolving himself of the consequences while stacking up the guilt on your end.

4. Character Assassination

Emotional manipulators or abusers will often diminish the feelings of their victims or diminish the effects their victims have, claiming that their partner is overreacting or is overly sensitive. They will make their victim feel like their actions are unjustified and that there is something wrong with how their victim reacts rather than how they act toward their partner. They will also ignore whatever it is their partners are feeling or whatever problems their partner may have.

Chapter 31: Manipulation in Business

The best marketing plan for any business is to find out customer preferences and deliver it. This way, such a business ends up promoting customer loyalty and also increases customer references as a way of advertising. The values that most customers hold dear are easy to identify since they are almost universal. These include but are not limited to; best quality goods, good customer service, affordability, and other customer incentives such as loyalty discounts and flexible return policies. It would be in a good sense for any company to try and abide by these and other customer preferences. However, this is not always the case.

Company priorities may not be in sync with customer preferences. This is because often the central goal for most businesses is to widen their profit margins as much as possible. As such, paying so much attention to their customer preferences may prove counterproductive. This is because producing the best quality products at low prices while offering good loyalty discounts may not make for the best business strategy. It is for this reason that many business holders have developed clever ways of 'tricking' their customers so that everyone goes home satisfied.

Advertising and miscommunication is often the area of target in manipulating clients. A well-designed advert holds the potential of significantly increasing the sales of a particular product. As a matter of fact, a well-executed advert can have the capacity of causing you to purchase something which you had no prior plan of purchasing. Such manipulation schemes are often executed in batches. This is to say that it is rare to have a single fool-proof plan to sway customers, but rather, separate methods are executed in conjunction with each other in order to achieve the best results.

The methods through which business people manipulate their clients are numerous. While some may be considered prudent business measures, others border on the downright shady and illegal. Some business owners have been known to pull no stops in their efforts to milk the clients of their bottom dollars. As such, it is important to learn how some of these methods are used, how to spot a manipulative businessman, and best of all, how not to fall prey to their scheming minds and tactics.

Persuasive Advertising (Misleading)

In business, there are two types of advertising. The first kind is the straightforward type, where what you hear or perceive is what you get. This is the honest type of advertising that is void of any trickery or manipulation of potential buyers. Seldom has this type of advertising brought profits in the form of improved sales. This is because customers need to be given reasons why they want to buy an item rather than just being given the specifications of various items. This is where the second type of advertising (persuasive) comes in.

Non-Specific Type

How many times have you run into adverts that are seemingly very attractive but are non-specific when you consider them deeply? Such adverts are usually connected with post-purchase advantages of various items. A good example that I am sure you have come into or will in the future is "Buy this item and benefit from a ten percent discount and an extended warranty." I have no problem with the first part of the advert. In fact, it seems genuine enough as a result of its specificity. However, the part on the extended warranty is where my problem with the advert lies. Just what is this extended warranty? It would have been much more helpful to specify in the advert the exact amount of time covered by the warranty.

You will be surprised to learn the extent of such and other forms of treachery in adverts. Other examples you might find to this effect are; "this product has a long shelf-life," or "Buy this item at a now reduced price of…" Both of these statements are certainly appealing but non-informative. They would be far more informative and trustworthy if they were more specific. The first one, for instance, should have expressed the shelf-life in exact time, while the second one should have stated the initial price of the item.

Although not all advert statements similar to these are designed to mislead, a significant number of them are.

The primary targets for such adverts are those shoppers who may be in a hurry to purchase items. Specifically, they target those people who may not be loyal to any brands and are therefore dependent on adverts to make their choices. When you are in a hurry and have to purchase something, it would make perfect sense to settle for the one with the "extended warranty and shelf-life" even though you may not have a clue just how extended they are.

Chapter 32: Manipulation in Relationship

It doesn't have to be hard to manipulate your significant other one to get what you want. The most archaic way to do that is to turn him on and then press for the favor, meaning that if he doesn't give you what you want, he won't be able to get it on. But there are a variety of more discreet ways to manipulate your significant other if you don't want to follow this drastic path. Whatever the strategy, as you make your submission make sure that you look sexy, if your significant other is reminded of how sweet or hot you are, you'll be more able to get what you want.

Here are some most widely used manipulative techniques that are used by partners to manipulate each other:

- Guilt

- Martyrdom

- Using others to "present' your idea

- Hiding your errors

- Presenting the wrong reasons for behavior

- Overreacting to make your partner feel wrong about his or her emotions

- Giving something as a gift

- Making Excuses

- Passive/Aggressive Behavior

- Compromising at a time to get what you want

- Padding a request

- Hiding something you have done wrong to fix it before it gets discovered

Guilt

People feel bad when they don't live up to people's expectations, which are vital to them. They use emotional blackmail because they know what makes your partner feel bad about him or herself and use this knowledge to get what they need.

Martyrdom

If you regularly give your partner too much, you might be trying to make an emotional bank balance that makes your partner feel obliged to pay when you want something — even if he or she would rather not be willing to do so.

Using Others to Present Your Idea

This form of manipulation happens when one spouse uses skewed sources in order to get the other to obey. "Everybody believes ..." or, "our best friends still take a minimum of two holidays a year," or, "new research shows that."

Hiding Your Errors

If you fear critique or disappointment from your partner, you may find yourself hiding something that you have done wrong. Waiting a moment when you are going along well is normal to reveal the truth and soften the blow.

Presenting the Wrong Reasons for Behavior

If you're caught doing something that upsets your partner, you're building a more trustworthy narrative to shift your partner to your side. When, under these conditions, he or she "understands" that your conduct was right, you may be able to neutralize a potentially harmful response.

Overreacting to Make Your Partner Feel Wrong About His or Her Emotions

Making chaos is a typical way to get your partner back down, whether they hate situations, emotional turmoil, or dramatic results. Even if you feel something intense, you rely consciously or unconsciously on the fact that your partner is going back down to avoid the situation's intensity.

Giving Something as a Gift

One example is telling your partner that a great deal arose that you know he or she would really like when it's something you really wanted but didn't think you could get it.

Making Excuses

Making excuses such as I've got a headache "or," it was a really rough day. I've just not expected that much stress. Tomorrow, I'm trying to get to it, "or," I'm so sorry, I just skipped. I've had too much on my mind.

Compromising at a Time to Get What You Want

That's one of the most popular deceptive forms. Most romantic partners know what their partner likes, but they can't comfortably refuse to put on a momentary charm in anticipation of a potential appeal.

Padding a Request

This strategy requires you to inquire deliberately for much more than you think you'll receive, realizing your partner's going to offer nothing, which is what you always desired. "Honey, it would be my wish to get the latest Tesla. What are you thinking?"

Hiding Something You Have Done Wrong to Fix It Before it Gets Discovered

It's normal that you don't want your spouse to be unhappy with what you've done, so you're trying to hide or correct it before it's figured out. You play against the clock, so you've got to get very good to keep him or her off the track until you've cleared it.

Keep in mind that most intimate partners only resort to manipulative behavior when they genuinely believe that by being more open and direct, they can't get what they need. Very often, in adult relationships,

Chapter 33: Manipulation in Friendship

It can be a bit tricky to exploit your mates as they will know you well enough to call your bluff if your persuasion abilities are not up to par. But don't forget—you can still have your mates do whatever you want. You've got to butter up your mate first. Be sweet, do little favors for her the week before you need significant support, and try to note what a great friend she is. Do whatever you need to do to be a fellow student without going overboard.

Put the thoughts to use: Your mates are concerned for you, and they're not going to want to see you angry. Use those acting abilities to look a lot madder than you are.

Always note what a great friend you are: Be armed for stories of occasions when you have done amazing stuff for friendship's sake.

Place shame down: You don't have to play the "poor friend" trick, but you can say a couple of more occasions politely that the partner has let you down. Make it sound like you're used to your friend's uncaring actions without being too accusatory.

Manipulating Friends in a Noble Way

Manipulation is generally a bad technique to use to get what you want, but when you have a noble cause, it is sometimes justifiable. Maybe you're trying to get someone to lead a healthier lifestyle or have Fun with you on an outing. If other methods fail you and it's time to turn to a touch of manipulative behavior, here are specific tactics you can use to get what you want without sacrificing your principles entirely.

No one enjoys being fooled, so you don't want to use anything you know for evil purposes here. Much of what we're going to talk about is just about building a situation in which it's more possible that anyone you're trying to manipulate will be happy and appreciate themselves more. This is not just about getting what you want but creating a positive manipulator and manipulates experience.

Step 1: Convince Your Friends to Do Things That They Don't Want to Do

It's nice when you've got someone you could share an activity with. The thing is, you can enjoy interpretive art, but it's going to be challenging to offer your mates the happiness they will be provided.

Luckily, under the right circumstances, most people can get around. You probably thought you'd hate last spring's ass pinching festival, but, as things turned out, you're going back for the fifth time in expectations to carry a blue-ribbon ride. What we end up like is often, in all seriousness, a matter of circumstances. If you want your partner to engage in something you like, under the right conditions, they will be more likely to join in.

You have to convince your friend to go with you first. Rather than trying to convince them that they're going to want to follow you because that will encourage them to come up with counterarguments, ask them to join you as a favor. It is because while we believe we do good things for people because we like them, our minds prefer to process items in the opposite direction. The reality is we tend to like somebody because we were doing something beautiful for them. If your friend sees the particular activity as a favor, if you try to drag them along, they'll feel better about you.

Step 2: Make Your Friend Have Fun

There are specific ways that can help you to make your friends have Fun:

- Handle Challenges Together

- Boost Your Friend's Mood

- Choose a Familiar and Comfortable Environment

- Reward your Friend's Competency with Compliments

Handle Challenges Together:

First, it can improve if there is anything about that game that is potentially difficult. Do it with them, and it can become a bonding experience? Even if they haven't appreciated the activity, they will lovingly look back on it afterward, because it got you all together.

Choose a Familiar and Comfortable Environment:

If the activity surrounds the person with familiar things and the types of people they like, it can help. Although we like to think that we are open to new ideas and value the distinctions among others, we don't really do that. If you want someone else to like something else, it helps if you can make them feel comfortable in as many different ways as possible.

Boost Your Friend's Mood:

At last, get them in a good mood in advance. This may seem complicated, especially if the person in question is a wrong and pessimistic individual you have come to love in some way, but it is easier than you think. There are a few simple ways, as noted in our brain hacking guide, to manipulate a person's brain to have the specific behavior for a given situation. While there are small things you can do, like reciting a list of positive phrases, that's kind of a strange thing to do in other people's company. You can also use the passion to place them in a better mindset. Having them chuckle is one of the best options, but if you're not naturally funny and reluctant to get the tickler out, you can do the trick with repeated smiles. Note how you will smile in return the following time you see someone smiling. It is difficult not to mirror happy expressions, as this usually happens without our full knowledge. Small things like smiling and humor can go a long way, even when they are unrelated to the activity being given.

Reward Your Friend's Competency with Compliments:

And don't forget the compliments. Let other people know that you think they're doing a great job once they're finished. People tend to like something more when they praise their actions in terms that stress their integrity.

Chapter 34: Manipulation Techniques

Impose an Unreasonable Request, and Then Present a Reasonable One

This is a technique that has proven to be very effective, and many manipulators often use it. It is also shockingly simple. Whenever a person wants to manipulate someone, they come up with a request that is not reasonable. The other person will reject the unreasonable request, and in that instance, a reasonable request is presented. The new request should be appealing to the individual who is being targeted. The best example to use in such a case is when an employee may not accept a permanent request to arrive early at work, but they will voluntarily accept a request whereby they are supposed to arrive at work early over a specific period of time to handle various urgent duties. The employee will prefer engaging in a short-term request, since it is less cumbersome when compared to the long-term request.

Inspire Fear, and Then Ensure That the Victim Has a Sense of Relief

A manipulator may have chosen their victims carefully, based on who is the most vulnerable. In this case, a manipulative person will make sure that a victim's worst fears have come to life. In the process, they will then focus on ensuring that these fears are relieved, and the victim will be happy enough to give them what they want. This kind of manipulation is dangerous, and you should reach out to people who can help to keep you safe from an abusive dynamic like this.

An example of how this kind of behavior might begin – assume that you have a car. Your friend might try to shock you by telling you that the car was producing some funny noises and that the engine might be dead. At that juncture, you will be in fear. After that, they inform you that they realized the strange noise was being produced by the radio.

You are relieved. Since you are relieved, your friend may go ahead and ask for another favor, such as – they want to borrow the car again.

Ensure That a Person Feels Guilty

A manipulator may try to get what they want by invoking guilt in another person. For starters, they might carry out an evaluation and learn more about how to make someone feel guilty by making that person feel bad for a variety of reasons.

If the manipulator is targeting their parents, for example, they would showcase that it's their parents' fault that they are the way they are in that moment, if invoking some form of guilt among one of their friends, they may make sure that they have enlightened their friend about the number of times that they have been let down by them.

Bribe a Person

When a manipulative person is after something, they may issue a bribe. In such an instance, they do not have to use tactics such as blackmail to get what they want. A reward may be given, but in the form of a bribe. The manipulator will learn more about your needs, but will try to hide the fact that they are issuing a bribe.

Pretend That You Are the Victim

When a manipulative person pretends that they are a victim, they will attract some sympathy. This is a commonly used method for some people who "play" the victim any chance they get. They usually make sure that they don't overdo the act in an attempt to get what they are looking for at the end of it all. Victims always appear helpless, and that means that the target will appear vulnerable as they offer to help them. They will pretend to be dumb, although they know what they are doing. They may pretend to be pathetic and helpless but will get more desperate and even enraged if you realize and don't give in to this type of emotional manipulation. You need to try to discern who is a real victim and who is manipulating you.

Use Logic

Logic is important in some of the day-to-day activities that you engage in. Always ensure that you have come up with a list of reasons as to why you would benefit from the things that you are asking for from someone. A manipulative person will always present their case calmly and rationally, but they will make sure to display some emotions, to get what they want at the end of it all.

Maintain the Character

Depending on the method that has been used, a manipulator will try to make sure that they have displayed some emotions that could relate to their current scenario. They may appear worried or even upset, depending on the matter at hand.

Manipulate Anyone in Your Life

As a manipulator, a person may develop different tendencies, including manipulating other people who are close to them in real life.

Manipulating Your Friends

When it comes to manipulating or being manipulated by your friends, you might realize that it is a tricky situation. Perhaps your friend has been making sure to flatter you, always making sure that they have been nice while also doing some small favors, in case they need a favor within a few days. If someone is a "real" friend, they won't need to manipulate you for a favor and vice versa. Try to stay away from toxic "friends." Some ways that the manipulation may be carried out:

- **Utilize your emotions** – your friends should be caring individuals; as a result, they will not want to see you upset. If you have any acting skills, make sure that you have used them accordingly to ensure that you will appear to be a very upset individual.

- **Constantly remind your friend about how good they are** – always ensure that you remember the periods when you have always done some good things for the sake of your friend.

- **Guilt-trip your friends** – you do not have to utilize the "bad friend" card. Always mention someone casually and remind them about how they have let you down. Always make it sound like your friend is uncaring without going overboard.

Manipulating Your Significant Other

If you have a manipulative partner, they may attempt to gain favors by turning you on and asking for the favor, so you understand you cannot get what you want unless you heed their demands. They may try "buttering you up" by asking for favors after giving you compliments or lightening the mood. These examples are the kind of thing that might happen before more damaging behavior escalates. You should try not to get too deeply involved with a romantic partner who is manipulative as it is possible they will be abusive in other ways.

The Impression You Use Determines Whether Your Manipulation Techniques Will Subdue the Target

A manipulative person will always make sure that they are deceptive and also swift. What matters most to them is ensuring that their image is still intact.

- **Utilize emotions** – look into what your significant other would do when they realize that you are wallowing in sorrow. In most cases, your partner will ensure that they have reignited the happiness within you.

- **Public embarrassment** – if your partner is determined to solicit a favor from you, they may have utilized the waterworks approach in a public place. The best example to showcase the effectiveness of such an approach is – when a child tries to solicit a favor from their parents in public, the child hopes the parent will give in to their demands. This technique will most likely be used sparingly.

- **Issue small bribes** – to encourage a favor, such as going out on a dinner date or to any other event, small bribes might be used.

Manipulating Your Boss

When dealing with professional relationships, for example, in an employee/manager dynamic, there are some things that can be done to increase the chance of a positive working relationship and of you being able to appropriately appeal to your boss for what you want from time to time. Use the approaches that are logical and rational when dealing with your boss. When you have some personal problems, do not discuss them in front of your boss. Also, do not appear at your boss's desk crying because of some personal issues. There is a high chance that you will be fired. When dealing with your boss, make sure that you are logical. Also, make sure that you have provided some good reasons regarding why you need some assistance from your boss.

- **Make sure that you are a model worker.** Such a technique will always work when you need to make a request. Also, make sure that you are working a bit late. Additionally, make sure that you are always happy and smiling whenever you are around your boss.

- **When soliciting a favor from your boss, make sure that you have done so in an offhand manner.** Always request casually. For instance, approach your boss in the office and tell them that there is an important matter that you wanted to discuss with them. When your boss hears that, they will issue you their undivided attention, and they will enact on your favor at the end of the day.

- **Try to ask for a favor at the end of the day.** Do not engage your boss early in the morning. First, make sure that you have observed their mood. If they showcase that they are stressed, you could opt for another moment. If you want to approach your boss during a break, you can do so as they go to look for lunch. They will want to quickly deal with your requests, and they will not also argue with you.

Manipulating Your Parents

It is evident that your parents should always love you unconditionally. As a result, they may be more susceptible to manipulation techniques. The main fact here is that your parents love you, and they will always support you in every way possible. You have to ensure that you are a model offspring for some time before you can make a request involving certain favors. Always make sure that you have not missed your curfew. Also, make sure that you have spent most of your time studying and assisting in handling some house chores. Afterward, you can go ahead and request a favor.

- **Ensure that your request is reasonable**. For instance, you may want to attend a concert and the following day you should be attending school. When making such a request, make sure that you have done so casually. Always make sure that your parents can see the possibility in the situation, and they will not reject the proposal in the long run.

- **You can also pose a question to your parents while you are folding laundry**. When handling such tasks, your parents will remember that they have a great son or a daughter, and they will be more likely to comply with your wishes.

- **Talk more about how you will engage in some of these activities together with your friends**. When your parents hear that you will be engaging in a specific activity together with your friends, they will be more inclined to issue you the go-ahead to proceed.

- **Ensure that your parents feel guilty**. For instance, you may have wanted to go to a concert. If your parents deny you the opportunity to take part in such an event, you will just tell them that it's okay. Always make sure that your parents will feel guilty since you may be missing out on an opportunity to take part in a major event.

Chapter 35: NLP

The first step that you need to use in order to gain a level of influence over someone is to figure out what their secret blueprint is that makes them who they are as a person. There are going to be several aspects of a person you need to understand in order to gain control over them that you want. This blueprint is going to show you their doubts, hopes, fears, and the things that they like and dislike about them. You will now be shown how to figure out all of these aspects of a person's blueprint and how to take action based on this information to increase the amount of influence you have over the other person.

To help you understand more about the fears that someone has, there are two main methods that work the best for that. These can either be used on their own or in conjunction. The first method that we can take a look at is the passive method. This method is just going to involve you simply paying close attention to the other person, listening to how they talk and what they talk about, in order to determine the things that worry them the most. You will find that different people are more or less obvious in the way that they reveal this aspect of themselves. Some people talk about things and clearly state they are worried by them, while others are not really all that explicit about it, and instead they are going to use some hints at it with the general demeanor and tone of voice that they use when it is time to discuss certain issues.

The second method that you can use is a more active method. For this one, you can listen for a bit and then try to lead the other person to the responses that you are looking for. For example, you could causally lead the conversation over to the topic of health with a particular person. Depending on how willing the other person is to talking about the topic, their tone of voice, and how physically comfortable they are with it, you will be able to figure out how much that particular person worries about health. You can use it for any topic in order to gauge the fear that the person has on that issue.

Uncovering the hopes of another person is often going to be easier than determining the fears that they have. This is because you will find that people are more willing to disclose their hopes rather than their fears. Many people like to give away what they aspire to in life by disclosing their aims for the future. Even some of the aspects that seem trivial amount a person, such as the purchases that they choose to make, can indicate the way that they are going to see themselves and how they like to be seen by others.

If you are looking to encourage others to open up about their hopes is to start talking about some of the hopes that you have. This can help make it so that the other person feels more candid. A manipulative and dark NLP spin that you can use is to disclose some of your hopes, ones that aren't sincere, that are specifically intended to increase the comfort level towards a certain topic. For example, if you tell the other person that you have some money worries, even though you don't have those money worries. This makes the target feel that money worries are acceptable to talk about, and they will then open up to you.

NLP, Manipulation, and Mind Control

Can NLP help you avoid negative manipulation and mind control? Yes, NLP can help anyone to fight manipulators. Often, we move along life on autopilot-responding to life in an extensively automatic way. This leaves us vulnerable to manipulation because we hardly analyze situations critically and make strong decisions. When living life on autopilot, we tend to follow what other people are doing (social proof) and also allow other people to influence our choices. Sometimes go through life drive by those subconscious programs which we have learned and practiced for years – some of them we practice since childhood.

Some self-development advocates and personal change ambassadors can fail to explain to us how we can avoid the specific tools we should apply to improve our lives. On the other hand, NLP lays out the tools you need to implement that change. It informs you that you are responsible for your actions, reactions, and responses to the situations in life. NLP allows you to get behind the steering wheel and take charge of your life instead of having another person drive you around.

NLP is practiced more because of its practicality – The tools are functional, and a wide range of challenges can be addressed through NLP. Include;

- Developing better relationships,

- Becoming more healthy

- Overcoming phobias and fears such as fear of public speaking,

- Improving communication

- Being more successful and impactful in your career and family life.

Success in any field of life, be it career, sport, family, requires excellence. Neurolinguistic programming is a roadmap for this excellence. Although other factors like luck and innate ability play a role in the success of an individual, the majority of NLP tools must be applied. Success is a predictable result of behaving and thinking in a certain way.

Mind control, hypnosis, and brainwashing are all closely linked together as concepts, but it is important to keep in mind their differences so that you know which one is the best technique to use in whatever situation you might find yourself in.

Mind control is perhaps the most subtle out of the three concepts, but it is also easily the broadest as well. Mind control refers to any series of words, actions, or behaviors that you can speak or perform in order to take command of another person's mental processes and dominate them. Ideally, when you perform mind control techniques, your target should not be aware of what you are doing, both before they have been mind-controlled and afterward. Your target should not be able to trace mind control back to you. Instead, you should be able to use mind control techniques without being detected, which is made easier when you model your mind control techniques on concepts from NLP, the Dark Triad, and the principles of persuasion and deception. In addition, mind control is not a permanent procedure. While you can certainly perform mind control techniques on a particular target more than once, they will not remain mind-controlled by you for a very long time. There are ways to extend the amount of time that your target is mind-controlled, but they will never remain mind-controlled for incredibly long periods of time. Out of the three concepts, mind control is the easiest to pull off successfully and requires the fewest amounts of resources for you to use.

Mind control can be best thought of as an influence system significantly disrupting the individual on a very core level. The techniques used in mind control affect the identity of a person, which is, his beliefs, values, preferences, practices, behaviors, decisions, and relationships, among others, creating a new pseudo-personality or pseudo-identity. You see, Mind control can be used for the benefit of the victim, for instance, to help a drug addict overcome his/her addiction. However, in this case, we are concentrating on the unethical and inherently bad practices.

"Mind Reading" Other People

You will also find that the choice of language that the other person chooses to use is going to be a really powerful indicator of what drives them, as well as how they see the world. For example, there are those who are going to show that they agree with you by saying something like "that feels right," "I know what you mean," or "I hear you." Their choice of language is going to show how they perceive the world, and whether that is through their logic, touch, or sight. When you know what the perception is for that person, you can then draw upon that and explain ideas you wish them to disagree with in a language that isn't in alignment with that system. You will also find that by listening to the other person, they are going to start disclosing words that have a special level of meaning or some significance for them. For example, you may find that when the person is talking about someone they have a lot of admiration for, they may use the word brilliant. And this word is only going to show up when their emotions are heightened. This is a good sign that the word has some kind of significance to that person. You can then use this information to your advantage and deploy the word in some of the statements that you make in order to trigger an agreement from the other person. However, make sure that it is used sparingly. If you overuse it, this is going to seem obvious and can come across as an unnatural thing.

Chapter 36: Mind Control

Have you ever had the desire to manipulate and control other people's minds? Have you ever wanted to try these things and see how they really work? Well, you're in the right place now.

Let's begin by saying that, of course, you can't completely control your friends, partners, customers, or whoever you are in touch with to do exactly what you want or to transform them into mindless robots. Well, maybe we'll be able to do that one day in the future, but not yet. What you can do is subtly influence them without them being aware of it.

It's known that humans are often not in control of their actions, decisions, and behaviors, even though they believe the opposite is true.

For instance, most of us have the deep belief that we have a stable sense of self that remains consistent and that we can predict how we would act in the future. Could we really be so sure of how we'll behave in extreme situations? Are we masters of our state, actions, and behaviors, or are we slaves, subject to others' control?

Most people would believe that, during a crisis, they could remain calm, cool, and collected; lead others, behave heroically, or maintain their core beliefs no matter what happens. Ask yourself: would you still be "you" during the zombie apocalypse? Would you stick to your moral code? Could you resist controversial orders from an established authority figure? I'm not sure anyone could, and here's why.

The truth is, very few people could accurately predict how they'd act in extreme situations. To find the reason behind this, we have to look inside your brain: when you find yourself under heavy pressure or in a stressful situation, your brain releases a hormone cascade that makes you experience a flight-or-fight reaction.

This physiological reaction helps us survive in dangerous encounters but shuts down a lot of higher functioning. This might have been a great system for surviving a saber-tooth tiger attack, but in our modern world—where we actually need our higher functioning in dangerous encounters—it's not so effective to defend ourselves from others' control. So, in other words, when we experience extreme situations or our survival is threatened, we may not think clearly or act in typical ways.

To prove this point, two psychological experiments were done in the 1960s and '70s. The first was a highly controversial study by Stanley Milgram, a psychologist from Yale University, exploring the phenomenon of obedience. They were seated at a panel with a microphone, a speaker, and a dial.

The experimenter was in the same room, wearing a white lab coat, which is a traditional symbol of authority (Just think about your doctor, would it feel the same to you if he wore a tank top and shorts during your visit?).

Participants were told that the "learner" (an actor selected by Milgram) was in another room; they would be required to ask the "learner" pre-scripted questions using the microphone, and they would hear the response on the speaker. The dial had labels ranging from mild all the way through to extremely painful and even fatal.

Here's the scary part: although they experienced extreme stress, an astonishing 65% of volunteers administered the lethal shock, and those who insisted on ending the experiment didn't ask to check the wellbeing of the learner. Most volunteers claimed they would never behave this way but couldn't stand up to the "authority."

The other disturbing study was the Stanford Prison experiment run by Philip Zimbardo, which showed how people are easily manipulated into behaving in sadistic and cruel ways. A basement at Stanford University was modified to look exactly like a real prison, and a group of students volunteered for the simulation. They were randomly assigned to the role of prisoner or officer.

Originally planned to run for two weeks, the experiment was shut down after only six days because of the ruthless, vicious behavior by the officers, who started behaving in sadistic ways toward the prisoners.

Not only does this research demonstrate how easily and rapidly we can change our minds, but the scariest thing is the rationalization that we practice. After the act, most people will rationalize their behavior, convincing themselves that they actively chose the action and refusing to acknowledge or believe they were manipulated.

Not only that... now, has it got scarier. Our perception is limited, which means a part of what goes on isn't consciously available, especially when we are focused on something else. Two studies demonstrate this phenomenon clearly.

When focusing on the instructions—counting the passes by the people in white—most people didn't notice the gorilla running by and insisted that it wasn't there. Most of the time, the person giving directions didn't even notice.

It's not just gross inattention, manipulation, and post hoc rationalization that modifies our behavior. You can use the great power of priming to change people's actions without any conscious awareness from them. For instance, read this sentence: "The house is old; it creaked and groaned, struggling on its foundations." Now, try standing up. After reading that, did you move slower than normal? If so, you were primed by these words to think of 'old age.' In a similar way, you can be primed to change your voting preference just based on the location of the polling booth. You can be primed at the grocery store, where the most expensive products are located on the shelves at eye level.

You can now understand how these principles have been applied throughout history.

This is not a conspiracy theory at work but represents the innate desire to persuade and even manipulate others to achieve our ends.

Next time you see an effective TV ad, meaning you want to buy the product, you can bet you've been manipulated.

A lot of the messaging that successfully "manipulates" works at a level far removed from our conscious attention, but you should always remember that disciplined, conscious attention towards your actions allows you to stay in control. When you notice yourself acting or feeling persuaded to act, in ways that aren't typical, use your new awareness and try to determine which technique is at play.

Mind Control in Marketing

There are many other records concerning mind control, one above all is Dr. Robert Cialdini's Influence: The Psychology of Persuasion that shows clearly the scientific proof of mind control.

The most important thing in marketing can be summed up with just one word: YES. If you ask a commercial partner to promote your product, and he or she says "Yes"; if you ask your customers to buy your new product, and they say "Yes"; if you ask a blogger for a link, and he says "Yes," well, then your blog, activity, business is working in the right way and you can really succeed. And the most important thing here is that you can learn how to do that. Here is a concise guide to mind control. Read it and then use these tips carefully for your advertising and non-business efforts alike.

The first part of this strategy is to not ask them to think and instead do it for them. Here are some guidelines:

1. Have an idea for an event or learning opportunity rather than seeking prep work from your customers, do it for them; plan the event, complementary web pages, and email campaigns needed.

Then, provide them with those complete products, with everything already working, and ask for their assistance in finalizing the event.

2. Online evaluations can make or break a product or service. Rather than waiting for customers to write the appraisals you need, provide a handful of clear, customizable examples and a strategic list of where they could be posted.

3. Be specific and clear. Explain yourself and show proof. Tell them exactly what to do step by step and why, and they will be more than happy to tell you "Yes" for everything you are going to ask them.

4. Start from a little snowball. A successful marketing campaign always starts from something little to then grow bigger and bigger as things go on. To achieve your ideal "Yes," the hard part is to obtain the first one. But if you get it from the right person, then getting all the other "Yeses" will be very easy.

It's like an avalanche, you get a little snowball going down from the top of the mountain, and then it becomes a huge and powerful wall of snow. Here are some guidelines:

Again, if you can persuade (maybe with some mind control techniques) a public figure, or a celebrity, to create a testimonial for your product or service, which is very hard work, then you will see your sales increase so fast you can't even imagine, and you will find many other testimonials with little effort.

5. Ask for a little thing, take a big one. Have you ever heard the expression "give them an inch, and they will take a mile"? While it's usually given as advice, a warning against others' greed, it can be great marketing.

If you want to obtain something, don't jump for the whole thing right away. Remember the snowball from point #2 and getting that first, "Yes." It's the easiest way to get started and reduces the risk of wasted time or effort. Then, you can start asking for more (and more, and more) when the results of your effort reveal themselves.

And it's not really unethical or even manipulation if you think about it. Why wouldn't you push for more if things are going well?

6. Establish a real deadline. As you know, deadlines are important because they create a sense of urgency.

But always remember: the important thing is that the deadline you set should be real.

How many times has a salesman told you to come back as soon as possible when he or she sees that you're not very convinced, maybe telling you that there are other people coming advanced and you could lose your opportunity by not acting now.

This happens so many times in our life. People lie to you or simply pitch you with artificial deadlines, thinking that this will really motivate you to act. Everyone uses this technique: teachers, bosses, wives, and husbands. It's very likely you've used this technique, too. The takeaway here? Don't take this ineffective route.

You should, instead, concentrate on generating real urgency. It's not hard and can be built up with your current marketing plan. For example:

- If you create content, don't leave free data on your page or blog for an indeterminate time. Consider employing scarcity here, and say that it will be available for a limited time, after which, you will start charging a cost for it. The specific deadline will boost the number of downloads you receive, and fellow bloggers can boost promotion efforts while your report is still free.

7. Be generous—give more than you take. This concept takes us right back to reciprocity, but the takeaway here is how much you should do. It goes beyond a one-for-one ratio; think ten-to-one. For example, if you're going to ask for a link, you should have already given ten links. If you're going to ask for a promotion, you should have already given ten promotions.

If you're going to ask for 100 visitors, you should have already sent 1,000 visitors. If you're going to ask for $1,000 in products or services sales, you should have already sold $10k of their products and services. This is about generosity, and it's a nice way to be sure they always lean closer to "Yes."

And I know it's a lot of work to do, but trust me, it works, and it's worth it. This is the price of influence, and you will see real results and income.

Chapter 37: Difference between Manipulation and Influence or Persuasion

When you call someone manipulative, it is often a criticism. If you say that you are being manipulated, then that's a complaint against the treatment you are receiving.

Manipulation is a dodgy concept at best and immoral at worst. Why is this? Why is manipulation undesirable? Human beings tend to manipulate each other in different ways, and most of us tend to do it unknowingly. What differentiates manipulation from influencing, and why is it undesirable?

Almost all of us are regularly subjected to some attempt at manipulation. The gaslighting technique is often used to plant a seed of doubt in someone so that they start to question their judgment and, instead, decide to rely on the manipulator's advice. Guilt-tripping is when someone makes you feel guilty about doing or not doing something that the manipulator desires of you. Peer pressure can force someone to care too much about the manipulator's approval; so that they do what the manipulator wants them to. Advertisements actively try to manipulate viewers by encouraging them to form false beliefs. For instance, when the advertisements portray fried chicken as a healthy food or encourage faulty associations—as when cigarettes are wrongly associated with the rugged vigor of masculinity—we have manipulation. Phishing and other similar scams try to manipulate their victims by using some method of deception, playing on basic emotions like greed, fear, or even sympathy.

Then, there are other instances of manipulation that are rather straightforward—for instance, a popular example of manipulation is when Iago successfully manipulates Othello and plants seeds of doubt about Desdemona's fidelity by preying on his uncertainties and making him jealous. It works him up into a murderous rage, so much so that he murders his beloved.

Manipulation is probably wrong since it harms the victim. At times, if it is successful—such as with a manipulative cigarette ad—it can even cause death or a dreadful disease. Manipulative scams like phishing lead to identity theft and fraud; social manipulation can result in abusive and toxic relationships.

However, manipulation isn't always harmful. At times, manipulation is even desirable. For instance, let us assume that an individual has just gone through a breakup and is out of a toxic relationship, but in a moment of weakness, she wants to go back to her abusive partner. Now, imagine that her friends start to use a technique that's similar to the one that Iago used on Othello. The friends are trying to manipulate her into a fit of rage that will discourage her from resuming a toxic relationship. If this kind of manipulation prevents her from any form of reconciliation, then she will certainly be better off than she would've been had her friends not manipulated her. To many, this might seem a little sketchy, morally.

There is something that is still morally undecided about manipulation, even when it helps. So, if you use harm as a criterion to define manipulation, then it isn't right.

Perhaps manipulation is considered to be wrong because it uses techniques that are immoral based on the way it treats others. This idea might be quite appealing to those who believe that morality is essential and that we must treat each other as rational beings instead of objects. The only right way to influence someone else's behavior is through rational persuasion, and anything that doesn't fit in the definition of rational persuasion is undesirable. Even this answer tends to fall short; for all intents and purposes, it will condemn even those forms of influence that are morally well-intentioned.

For instance, the manipulative tactic that Iago used was to appeal to Othello's feelings and emotions. Emotional appeal isn't manipulative at all times. Moral persuasion often appeals to certain emotions like empathy, or at least it tries to convey how it will feel to have others do something that you are doing to them.

Likewise, if you get someone to fear that a specific thing or act is dangerous or even harmful, then to experience guilt for doing this might not seem fair. Even an invitation to doubt one's judgment is not necessarily manipulative in situations where there is a good reason to do so. All forms of non-rational influence don't necessarily have to be manipulative in nature.

So, what is the difference between influence and manipulation? It might seem like there is a fine line to tread between these two. The only difference is the intent with which either is used. Iago's actions were certainly manipulative and even evil, since he intended to make Othello think in the wrong way. Iago was fully aware of the fact that Othello did not have a reason to be jealous, but he led him to believe it anyway. This is a form of emotional manipulation that's similar to deceptive ways used by Iago to trick Othello into forming such beliefs that Iago knows are false to begin with. Emotional gaslighting takes place when the manipulator tricks the victim into doubting what the manipulator believes to be good judgment.

If a conman tries to make you feel empathetic toward a non-existent African prince, he is clearly manipulating you to elicit a pure emotion—like empathy—for someone who doesn't even exist. On the other hand, if someone tries to make you feel empathetic toward the suffering of people who are real and the appeal is sincere, then it results in moral persuasion and not manipulation. For instance, if someone starts a fund-raising drive to help all those affected by a terrible natural disaster, then their tactics amount to moral persuasion and not manipulation. If an abusive and unfaithful person tries to make their partner feel bad or guilty for raising any suspicions about their fidelity, then such an act is manipulation because the abusive partner is preying on the victim's misplaced guilt. However, if a friend tries to make you feel guilty for abandoning her in her time of need, then that's not manipulative—that's just a means of making you understand how your acts affected her.

There is a common characteristic that makes influencing and manipulation morally wrong—the manipulator tries to get the victim to adopt what the manipulator knows to be a wrong belief or emotion. In this manner, manipulation is quite similar to lying.

The factor that makes a statement a lie and morally wrong is oneself—the speaker trying to get the victim to believe what the speaker knows to be an immoral belief.

In both these instances, the person exuding influence intends to induce the victim into believing something wrong or inducing them to make a mistake. The liar will try to make you believe something to be untrue and, therefore, enable you to form a wrong belief. The manipulator certainly does what the liar does, but apart from this, the manipulator will also make the victim feel an inappropriate emotion (doubting and misjudging someone else, feeling weak or unworthy, and so on) that's completely baseless.

The main difference between manipulation and any other form of non-manipulative influence depends on whether the person exuding the influence is tricking someone into making a mistake. Manipulation trickles down to immorality. The manipulator does it with the knowledge that they are leading the victim down the wrong path—they're trying to deceive the victim into believing something that the manipulator knows isn't true.

It is a primary trait of the human race that we all influence each other in different ways, apart from rational persuasion. At times, influencing can help improve a person's decision-making ability by leading them to believe, critically analyze things, or even encourage them to pay attention to the right things. At times, influence can also throw a spanner in the works by leading someone to pay attention to the wrong things or even by discouraging them. Manipulation involves the deliberate use of influence to hamper a person's ability to make the right decision, and that's the reason why manipulation is immoral.

So, when your heart is in the right place, and you have good intentions while exuding a little influence on someone else, and you know that this influence will help the other person to make a good decision, then that's not manipulation; however, don't just assume that you always know best. For instance, if your friend is drunk and is intent on calling up his ex, and you know that it's a bad idea and you discourage it, then it isn't manipulation—it is persuasion, and you can let your friend decide for himself once he sobers up.

Chapter 38: Persuasion Tactics

Persuasion is perhaps one of the most innocent ways to control the mind of someone else. In a sense, it qualifies as mind control because it is literally causing someone to shift how they are thinking in line with what the persuader thinks is right. When you are able to master the art of persuading others, you will be able to yield that power when it is necessary, in ways that can be beneficial to both you and those around you that you seek to persuade. Of the different forms of dark psychology, this one is the least insidious. It does not hide and does not attempt to force someone else into doing something. Instead, it is open and honest—advertising its purpose and seeking to encourage those around the individual to do something because they want to rather than out of coercion. The persuader wants everyone to agree with him or her, but not badly enough to force the point or coerce others. When attempting to persuade someone, there are six principles that should be remembered. Understanding and utilizing these can be incredibly useful when it comes to influencing other people. These six tactics are reciprocity, consistency, social proof, likability, authority, and scarcity. Take the following several moments to familiarize yourself with each of these.

Reciprocity

Reciprocity is the concept of people wanting to give back when they receive. When you help someone, the other person is far more likely to help you. Reciprocity seeks to harness that concept, recognizing it as a truth of humanity and seeing how useful it can be in encouraging others to do as a persuader desire. This can be seen even in restaurant settings—when the waiter or waitress brings you a few chocolates or a complimentary treat like a fortune cookie at the end of your meal with your check; you are far more likely to want to give a larger tip than if you had received nothing instead.

This explains why so many restaurants do offer up that cheap mint or cookie in response—they want to earn that extra tip.

You can utilize this concept yourself by always making it a point to consider what you can do for other people before seeking the other person to do something for you instead. If you stop and ask what they can do for you, you are not likely to get as far as if you stop and ask what you can do for someone else first. Your mind will be blown the following time you try this.

To start, try doing this in a relatively low-stakes environment. Perhaps ask your spouse how you can help one evening, and after the fact, ask your spouse for a favor. Your spouse, if the favor is reasonable, is likely to concede!

Consistency

Consistency is a bit trickier to understand. It is the idea that people make active commitments to the world around them, and they feel obligated to follow through with it.

When you have a commitment, you feel the drive to follow through, simply because you want to be considered reliable and committed. While this may not necessarily seem relevant to persuasion, consider this point: If you can get someone to offer a commitment to something, you are more likely to get them to follow through after the fact. People are innately driven to complete whatever they have promised to do so.

If you want someone to do something for you, then you should always seek to get it put into a commitment of sorts in order to ensure it is completed.

With the commitment made, you should then make it known to those around you. By publicizing the individual's commitment, such as telling people at work that John over there has agreed to help you with your copying all week, you add an extra layer of pressure to the individual.

John is far more likely to try to follow through simply because he wants others to see him as reliable as well.

When there are multiple people's thoughts about him on the line, he is far more inclined to push through and complete whatever he has agreed to do so.

Keep in mind, however, that this has to be voluntary. The other person has to want to do whatever it is you are asking them, or they are not going to really feel compelled to follow through with finishing the task.

For example, if you attempt to coerce the other person into doing your copying, and they reluctantly agree just to get you off their back, they are not going to feel that same innate drive to finish the work as if they had volunteered to do so on their own.

Social Proof

When is the last time you have walked into a room, looked around, and been entirely unsure what you were supposed to be doing?

If you are not sure, think about the last time you went to a busy public building for the first time—you may have been entirely confused as to what you would be expected to do or where you should wait. Instead of standing there without doing anything, you likely looked to the cues of those around you—you appealed to social proof. You wanted to fit in, and so you chose to do what those around you were doing, even though you were still unsure that that was the right thing to do.

People oftentimes rely on the social cues from those around them to understand what they should be doing, thinking, or feeling. Specifically, people want to follow their peers rather than authorities or subordinates.

Understanding this concept can be incredibly important when it comes to persuasion—if you are going to be getting a new group of charges at work, the easiest way to get everyone in line is to get a single person on-board first and allowing everyone else to follow that one particular person's example.

You just lessened your own workload and allowed for those around you to be trained quickly and easily.

Likability

Ultimately, people are far more likely to be persuaded when they like the person who is attempting to persuade them. It is a simple fact of life—people naturally reach out to those they know and trust and are more likely to take the advice of someone they trust than someone they do not. This can be used in a wide range of ways, and even if the other person is entirely new to you or does not know you well enough to like you, there are ways you can persuade them to like you so you can then persuade them.

There are three things that cause people to be more likely to like someone. These are reliability, praising, and being able to cooperate toward a common goal. If you can harness these, you are far more likely to get someone else to like you.

When you are relatable, people are likely to get along better with you. When you can relate to someone, you are better able to empathize, which can allow them to better see that they do like you. The easiest way to make yourself relatable in situations in which you are, for example, a salesperson, is to share a small detail about yourself early on or decorate your room or office with pictures or items that are relevant to you. Maybe you have pictures of your children up, or perhaps you decide to add a photo of yourself engaging in a hobby. Anything goes, so long as it personalizes you. Secondly, when you want to be likable, you should always make it a point to praise the other person. However, you cannot just make something up or say something that you do not mean—you need to make genuine compliments to the other person. When you lie about praise, you are often seen as doing so manipulatively and, in an attempt, to convince them to want to help out of sheer flattery. Even though you may actually be complimenting them more to get them to agree than out of kindness, you should still make sure that whatever you do say is genuine. Lastly, you want to make sure you and the other person are working toward the same goal. When you are both working together toward a common goal, the other person is going to be far more likely to want to work with you. Even in situations where you stand to benefit far more than the other person, such as in a sales job when you are trying to sell a car, and you will literally make a commission based on the cost of the car bought, you should make it clear that you are working toward a common goal. You can do this by pointing out that you want to help the other person or through phrases such as "help me help you" that make the other person feel like you are on their side. After all, you are—you want them to get what they want while also wanting what they want to be mutually beneficial.

Authority

People naturally want to defer to authorities when it comes to certain situations and decision making. This is why people will go get consultations from lawyers or doctors, or they will go to a professional to help with taxes. When someone else is seen to have all of the pertinent information on something simply due to experience or education, it becomes far easier to just defer to whatever that person is thinking or suggesting. By recognizing the authority vested in someone else out of experience and education, people are able to avoid making the wrong decision due to a lack of experience or not knowing how something works. After all, would you want a daycare teacher to decide which surgery you should get to repair an issue? Unless that daycare teacher happened to also be certified as a surgeon, the answer is likely no.

This is incredibly relevant to persuasion—if you can establish yourself as an authority on a topic somehow, people around you will be far more willing and happier to go along with whatever it is that you are requesting of them, which will serve you well. Luckily, there are several ways you can establish authority simply and quickly.

The simplest way to do so is by making sure you keep your credentials visible.

Place them on your nameplate, or hang your diploma on the wall right behind your desk. You could also make sure that when your clients come in, your secretaries offer some sort of detail that appeals to your authority. If you sell cars, your secretary may say something about how you are the top seller of the month, or if you are a dentist, the receptionist might sing your praises to the person making the appointment.

You could also do this yourself by offering small snippets of details about yourself when the client first enters your office, such as making a comment about that one time you were in school at such-and-such prestigious university studying your major.

By dropping your credentials subtly and naturally, you set yourself apart as an authority, and you will gain all of the persuasive power and influence with it.

Scarcity

The last of the principles of persuasion is scarcity. This one is also quite simple—it is literally supply and demand.

When things are less readily available, people see them as more valuable, and when they are more readily available, they are seen as less valuable simply due to the ease of access. You can introduce scarcity in several different ways, depending on the context.

Chapter 39: Tips and Tricks

As soon as you have realized how knowledge of certain truths about yourself can enlighten you to notice manipulative tactics by other people, you will start to divulge from what you are to what a manipulator can do. With that in mind, if you wish to overcome manipulation, you need to be wary of the basic tactics used by manipulators. Once you have a firm grasp as to what you want and what you do not want, you can go head-to-head with a manipulator and even counter some of their most-used techniques. Nevertheless, always keep in mind that as soon as you realize that you are being manipulated, the manipulator loses. It is simply a matter of whether or not you wish to turn the tables and become the manipulator yourself. The following are the tips and tricks manipulators use:

Accusing Your Rival of What He is Blaming You For

This is often referred to as the act of pointing to another person's wrongdoing. When enduring an onslaught and experiencing difficulty regarding safeguarding themselves, manipulators tend to reverse the situation. They blame their rival for committing the exact things that they are being blamed for. "You state that I don't love you! I think it is you who does not cherish me!"

Appealing to Power

Numerous individuals are in wonderment of those in power or authority, or those who have status. What's more intriguing is that there are various images to which individuals experience extraordinary dedication. Remember, those who are easily manipulated admire those who are in power. Moreover, those who are in power are aware of their ability to control others by never criticizing them. Instead, they use complex misleading tactics to maneuver their thoughts and alter their decision-making process.

Appealing to Encounter

Gifted manipulators and con artists, as well as politicians, would often state that they already have experienced or encountered certain situations in their life, which makes them someone who is in power. Nevertheless, this appeal to experience provides them with an image of someone who is capable; this may be used to attack their opponent's lack of experience, even though they themselves have experiences that are limited. You can easily identify this manipulation tactic at times when someone is trying to distort their capabilities about a particular subject.

Appealing to Fear

People have fears. The unscrupulous manipulators realize a reality that individuals will, in general, respond crudely when any of these feelings of dread are enacted. Subsequently, they speak to themselves as being able to ensure individuals against these dangers, even when they are not capable of doing so. This is the same for when we talked about giving the target a glimpse of how their most desired outcome is achievable without providing it to them. Nonetheless, there are politicians and legislators who frequently utilize this methodology to ensure that individuals line up behind administrative experts and do what the legislature – that is, the thing that the government officials – need.

Appealing to Sympathy

Manipulators can depict themselves and their circumstances to the public in ways to make them feel frustrated about their current situation.

Utilization of this ploy empowers the manipulator to occupy consideration from those individuals who may be going through the same thing. Nevertheless, appealing to sympathy is a tactic that most politicians would use to redirect the attention of the public to matters that do not affect their demise.

Appealing to Well-Known Interests

Manipulators and tricksters are always mindful as to how they introduce themselves as persons who possess the right qualities and perspectives among the group of spectators, particularly, the sacred beliefs of the crowd, everybody has a few partialities, and a great many people feel contempt toward a person or thing.

Appealing to Confidence

This technique is firmly identified with the past points; yet, it stresses what appears to have breezed through the trial of time. Individuals are regularly oppressed by the social traditions and standards of their way of life, just as social conventions. What is conventional to most tends to appear as if it is the correct decision? You must note that manipulators infer how they regard sacred the ideologies and beliefs that the group of spectators is familiar with. These individuals suggest that their enemy aims to obliterate the customs, as well as social conventions. Moreover, they do not stress over whether or not these conventions hurt guiltless individuals. They make the presence of being autonomous in the crowd's perspectives; yet, it would typically be the exact opposite thing. There is a realization that individuals are generally suspicious of the individuals who conflict with present social standards and built up conventions. They realize enough to stay away from these. As a result, there is a kind of restriction on how social traditions are unwittingly and carelessly bound.

Creating a False Dilemma

A genuine problem happens when we are compelled to pick between two similarly unsuitable choices. A false dilemma happens when we are convinced that we have just two similarly inadmissible decisions, when we truly have multiple potential outcomes accessible to us. Think about the accompanying case: "Either we will lose the war on terrorism, or we should surrender a portion of our traditional freedoms and rights."

Individuals are frequently prepared to acknowledge a false dilemma since few are agreeable with the complex qualifications. Clearing absolutes is a part of their manipulative tactics. There is a need to have clear and basic decisions.

Hedging What You State

Manipulators frequently hide behind words, declining to submit themselves or give straightforward replies or answers. This enables them to withdraw at times of need. Whenever they are found forgetting data significant to the current situation, they would think of some other reason for not being able to come up with said information. At the end of the day, when forced, they may be able to give in; however, to be an excellent manipulator, you should renege on your missteps, conceal your mistakes, and gatekeep what you state at whatever point conceivable.

Oversimplifying the Issue

Since most people are uncomfortable at comprehending profound or unobtrusive contentions, there are those who are fond of oversimplifying the issue to further their potential benefit. "I couldn't care less what the measurements inform us concerning the purported abuse of detainees; the main problem is whether we will be tough on crime. Spare your compassion toward the criminals' victims, not for the actual criminals." The reality being overlooked is that the maltreatment of criminals is a crime in itself. Tragically, individuals with an over-simple mindset could not care less about criminal conduct that victimizes criminals.

Raising Only Complaints

Your adversary is giving valid justifications to acknowledge a contention; however, the truth of the matter is that your mind is made up, and nothing can change it. Gifted manipulators would react with objections after objections. As their rivals answer one protest after another, they would proceed again to object and object. The implicit mentality of the manipulator is that "regardless of what my rival says, I will continue to object because nothing else will convince me otherwise."

Rewriting History

The most noticeably awful acts and outrages tend to vanish from chronicled accounts, while false dreams can be made to become facts. This phenomenon is often observed with Patriotic History. The composition of a contorted type of history is supported by the adoration of the nation and regularly defended by the charge of antagonism. The truth of the matter is that our mind is persistently attempting to re-portray occasions of the past to absolve itself and denounce its spoilers. Chronicled composing frequently goes with the same pattern, particularly in the composition of reading material for schools. In this way, in recounting to an anecdote about what has happened, those who perform manipulative tactics do not hesitate to contort the past in the manners in which they accept they can pull off. As usual, the manipulator is prepared with self-justifying excuses.

Shifting the Burden of Proof

This act alludes to when an individual has an obligation to demonstrate some of his declarations. A good example would be the instance that happened inside a court. The examiner possesses the obligation to prove guilt past distrust. Furthermore, the defense should not claim the responsibility of having to prove innocence. Those who are capable of manipulating others do not have the need to assume the weight of evidence for what they attest to. Along these lines, they harness the right tool in shifting the burden of proof to their rivals.

Talking in Vague Generalities and Statements

It is difficult to refute individuals when they cannot be bound. As opposed to concentrating on specifics, those who are capable of manipulating others tend to speak in the most unclear phrases that they can pull off. We have already talked about how certain statements and generalities can put another person in a daze, which makes it easier for them to be manipulated. This misrepresentation is well known with politicians. For instance, "Overlook what the cowardly liberals say. It's the right time to be tough, to be hard on criminals, to punish terrorists, and be tough on those who disparage our nation."

Manipulators ensure they do not utilize particulars that may make individuals question what they are doing in the first place.

Telling Enormous Falsehoods and Big Lies

The majority of the people are liars, even about the little things; yet, there is still a reluctance to say things other than the truth. In any case, these individuals realize that in the event that you insist on a lit long enough, numerous individuals will trust you – particularly, on the off chance that you have the tools of mass media to broadcast a particular lie.

Every gifted manipulator is centered around what you can get individuals to accept, not on what is valid or false. They realize that the human personality does not normally look for reality; it looks for solace, security, individual affirmation, and personal stake.

Individuals regularly would prefer not to know the reality, particularly; certainties that are agonizing, that uncover their logical inconsistencies and irregularities, and that uncover what they hate about themselves or even their nation.

There are so many manipulators that are exceptionally gifted in telling huge lies and, in this manner, causing those lies to appear valid.

Chapter 40: Developing Manipulative Behavior

Manipulation is all about making people do what you want rather than what they want. It requires you to be so scheming so that they believe and think that what they are doing or what they believe was their idea all along. To do this, you must first learn what their true desires and then re-engineer them to suit the goal you need to be accomplished. You will find that the easiest people to manipulate are those that are closest to you because they have grown to trust you, hopefully, and cannot suspect a thing.

One most important fact you must keep in mind as you go about it is that men desire perfectionism, while women are carried away by wholeness. As such, a man will be more carried away by mastery of skills and the ego that comes with perfection. Therefore, approach the man by creating some uncertainty about whether or not the man can improve always taunts his ego and puts him up to give it a shot, which means success for the manipulator. Women desire to be balanced in various areas of their lives, especially when it comes to their relationships with family and friends. Therefore, suffocating some impact on their close relationships often brings out a desire to do something about it to achieve some balance, and this amounts to success for the manipulator.

Here are a few more laws to follow to develop manipulative behavior:

- **Emotion versus logic**: Manipulation is hedged on emotion rather than logic. If you allow your subjects some time to think, the chances are that logic will set in, and they will be less inclined to follow your commands. You need to guide the subject to begin to feel in a way that will benefit you because once this is achieved, issuing instructions will not be difficult.

- **Be flirtatious and charming**: Tantrums and crying don't work all the time; sometimes, you need to bring out the 'big guns'; you need people to like you. If people find you ridiculously likable, they are likely to respond positively when you react to situations with extreme emotion. However, the trick is to keep your emotions in check until the time is right.

- **Have a hold of your emotions**: Most times, your target will not have control over their emotions, but you must have a grip on them. A manipulator must know how to act. Sometimes, you will need to hold back emotions like sadness and joy, while other times, you will need to shed a tear or be extremely angry, whatever the situation calls for. Do all you can to incite the fear or the sympathy you need.

- **Disguise evil in altruism**: The art of manipulation calls for you to appear good and vulnerable, even when you are not. For example, when you want to lay blame on another, or criticize the behavior, find a way to wrap it all up under altruism. People find it very hard to hate an altruist, and it will work in your favor if you paint yourself as one. If you yell at a colleague for failing to do something that you wanted them to do, calm down and tell them that you were acting in their best interest because you care about them. Tell him or her that it worries you that they do not have their best interests at heart. Remind them that you are always there, no matter what others do to your target.

Of course, some people will see through your manipulation and call you out for it. Therefore, to ensure that you succeed at your game every time, take note of the kinds of people you can manipulate. The best type to manipulate are people who have hard it rough in the past, those with a childlike naïve trusting demeanor, those who tend to be too generous, those who crave attention, and those who claim to be sensitive to fads.

Once you have identified your target, the following thing is to acquire some insight into who the person is and what he or she believes or thinks about him. Commonly, people think of themselves to be smart, cool, sexy, generous, kind, confident, funny, hardworking, beautiful, and intuitive. Now, use those qualities to your advantage.

For example, if you wanted someone who thinks he is fun to be around to come help with your cleaning, you could say, "Come help me clean my house. It will be fun. We will be playing some loud, cool music and dancing to it." If the person declines the offer, say to him, "I thought you were a fun person who can draw fun out of anything. I didn't know you are so dull you would rather sit here by yourself than join me in cleaning my house." You see, you will have tweaked the fun-loving nature to your advantage, and the chances are that you will have won yourself a maid for the day. Besides taking note of the beliefs your subjects hold about themselves, you also need to take note of their fears or weaknesses, emotional triggers, things that make them happy, reactions to different situations, likes, and any other information that could help you learn and predict their behavior or tendencies.

How to Discover People's Thumbscrews

Below are tips to help you figure out your targets so that you can use your knowledge to get an edge over them.

Take Note of the Unconscious Movements and Gestures

The most basic way to know more about a person is to watch them, to see how they behave and react to things. However, you got to know what to look for, where to look, and how to look. You also need to have excellent listening skills so that you grasp the weight of every word spoken and of other verbal nuances. Even if you are not interested in what a person is saying, you need to fake it. Appear eager and sympathetic because these two qualities will get anyone to speak. Your eyes should be very attentive at this point as well. See how the person reacts to others around him or her, such as traffic officers, servers at the restaurant, colleagues at work, and family members. See the conversations that delight or spark some interest in the person. Also, take note of the hidden messages, their clothes, jewelry, and style could be communicating. One way to get into the core of a person is to share with them a secret. Once you have been observing them for a while, reveal something, even if it's made up, and watch the response that this elicits.

The answer given will allow you to see into the person's weak points, and you could use those advanced to manipulate them.

It is essential that you also discover people's idols. Get to learn the things they worship, especially the things they can do anything to get. Once you secure this information, now work on fulfilling their fantasies.

Discover the Helpless Inner Child

You can trace the majority of the weaknesses in human beings to their childhoods before the person learns to create compensatory defenses. It could be an unmet emotional need such as parental support, a secret taste or indulgence that developed from being pampered or indulged in that area, or a childhood weakness. One way to spot the childhood weaknesses is that whenever you touch on that area, the adult begins to behave like a child. For each of these scenarios, step up and fill the void, and you will see that slowly, the person will start dancing to your tune.

Discover the Weak Link

Sometimes, weaknesses do not point to a thing or place, but a person. There could be a person behind the scenes who has tremendous influence over your target. If you win the favor of the one behind the scenes, you could easily influence your target's will. When dealing with a group, they fine the weakest one and use him as your way to get to the rest of the group.

Take Note of Any Contrasts

We already noted that one group of people that you can easily manipulate are those that claim to be very sensitive to fads. They always claim that their antennas are still up, but the reality is that they do so to conceal the opposite. Most times, people who thump their chests are the biggest cowards; the uptight are always looking for adventure; the shy who do not like the limelight are often screaming for attention. You will be intrigued to learn that there are many contrasts among people, and you only need to probe beyond the appearances to see them.

Meet the Unmet Needs

The emotional voids in all human beings are either the lack of happiness or the lack of security. The insecure are suckers for any form of social validation that comes around, while the unhappy are continually working to find things that could make them happy. Fortunately, insecurity and unhappiness cannot be disguised, and you can smell them a mile away. If you can find a way to meet these unmet needs, you will be well on your way to exercising power over your target's will.

Control the Irrepressible Emotions

Besides unhappiness and insecurity, human beings suffer from other uncontrollable emotions that render them to be ripe candidates for manipulation. Some of the key emotions are uncontrollable fear, greed, hatred, vanity, and lust. People on whom these emotions have a grip cannot control themselves, and your role will be to control these emotions for them.

Taking in and practicing the tips provided above will help you develop manipulative behavior so that you can get to bend people's will. Needless to say, it is inhumane to ride on other people's weaknesses to get them to do your bidding.

Chapter 41: Identifying Hidden Manipulation

There are different types of manipulation that you will encounter during your life. When we are talking about covert manipulation, we are talking about a kind that occurs under the level of your conscious awareness. If you are a target of this type of manipulation, you probably will not be aware of what is going on, which makes it the most difficult type of manipulation to spot and deal with.

Some of the most skilled manipulators will be able to make you doubt your emotional well-being and self-worth, which makes it easier for them to be able to control you. When you fall into this trap, the manipulator is then able to take away your identity and a lot of your self-esteem. This does take a lot of time to accomplish, but then they have time to get you to do what they want.

Most experts will refer to these skilled manipulators as covert-aggressive people. They will have a tool belt of tactics that they can use to get their target to do their bidding. And they are usually so skilled at what they do that the target will fall prey without ever noticing. Some of the tactics that a covert manipulator will use include:

- The ability to hide their aggressive intentions,

- Make you afraid, make you doubt yourself, and more, until you are willing to concede or give in to them.

Dangerous Manipulators

Good emotional manipulators can use almost any type of behavior to accomplish their goals. They are even more dangerous when they can read behavioral patterns and the actions of their target. When they can read their target, they will soon know their target inside and out, such as their level of conscientiousness, weaknesses, fears, insecurities, and beliefs. And in the hands of a manipulator, knowledge is a power that they can use against their target.

In some cases, the manipulator can even become known as a psychopath. There are many manipulators who do not fall into this category, but still, manipulators are really hard to have real relationships with. They will take a lot of time to study people, and then they will never think twice when they use that information against their target. They are more concerned about being able to get what they want in every situation that they will not stop to consider their target's feelings or how they should be acting in a real relationship.

One factor that you need to keep in mind is that manipulators have a need to be in control. They are power-hungry, and they will do whatever they need to achieve that goal. They will often hurt people in the process, and it will not bother them at all. If you ever feel that you are less superior, less intelligent, less strong, or less confident in your life, especially if you are around a specific person, then this person may be manipulating you.

Think about the relationship that you are in right now. Are you able to remember backing when you first met them? Was it something magical, something that swept you off your feet? You will find that most manipulators are sweet talkers. They are experts at being able to hide their real personalities and real plans from their target. They already have plans to trick you into getting what they want, and they will start from the first moment that they meet you.

In the beginning, this person will make you believe that they are willing to do anything for you, and they will keep up with this act until you are hooked deeply and until you show them your vulnerability. Once you have done this, they will start to bring out the manipulation, and sometimes the extreme abuse will start if you let it.

Over time, usually pretty slowly, so it is hard to pinpoint when it actually started, you will be able to notice that your ideal relationship has changed. It has become more confusing, exploitative, and demeaning. You will notice that the self-esteem that you had in the beginning (whether it was strong or not) will start to turn into doubt, and it is likely that you will start to blame yourself for this issue.

At this time, the manipulator will have full control. It will not be long until you are fine with just getting crumbs out of all the interactions in the relationship. You will be blamed for everything that goes wrong, even if you had nothing to do with it. You will have to take care of all their needs and care about them all the time, while they will no longer care about you or your fears, needs, and emotions. These manipulators do not really care about any of these things; they only pretended to care in the beginning to get you hooked on them.

It is amazing how quickly things can change. Once a target is under the control of their manipulator, even those with very high self-esteem will turn it around. They will start to blame themselves for anything and everything that goes wrong in their relationship. They will start to overanalyze things that happen in their lives, and usually, they will do this until they are so confused that they do not know what is going on in their lives. Every part of their day can start to suffer because of this confusion and the tactics of the manipulator, such as their mental health, physical health, social relationships, and career.

The sad part about all of this is that the manipulator will be able to do all of this without you seeing where it started. It is not something that happens one day, and then you can see it and leave. It starts out slowly, usually with a few little remarks or tactics that are used. Then one day, the manipulator will have taken over all the control, and you don't know how to handle the issue at all or to understand what is going on.

Chapter 42: Consequences of Remaining in Manipulative Relationships

At this point, you are better equipped to recognize the symptoms and causes of manipulative behavior in your partner. You may already be sure that he or she is definitely manipulating you. However, even with that knowledge, it can still be difficult to convince yourself to make the difficult decision you need to make.

In order to help encourage you to take action, this will focus on the consequences of sticking with a manipulative partner without hope for improvement. In all likelihood, you will probably already recognize some of these problems and consequences already. This is all the more reason to take control of your life and deal with this situation.

General Relationship Problems Which May Be Caused by a Manipulative Partner

Lack of communication: a lack of communication can stem from many different causes. Typically, it results from a feeling as if you are unable to honestly express yourself to your partner (and your partner feels unable to express him or herself to you).

Lack of communication can lead to small problems growing into overwhelmingly huge issues. The longer the communication line between you and your partner is cut off, the more distant you two will become. It is difficult to live with a person when you feel so distant from them. Your partner can start to seem like a stranger, and this can damage the relationship irreparably. You need to restore healthy communication to your relationship as soon as possible or risk it falling apart entirely.

Every fight turns into a shouting match: if you and your partner are unable to disagree or argue without shouting over each other, this is a serious problem. The point at which either of you begins shouting is the exact same point at which you both stop listening to each other. And if neither of you is really listening to what the other person is saying, you can shout until your voice goes out, and it will be useless.

No matter how emotionally sensitive the topic of the argument is, you and your partner need to work on discussing things with each other calmly and try to understand where the other person is coming from. This is difficult, but if you are both willing to work at it, it will become easier with time, feeling as if you are putting in all the effort: if you feel as if your partner puts little effort into maintaining the relationship, this can be exhausting. Relationships need two people. If you are the only one working at it, then it's not really a relationship anymore.

Sometimes, this imbalance comes from your partner's apathy or lack of concern for you. Other times, it may simply be a result of him or her not realizing what it takes to make a relationship work. This is particularly the case if he or she has never been in a serious or committed relationship before. If that is the case, be calm, open, and honest about what you need and explain that the relationship requires both people involved to put in the effort, feeling as if your partner does not care about your feelings: if your partner shows little or no regard for how you feel, this is an unhealthy relationship, committed relationships are built on a foundation of mutual respect, love, and trust. Without these ingredients, it simply cannot work. So if your partner does not seem to care about your feelings, you need to figure out what the cause of this is.

If he or she truly does not care, you need to end it so that you can work on finding someone who does care about you. On the other hand, if he or she simply has difficulties expressing his love and compassion toward you, then you need to find out if he or she is willing to work on that problem. If so, the relationship can still be saved. If not, you just need to end it there, feeling as if you get little in return for your effort: just as it requires two people to put in the effort for a relationship to work, it also requires a feeling that you are getting something out of the relationship you work so hard to maintain. Your relationship should provide you with a sense of safety and a feeling of being loved.

On the one hand, if you feel you are getting little in return, you need to consider what your expectations are from the relationship. If you are expecting too much from it, you will never feel satisfied. However, if you are open and honest about what you want out of the relationship, your partner can meet you halfway and help you determine which expectations are reasonable. If he or she is unwilling to meet any of your expectations, you should end it. Feeling underappreciated: with all the effort it takes to build a strong and healthy relationship, it is important that you feel that your hard work is appreciated. This appreciation is an extension of your partner's love for you and a sign that he or she values the relationship you have together. Without that appreciation, it can be difficult to find the energy to continue working at the relationship. Try to determine whether this lack of appreciation is simply caused by your partner's failure to show the appreciation he or she feels or whether he or she just really does not appreciate you. If it is the latter, you should leave. There is someone out there who can and will appreciate you. Feeling disrespected: just as with feeling appreciated, it is important that you feel respected by your partner. Does he or she encourage you to pursue your goals? Does he or she respect your opinions and thoughts? If not, then it will be difficult to maintain the relationship. You will grow increasingly dissatisfied. A lack of respect can even lead to low self-esteem and depression. So this is a serious problem that needs to be addressed. Whether or not manipulative behavior in your partner is ultimately to blame for the problems just mentioned above, you do need to make an effort to address these issues with your partner. Establishing an honest, open line of communication where both you and your partner feel safe from judgment is the first step toward resolving these issues.

Serious Risks and Dangers Involved in Manipulative Relationships

In manipulative relationships, they are almost a given. It is very likely that you will be experiencing all or most of those problems if your partner really is manipulative. We will focus on problems that are more specific to manipulative relationships and toxic relationships in general. These problems will not occur in a healthy relationship. If you are experiencing any of these, it is a sure sign that you need to end this relationship as soon as possible.

Developing a chronic emotional illness: remaining in a manipulative relationship for too long will often lead to you developing a serious emotional illness. The most common ones experienced by people who have been manipulated are depression, anxiety disorders, and even suicidal tendencies. All of these can be severely debilitating and sometimes life-threatening. Do not put yourself at risk for developing a serious emotional illness just for the sake of your partner.

Escalation to more serious forms of abuse: what started out as shouting matches could very well escalate to emotional, physical, or sexual abuse if your partner is manipulative? There is absolutely no excuse for such behavior. At the very first sign of such abuse, you need to get yourself out of the relationship and somewhere safe immediately. If your partner truly did love you, he or she would never dream of abusing you in any way. No matter what he or she says to convince you otherwise, that is all there is to it. People who love each other do not abuse each other.

Extreme isolation from your support circle: the longer you stay with a manipulative partner, the more and more isolated you will become from the people who truly love and care about you. Isolation is one of the techniques manipulative people use to control you and make you feel dependent on them. Do not under any circumstances allow yourself to become isolated from your friends and family. If you feel that you have become isolated from them, end this relationship immediately and go to your friends and family for support.

Even if you feel guilty for allowing yourself to be isolated from them, you can always go back to them. These are people who truly love and care about you and will forgive you for anything you may have done while under the influence of your manipulative partner, becoming severely codependent: as your self-esteem plummets and you become more isolated from your friends and family, your risk for becoming codependent increases dramatically. At the point of codependency, it becomes extremely difficult to end the relationship because you are so filled with fear and anxiety about leaving this person who has manipulated you into such a state.

This is exactly what your manipulative partner wants—completes codependency, meaning complete control over you. True love is not a power play. If your partner really did love you, he or she would not feel the need to completely control you.

Losing your sense of self and value: the more and more you become absorbed into this manipulative relationship, the more you will lose your sense of individual identity. You will forget what a wonderful person you are and all of the great things you used to do.

Your whole identity will become dependent on your relationship with your partner. This is extremely unhealthy because the fear of abandonment you may have felt earlier on while now not only be a fear of your partner leaving, but a fear of you losing yourself. You need to get out of this relationship and recognize that you are still a full and valuable human being, even without your partner.

Chapter 43: Convincing your Parents

Here are some ways that you can use to get what you want from your parents:

- Convincing your Parents
- Bargaining with your Parents
- Pleasing your Parents

Wait for the Right Moment

Take note of the moods with your parents. You may be upset with you for misbehavior, irritated with job issues, or unhappy at a friend's or their partner's troubles. If they are frustrated in any way, now is not the time anywhere to inquire for a present or a holiday.

Even if they're pleased, if you've been in trouble recently, it would be wise to wait for at least a couple of days or until the stress or awkwardness has disappeared between you.

Don't ask your parents when they are swamped. Imagine someone asking you to go to the store and pick them up some almond milk while you're doing a massive school project right in the middle. Such a proposal will seem greedy and irritating.

Show Gratitude and Thanks When You Ask

No-one likes selfish, privileged behavior. Imagine someone coming up to you, saying, "Give me the gift I've already asked for!" You'll most likely feel unpleasant and perhaps insulted. You want to reassure your parents that the presents you are getting are appreciated and that you adore the work they are doing to make money and get what you want.

Try to open the question like this, "Dad; you're always working hard to support us and treat us to the stuff we want. Thank you very much." This is not a trick to fool them. Don't pretend appreciation or put it on. Be sincere in your conversation, and it will go a long way.

Don't Use Hints

Making general remarks to your parent(s) like, "Wow, the Samsung galaxy s6 looks excellent! It has all these advanced features... "There is nothing promised. It is likely that your parents will not get the message. Or they're going to get it and do nothing. You do not understand what you want, anyway. Be straightforward with what you want. An example of direct communication is like this: "Dad, I want to go on a vacation to Florida so that I can learn to surf by the ocean." It is also good to have a more constructive intent. Take this scenario, "Dad, I really want to have a laptop, so I can spend more time writing and studying how to build websites so I can prepare for college."

Use a Delayed Response

Don't expect an instant, yes or no, from your parents. On the opposite, suggest something like this, "Dad, I'm going to ask you something, but I don't really want a quick answer." This will allow your parents time to consider whether they are willing to buy it as a present or to drive you where you want to go. Using this strategy shows patience because you're willing to wait for an answer for a day or more. This might please your parents and give you a better score.

Other Tips

1. Wait until you're doing something right, and use it as your reason why your parents should get it to you, what you want.

2. If you have been bad or wrong, do not ask immediately after the incident. This won't work, as you'll have been in their bad accounts for quite a while. Don't also say sorry and ask on the same day, because they'll think you're just saying sorry to get what you want.

3. Don't ask them when they are busy on the phone.

4. Make sure you do not expect an immediate reply. Before you get your final answer, you should try to impress them.

5. The more you speak, the more the idea remains in your head. Yet don't inquire too often. Request for the same for your birthday, Lent, Christmas, or any other holiday gift-giving don't investigate every day, arbitrarily.

6. Don't be nervous while asking, and Make no worries about it.

7. Show your parents you are responsible for getting what you want and don't give them a reason not to get what you want. It shows you can handle them.

8. Please focus on what you'll be doing. That way, you look like you should know what you're talking about, making your parents think that you seem mature.

9. Don't just go on and on about that. It is just getting annoying and making them less convinced.

10. Speak clearly, and don't feel the floor down. This is critical to understanding you from your parent's perspective.

How easily a person falls in your hands depends upon the impact you have on him or her. Be fast and agile about the projection of your image (be tricky).

Put the thoughts to use. Do you want to see you screaming or being very visibly upset by your other significant one? Obviously not.

Use the waterworks strategy in general if you want to get what you want. Just as an adult is more likely to give in to a kid who holds a public tantrum, when you're weeping in public, the guy will be more likely to give in — using this strategy sparingly.

Using petty bribes, if you want your man to take you out on a nice lunch, the following day, try to go with him to the baseball game. Then this turned out to be less like bribery and more like natural cooperation.

Take an acting class to help you hold your emotions under control.

That will come naturally for some people, so don't try too hard and strive not to be too noticeable.

Try to show the individual a curiosity and make it look as if you need anything. They'll feel ready to help you out.

Compliment people and comply (most) with what they're doing, unless it's illogical or makes you look like a suck-up

Chapter 44: Things You Need to Do to Manipulate People

You should be able to influence others with excellent verbal communication skills. If you want to manipulate people, it is important that you speak clearly and skillfully express your thoughts. There are a number of ways to improve your verbal skills, and we can't go into details, but we will keep listing a few so you get an idea.

Improved Verbal Communication for Better Handling

a. **Begin to read as much as you can**. A great vocabulary is important, and reading is the best way to improve it. You can read records on any topic when questioning you. Avoid simple texts that require little effort and can even handle the 5th grade. In addition to vocabulary, reading will expand your knowledge of various subjects and will obviously make things easier for you to think about. Many people hate reading, and maybe you are one of them, but we guarantee that once you read it, it isn't as bad as you think. In addition, we are usually forced to read boring classical literature when we are young. This is not the case in this case. You can read online contemporary novels, journals, magazines, and interesting articles. b. **Practice your voice before a mirror**. It's important to look at how you speak and to be confident with it. In the end, you will find things you don't like and change them. If you don't like the specifics, nobody else will. You can also speak to others you want to control and exploit. This is not the first time you talk about the subject when you meet them. You can make it like a play and repeat it a couple of times. It may not be 100 percent according to the script, but most likely, it will be the same, and you'll be set. c. **Work on your voice and your tone**. Everything you say is not the only thing that is important. How you do it is no less important. The document, listen to and evaluate your voice. Write down what you like and what you don't like about it. Learning about it will increase the mental manipulation success rate. Don't talk quietly and monotonously. Make sure what you say is transparent and secure.

How can you affect anyone if you mumble and can't even listen? Imagine yourself on stage as an actress. You practice more, and you're going to get better.

d. You will look good before the people you want to exploit. We include this in the skills list because one really needs to look good. Genetics plays a role here, but you must use this' Halo Effect' to your benefit as much as possible.

e. How to look good for a person to exploit. Crucial grooming is a crucial part of the good look (and smell). We all know this. They all know this. But so many people fail to do so. Human beings have an innate attraction towards clean people because they have been healthy throughout history. We still have those traits, and we just like the clean and smelling people. How can someone be fooled if you stink? This does not take much effort. Wear a deodorant, shower, and a good fragrance.

f. Have a haircut that's perfect for you and looks good. How your hair looks influences the whole wardrobe directly. If you talk to a guy you're trying to influence, and your haircut is one thing he sees. The fact that many people don't know their hairstyles and still want to look good is irritating. You also have to be rational. If the haircut isn't perfect for you, just let it go. Don't try to rock it when it looks awful to you, obviously. Have a feeling that one is for you, and never try to save a salon and visit the terrible one.

g. Don't go nuts and dress nicely when you can't rock it. You must convince a person that you exploit. You can't go wrong with an easy, classic look, and don't try unless you know what you're doing. If a person doesn't like your outfit, he won't take you too seriously, and it will be very difficult to manipulate somebody in this situation.

Learning more about neuroscience and psychology teaches you more about manipulating people. You must at least understand the human mind profoundly if you want to be a master manipulator. Of course, what we teach you here helps you, but you need a deeper and broader understanding of human behavior so that you can actually easily influence people.

How can you? How can you do that? First of all, browse our website and read general articles on psychology. Then watch some videos on YouTube. The following step is to begin reading actual records on psychology. If you want to learn fundamentals, there are always good manuals for the University of Psychology.

Chapter 45: Manipulation Games

Some manipulators are so hazardous that they could inflict so deep wounds that may take a long time to heal.

When you meet a charming person, it is not always applicable that they may be a sociopath, but if you feel that you are being gaslighted, manipulated, or messed up with an excessively loving person, then this could be possible that the charming personality is none other than a sociopath. Sociopaths are the people who are people who know how to manipulate people so well that they have a way of controlling others around them, be it any situation. They would know every tiny bit of you, from the way you dress to your mental ability to think. The main target of manipulators is the people who are vulnerable and easy to dominate. They judge you and then play with your emotions accordingly. Being in touch with a sociopath could be a disorienting experience for you, once you know all their tactics and games they play, you would not let them take over your advantage.

Here are some major mind manipulating games that manipulators play:

1) Flattering You Extensively

It is a fact that everyone who flatters enormously is not a sociopath, it depends. But in case they are a sociopath, they would do whatever it takes to win you over your trust and gain your confidence. If you know about this strategy of them prior, you may not become a target of these manipulators and would know in advance that the compliments and flattering remarks given by them are in-genuine.

The manipulators like these may say that 'you are the most amazing person, humble, charming, or intelligent person on this planet that I have ever met' or 'my life is incomplete without you.' Even though it has not been long that you have met that person, in those cases, if statements like these are being used it may be a hint or indication for you to understand.

2) Never Take Accountability for Anything

Usually, manipulators never take any kind of responsibility for their decisions, feelings, or behavior. Instead of being accountable for their actions, they blame others for such actions. However, the other person would want to make the situation better and would not even know that it was not their fault, but they are being targeted by the sociopaths. They will comply with all the demands issued by manipulators as they would feel insecure for such actions and with respect to bringing the situation to peace.

3) Enjoy in Messing You Up

Manipulators may enjoy messing with your head. They will not show any contrition, even for their mistakes. Instead of showing remorse, they will blame you and will take pleasure in doing so. For example- if you quarrel with your friend for any reason, the manipulator will take advantage of that situation by acting sympathetic and taking your side. He will criticize and highlight how awfully your friend treated you. This is one of the manipulative behaviors that sociopaths play with other people. Now that you are aware, you may not get caught up in their manipulating strategies.

4) Have a Full Control

The biggest manipulators play the manipulation games by keeping control over the other person. They would always turn the situation in their way and always want the ball in their court. If things are not going the way they want, they start argumentation and show aggression. They may even threaten you at some points as they start dominating you. Some manipulators use 'threats of suicide,' or some may say 'you will feel sorry for what you did.

5) Lying and Cheating

It is one of the common and blatant signs of a manipulator. The manipulators just want to reach their goal and always want to achieve what they have thought of, no matter what may come. Lying to a person or cheating on them is their biggest tool to take over your advantage. The sociopaths will not follow usual codes of conduct as that is why they are manipulators, so you have to be assertive to find out their 'not so good' games that they play and have that gut to feel the vibes of the other person is negative.

6) Gaslighting Your Opponent

It is one of the dark tactics that many manipulators use to confuse you, you feel like you can't win the argument after being gaslighted by the manipulator. It is something in which manipulators use your words against you even if you haven't said anything wrong or no matter how authentically you are doing something. They will let question your sanity, and you will defend yourself by ending up saying statements like 'I did not mean that way' or 'I am sorry if you felt bad.' They will make you feel guilty for what you have done (even if you were not at invalid). They would also provoke you through immoral actions and disturbing statements and then pretend to be over-emotional or sensitive, and irrational.

7) Manipulators Always Play on Your Good Side

Sociopaths always find and discover your weaknesses and kindness against something. They then use those weaknesses against you and find the reasons which will give you a benefit of doubt, which makes you an easy target. For example- if a man passes flirtatious comments to other women and his partner confront him to not use those comments, then he would say 'how could you even doubt that as there is nothing serious in it and I only love you' or maybe anything that it takes to gain your confidence and get back into her good records. After a while, you would stop saying that to him, and he would take the benefit out of that opportunity.

8) Make You Lose Your Self-Belief Power

Manipulators do certain things that may loosen up your morality and rationality, such as not letting you speak up against anyone, make you lose your confidence, questing yourself about your existence, assert boundaries, and degrading your self-esteem. And after a certain period, it becomes very hard to negotiate from within that relation without abuse or offending, or displeasing further confrontation.

9) Justifying the Immorality Done by Them

They would justify all their actions. Even if they break the law, they would rationalize it. Manipulators only focus on their needs, they are not concerned about anything else if their needs are getting fulfilled, and they are getting benefit out of it even if it is illegal. If you try to make them realize their mistake, they will cover it up by manipulating your reaction against that situation.

They will turn your mind the way that you will start feeling whatever has been done by them was not immoral, and maybe you are overthinking. One thing is universal with all manipulators that they would never admit ti anything they have done illegally. Instead of admitting and feeling guilty, they will make that illegal thing authentic and will justify the reason behind doing that action.

10) Back-Tracked Their Own Words

A manipulator is not a man of his words. They will never be up to what they say, which is enough to make you crazy as you will tell them about what they said and they will pretend that they have never said any such thing ever, moreover, they will force your mind to rethink and will make you fall under a doubt that they have never said such a thing what you were thinking.

11) Give You a Silent Treatment

Some manipulators may play silent games with you. If they want to abandon some action before you do one or they are upset with you regarding some action, they will neither say anything nor make any eye contact with you. Manipulators do not care whether the other person is ethical, they are self-centered and only care about their feelings. The silence is their way of attacking and making you feel guilty whether you are right or wrong.

12) Bully Intellectually

A manipulator may also try to use some technical facts and figures, which may not even be true just to win an argument with the other person.

If they use facts and figures against the topic you already know about, they won't be able to make you wordless, so the manipulator would know that against what topic to use the statistics to make you dumbstruck.

13) Treating You Differently

If a person has a bad reputation with the others and is being over-friendly and deeply emotional with you, then something may be dubious. If you are experiencing the same thing with a person, it may be a warning indication to be cautious. For example- if a person has a good reputation in the office and just because of that is being over-friendly with you. You need to be aware of how and why they are treating you differently and analyze the kind of interactions they are initializing with you at the beginning. You can judge and keep distance from them accordingly.

It may not be true all the time, as a person may be good to someone, but he may not be good to the other one. You cannot judge a person's behavior based on the other person's verdict. You can just be certain about it once you start getting familiar with that person. And yes, certainly, now that you are cognizant of all the manipulation games played by sociopaths with the other person to dominate, execute and take over the advantage of them, you will not let them do so. Manipulators cannot harm you until you are acquainted with all their dark psychological tactics.

Sociopaths think that this is their biggest strength to manipulate people, and this is what they use against the innocent ones. But if you can spot their signs, this will keep you safe as well as transform their biggest strength into a weakness.

Chapter 46: Reading Personality Types

Recognizing psychology in company management is an integral aspect of successful direction. What drives one individual won't inspire another. To boost productivity, efficiency, and functionality, it's crucial to comprehend character styles and social dynamics.

1) Avoidant Personality

Characterized by intense social anxiety, hypersensitive to some criticism, fear of people, isolation. This sort of worker can be quite reliable and compliant if positioned in non-invasive occupational functions, in which little to no communication and personal interaction is necessary. They're nonthreatening and non-demanding, typically have very few, if any, friends. They're secure and excited to take additional work often as they're too bashful and dislike confrontations. These kinds of people aren't antisocial, only intimidated by individuals and particularly authority figures. They don't have to be micromanaged or preoccupied. They generally accomplish all work in time and make a few errors. On the drawback, "avoidant" workers won't work well in leadership positions, and it can be a major mistake to set them in managerial functions. They may be readily manipulated and falsified and drown in prohibited practices. They're best fitted for tasks that require little interaction like clerical, administrative, computer technology, and web-based places, accounting. They lack human relationships and are motivated by simple compassion, training, and counseling. They fear being rejected. They get together with everybody.

2) Dependent Personality

May perform well with a narcissistic or borderline kind supervisor. They're always in need of direction and guidance. Their questions never cease, and have to be reassured at each step along the way. Since they're in a continuous need to be informed what to do, they make great assistants and, if trained nicely, can become great faithful employees. Dependent personalities want people and dread being lonely. They're ready-made followers.

3) Histrionic Personality

Reveals a pattern of a continuous need for attention, enthusiasm, enthused, and go-getters. They're excellent in direction; create good salespeople, speakers, celebrities, and teachers. Their life is a psychological roller-coaster; they rely on their own instinct and go with their gut feeling. They love to be in front of audiences of people, always the life of the party, are generous and likable men and women. When they're happy, everyone is happy, but working with them may be a joy or a distress.

4) Borderline Personality

Believing is "that is the best job I will ever have and the worst place I have ever worked." They're dangerously unstable, overly emotional, irrational, and spontaneous. They make decisions that they regret. If you're able to detect borderline character, you would like to prevent employing this individual at any cost. They expect you to think whatever they think, and if you do not, they'll get mad. They move from a high-manic country where they're filled with energy, enthusiasm, intense happiness to a stone bottom where they're depressed and suicidal. They could act mad, neurotic, and require medical care. They feel entitled to control individuals and expect them to follow along. They either love you or hate you. There's not any grey area- it's black or white. They're unpredictable and behave according to what they believe right now. Their private lives are often busy with stormy romances, play, mood swings, impulsive spending, substance abuse, and poor health. Some borderlines may be educated and capable and may be a trusted worker if you're on their side.

5) Narcissistic Personality

Possesses feelings of entitlement, doesn't live by rules, believes they are smarter and larger than everybody else and has a feeling of grandiosity. They generally believe they are more capable and unappreciated. "It is my way or the street. I am unique and deserve to be successful; others don't like me because they're jealous of my talents." They don't operate well inside a corporate arrangement and occasionally make enthusiastic and aliens with their own schedule. They like to feel great at the cost of others and think that what is good for them is great for others. While they could be proficient, vibrant, and remarkable, they tend to take things personally. It is not unusual for them to participate in vindictive behavior whenever they are feeling betrayed. They have a natural attribute to control other people and exploit for their particular function. They generally state more than they are and use intimidation on others. They often engage in prohibited practices and could be a massive liability risk. Since they believe that the entire world orbits around them, they see little use in continuing or self-improvement education. They have to be handled carefully in a diplomatic manner and frequently with ass-kissing. Beneath the surface of the bloated ego lies brittle self-esteem and an extreme sense of shame and inadequacy. Narcissists probably resort to aggressive violence and litigation when sanctioned or terminated. Disciplining and firing need to be performed carefully, tactfully, diplomatically, and well-documented.

6) Antisocial Character

Would be the most damaging kind in a functioning atmosphere. This sort of individual would do anything to make their ends meet at the cost of everything and everybody with no respect or conscience. It's not always detectable and may ruin the entire firm. They'll do the minimum on the job and make the most of each advantage, drive customers away, ruin standing, manipulate others into their own unethical practices, and prohibited actions. A number of them become cutthroat entrepreneurs using usually shady strategies and predatory methods of moving over everybody else. They are sometimes confrontational, violent, destructive, and spontaneous. An extensive criminal record could likely rule them out from being hired.

7) Obsessive-Compulsive Personality

Is a kind that ignites everything to perfection and focuses on details. They generally excel in their job at the cost of their social life. They're scientists, planners, engineers, economists, editors. They could work nicely with virtually every personality type since they're getting the work done, and that is their sole obsession. They aren't confrontational or violent, and many are often calculative, organized, and concentrated on their undertaking. The dependent character would be a great helper to an obsessive-compulsive manager. They have high expectations of themselves and create demanding managers. Everybody is going to be expected to maintain speed. They consider there is always space for improvement and take their job seriously. As workers, they frequently spend too long "perfecting" the job, which can result in distress and have to be reminded of deadlines. They're motivated by the feeling of accomplishment and give it 110%. Sometimes they will need to be provided a sense of leadership and deadlines because they may get stuck on particulars and be indecisive regarding the leadership of this undertaking. It's the simplest and most satisfactory kind of individual to use. The task is always performed and no play.

8) Paranoid Personality

Characterized by continuous distrust and suspiciousness. They keep up their guard and don't open easily. They believe that individuals cannot be reliable. The world is filled with mean and selfish men and women that will hurt and betray them. Should they concentrate on work, they could achieve substantial success, particularly in complicated strategic planning. In addition, they have a knack for technical specifics, fantastic memory, and strategic visions. They could make excellent leaders as soon as they gain confidence and relaxation in their job environment. Anticipate suspicious questioning of different people's motives and motives of homework. They prefer to listen to calm logical explanations and react well to logic instead of assurances or guarantees. Constantly be fair to gain their confidence. They generally have sharp instinctive abilities and may tell lies straight away. The paranoid mind is pushed by a sense of entitlement and superiority, frequently in reimbursement of the private inferiority feeling. They see business as a combat area and have a defensive strategy. They are prepared to beat you in your game, maintain their friends close and enemies closer. You will never know their schedule. In extreme cases, it may be difficult to utilize diehard employees, and it may create a hostile and stressful work environment.

When betrayed, the paranoid will hunt you down and punish. A planned out way once about the hit record, your destiny is sealed. They think that nothing is their fault.

9) Passive-Aggressive Personality

Think that life isn't honest, nothing is their fault, what bad happens to them even though they do all right. They're a victim and constantly have "perfectly explainable" motives. They never take responsibility and behave like an injured party. They can be passive in their job, masters of procrastination, and utilize "self-handicapping" techniques they use as a justification for work not being performed. They're competitive, malicious and may be involved in sabotage, corporate espionage, and malicious whistle-blowing and may elongate any provider. They're notorious for filing civil lawsuits. Be mindful of firing that sort of individual, record and communicate the grounds for this choice, and extend a face-saving manner of leaving the corporation. This individual will become somebody else's problem. Be cautious with recommendations to prevent additional litigation.

Handling Individuals - The Challenges

Everything may be handled readily with a few attempts except "individuals." Why has handling people gotten so difficult in contrast to handling different tools like currency, time, machinery, equipment, etc.? All resources interact with the surroundings, but people get easily affected by the environment and alter their traits, attitude, and behavior dynamically to a significant extent.

Handling People Becomes Difficult

People mostly get affected by their parents, relatives, and friends, the way in which they are brought up in youth, by their environment, the group that they socialize and mingle, their own encounters, by different Medias such as television, internet, and newspaper, etc. This list is unlimited. If you carefully analyze, individuals are the only beings that may be affected in a variety of ways and may be forced to act so dynamically within this world. It is now hard to predict people's response and behavior to any kind of specified situation or surroundings.

From the situation of altering characteristics of individuals, it gets really challenging and hard to handle people. There's a strain on us on the technique, which we have to manage individuals. Individuals can't be blamed for this changing mindset and behavior, as they're also required to handle many individuals and connections in their own life, and it will become hard for them to keep exactly the identical manner they used to deal with other people.

The Best Way to Overcome This Circumstance?

We are social beings, and we can't isolate ourselves from individuals or society, even if we would like to. We can't steer clear of people, and there cannot be any circumstance that makes us not socialize with any individual. The way to overcome the circumstance? The solution is "listening."

How Do You Know the People in Your Lifetime?

To get a moment, let us have a brief journey in the brain of a special individual. As we step within this thought, we start to grasp a photo of the individual's likes, dislikes, fears, ideas, customs, beliefs, perspectives, tastes, principles, values, and so on. We see them for who they are, for what they stand for without camouflage or emotional disturbance, and we wonder... about the indications that their body leaves behind. This will give us a profound unprotected insight into the recesses of the mind.

Inside the discussion, we'll concentrate on unlocking the emotional components that piece together the individual character. The wisdom and comprehension you'll gain from this investigation will offer you a profound insight into people's ideas and motives, regardless of what their verbal speech may indicate. This may fortify your persuasive and powerful abilities to convince other people to a way of believing.

Chapter 47: Strategies in Seduction through Manipulation

When you know how to get into someone's mind with sultry, emotional manipulation, it doesn't matter who you are or how much is in your wallet, despite what some people may say.

At the end of the day, the thing people will listen to the most is their emotions, and we will tell you how to handle someone's emotions just the right way, so they go crazy for you.

First, we have state control. State control on your end means not being bothered by rejection. Being rejected doesn't reflect on you in any way. It only reflects on the situation, the disposition the subject had at the time, and your own delivery. If any of these things change, you can turn a rejection into a date. But if you don't manage your state control, you will lose hope with this person and never get anywhere. Be sure not to take state control for granted in seduction.

But don't forget that state control is also controlling the emotional state of the subject, and this is everything in seduction. Now, it is a little different here, because you don't want them to feel a negative emotion.

In other cases, it is fine for them to feel a negative emotion for the purposes of them seeing things your way in the end. But in romantic affairs, our senses are too fragile to be too negative valences. Therefore, you need to control their state in a more gentle way. As we move through the rest of the seven foundations, you will see what we mean.

Next, there is sensory acuity. Especially when it comes to seduction, the senses are everything. You need to make sure your love interest in experiencing positive sensations around you. Are you making sure they are drinking a sweet drink? Do you smell good?

Does your skin look soft to the touch? Is there music playing, or is there a lot of noise? We understand that some of these things are outside of your control, depending on the social environment, but some of them are in your control.

Of course, the most obvious part of sensory acuity here is managing your looks. But we all know what we do to spruce up our appearance

Make sure you are paying attention to their unconscious body language. All of our lessons in that area apply to seduction as well. Use your insight to read between the lines when they speak.

Finally, use your imagination to strategize how you can change things between the two of you. And use your sense of imagination to get them to see you and them as a possibility. It may be that you are not even in their view. This doesn't even have to be a bad thing; sometimes, it is not personal. They might not even think they are looking for someone right now. Getting them to see you as a possibility might just mean seeing anyone as a possibility. But following all these other techniques will make sure it is you.

Next, the foundation of unconscious communication comes into play. Ask yourself what your love interest is doing with their eye contact. How are you responding to it? Does their body language look relaxed? Do they look like they are in charge, or like they are waiting for permission?

Voice and emotion in the voice can make the difference between knowing what is on your love interest's mind and being completely clueless. Sometimes, they give us clear signs of what they are thinking. Other times, they completely leave us in the dark. But we have to be sure to listen to these things either way because we can't afford to miss something.

The fourth foundation of neuroscience comes into it because of the mirror neurons. Remember that the best way to get mirror neurons to fire is to tell a story. Now, with a love interest, you can't just jump into a conversation with a story. You have to make sure it feels relevant to them. But this is what will seduce them. This is what will get them to have deeply felt emotions for you.

Psychology, the fifth foundation, plays its part in the dark psychology of social comparison. It is a forbidden truth that social standing plays a big role in the selection of mates in the real world. That means you may have to manage your social affrays before you can get with this person. It depends entirely on their goals. But dark psychology doesn't lie. The most attractive thing a woman can find in a man is the impression that other women want them. This may seem strange, but we see this isn't the animal kingdom, as well as in research on humans. It seems like when women think other women want someone, it makes them want that man, too. It is probably a good extrapolation to make that the same goes the other way around. Imitation is self-explanatory for seduction. Do whatever unconscious cues of communication they are doing, and they will let you deeper into their unconscious. Nothing changes here in the realm of seduction. The seventh foundation — framing — is where you finally land the date. After you have done so, you can reach the event step and frame yourself in a certain attractive light that can't be denied. They saw this was all true based on the rules you followed. If you go by all these guidelines, you will have anyone worshipping you at your feet, because everyone loves to be emotionally manipulated, particularly in the context of seduction. Whether we want to admit it or not, it makes us excited, and it makes us feel thrilled. We like to feel submissive, sometimes. It makes us feel good to think someone else is in control. This applies to the area of seduction as much as it does anywhere.

Chapter 48: Social Manipulation

It is victim abuse by leveraging common social prejudices in one or more victims. Many of these prejudices can be viewed as shortcomings in the capacity of a victim to make reasonable decisions about their true place in society. Social manipulation is generally seen as manipulative and hostile towards a survivor. It can be used with the victim's best interests in mind or it can be indifferent to the needs of the victim. This is typically very confidential, but there are situations where the victim might be aware of some aspects of the deceptive action. Thus, social control can or may not constitute underhand coercion, depending on the context and motives.

Stamina: Short to Long.

Availability: Low to High.

Conditions / Opportunity / Effectiveness: A person or a group may be subject to social exploitation. It can be performed by a person or by a party. This may be driven by interpersonal, psychological, cultural, or political objectives. Some methods of exploitation of society are very powerful, some less reliable. Many of the styles are long-lasting, and others are only short-lived.

All of us are susceptible to social prejudices, and a deceptive action provides fertile ground for their use.

Methodology / Refinements / Sub-species: There are a variety of so-called social prejudices that a manipulator can use against one or more victims. Some are more favorable for the manipulator than others. Here are some typical social biases:

Actor-observer bias: This is a propensity to interpret other people's actions as a consequence of their personality rather than context. On the other side, we frequently exaggerate the effect of our own surroundings and downplay our own personality's effect on our own behavior.

This propensity blames others for their actions because they are inherently "evil" but justifies our own actions because we are merely powerless victims of poor surroundings.

When attributing their poor acts to their innate evil nature, a manipulator uses this tendency to alienate and demonize victims. The manipulator stays above such responsibility by alleging a negative climate for some possible moral crimes of its own.

Egocentric bias: This occurs when individuals assert more moral responsibility for the result of a collective action than they should be entitled to by an objective observer. It's also a tendency to exaggerate shifts in the present and the past to make people seem better than they actually are. This very irritating bias happens rather often when one person takes more credit than is due to them, or when someone intentionally mentions their success despite the fact that other others were responsible for that achievement.

Given the negative nature of this viewpoint, a manipulator does have its benefits. Very often an egocentric person can be very useful when, for example, a manipulator needs to "hedge their bets" in taking a particular action.

If things don't turn out as planned, having an egocentric sort around who's able to boast of their responsibility for the undertaking can be very beneficial. This is a valuable insurance policy for the manipulator if things go wrong. The egocentric victim is a ready and eager fall-guy whose responsibility for the success-turned-failure has already been claimed by the scapegoat.

It is linked to the Self-serving bias, a propensity to take greater credit for successes than defeats. It can also manifest as a propensity for individuals to interpret ambiguous knowledge in a way that favors their interests (see also group-serving bias).

Hypothesis of defensive attribution: this tendency makes us more likely to blame others for a crime when it is significant. The risk is lower when it is less extreme. If a mishap is more extreme there is a stronger propensity to blame.

Any parallels between an outside investigator and the victim of the mishap often raise this propensity to assign blame. Therefore, in general, as the result is more serious, the observer may assign more blame to a harm-doer, and the victim is more comparable to the observer.

Example: men are statistically more likely to delegate any blame to a survivor of rape than women, as some men appear to have less sympathy for the victim than most women do.

Manipulators use this bias to either establish antagonism to the source or target of a mishap, or both. An effective source of manipulative influence is the stirring up of antagonism within a particular group.

For example, when a young woman dies in a country where abortion is prohibited during a miscarriage, then the response of many people in that country is naturally to criticize the laws that permit this. Many outsiders (men and women) would blame the woman's husband for sending her into such a morally backward country to give birth. But another community will use the event to reinforce their anti-abortion beliefs and the guidelines established to allow termination. The case is very bad, so blame must be given. A manipulator may use such an occurrence to fan an argument's flames in favor of allowing legal termination of pregnancy to save the life of a mother. The prejudice is a strong factor in persuading victims to take a specific moral stand, regardless of the moral concerns at stake here.

Dunning – Kruger effect: Sadly, people who are incompetent frequently fail to understand that they are incompetent because they lack the ability to differentiate between abilities and incompetence. People sometimes wrongly rate their success much higher than average.

Many of us would have noticed the odd phenomenon in certain people that manifests itself, namely the potentially dangerous mixture of ignorance and arrogance. This phenomenon is named for the Dunning-Kruger effect. It creates the sometimes puzzling combination by which a person may know almost nothing about a topic but yet proclaim great faith in their knowledge of that area.

A manipulator can take advantage of this trend when identifying a potential target and convincing them to take on more than they can handle in a subject area where they have little expertise. This may obviously put the victim at risk of making a major mistake, being exposed, and having to bear the consequences.

For any possible victim this will obviously not work. Some of us know our limits and would not be tempted to claim to have more experience than we do. However, there are plenty of suitable situations, given near total ignorance, that can and should adopt a mantle of confidence.

Extrinsic bias incentives: this is a phenomenon in which people believe that they are motivated by intrinsic motives (i.e., pure intellectual interest) but that all others are motivated only by extrinsic motives (money, prestige, etc.).

Motivation Types: Intrinsic motivation refers to motivation motivated by an interest or pleasure in the task itself, it resides within the person rather than depending on any external pressure. Intrinsic motivation is based on taking pleasure in an action instead of striving for an external reward.

Extrinsic motivation refers to the execution of an operation to achieve a result. Through extrinsic motives are money and prestige bonuses and/or threats such as physical punishment, exclusion, etc. Competition is usually considered extrinsic, since the competitor is expected to compete and beat others.

Manipulative uses: A manipulator may take advantage of this particular prejudice by persuading a person to be inherently superior to others because higher motivations drive their motivation. Therefore, the eager victim can be convinced to ignore their desires for more material benefits such as money and reputation.

False impact of consensus: This is a propensity for people to overestimate the degree to which others agree.

This is a readily useable prejudice in a deceptive context where a trusting target can be convinced to enter an antagonistic "lion's den" with the absolute assurance that the lion will agree with him.

Fundamental attribution mistake: There is a tendency for people to blame personality rather than external conditions for a bad situation. When something goes wrong, we are inclined to search out a person to blame rather than agree that it only occurred in a particular situation because of a combination of circumstances.

Politicians are frequently blamed for economic downturns, although many economic downturns are, in fact, just pure cyclical. Commodity markets, for example, are going through long cycle shifts due to long term shifts in global supply and demand. It is clearly unfair to blame a local official for such economic events. Nonetheless, depositing a regime that fails to deliver is common practice in Western politics, whether it is under their control or not.

There are fairly simple manipulative applications of this. A political opposition will often unleash its "attack dogs" to find a scapegoat if there is a crisis, an economic problem, or any sort of organizational issue or natural disaster, much to the public's applause. In blood calls, the tone of rational claims over long-cycle commodity price patterns is drowned out.

External agency illusion: this is the phenomenon under which people perceive a particular experience as the product of any 'external control,' 'insight' or 'benevolence.' This is the misunderstanding between the illusion of "the magic in here" and "the magic out there." In this delusion, rather than their own personal effect on real events, a victim sees a "moving eye" or an unseen external force.

For a manipulator, the illusion offers fertile ground. Every person suffering from this delusion can be convinced that what is happening is the product of some mysterious external force that may somehow be supernatural or mystical. For example, a person may be convinced that the reason they inherited a small fortune is a benevolent act, which has happened to support a religious sect financially with a donation, etc.

Transparency illusion: this is an illusion in which we overestimate the ability of others to know us and overestimate our own ability to know others. We prefer to assume that we are an "open book" to others and equally transparent to us. In reality, certain people will always say that humans are inscrutable.

We may not actually show any clear outward signs of emotion, even though we're rather depressed or quite content. In terms of emotional speech, human beings are simply not quite clear.

A manipulator can use this phenomenon to trick a victim into thinking that the manipulator is not feeling any form of strong emotion. Similarly, a manipulator may claim to feel extreme emotions just to trick the victim.

In-group bias: This appears to offer preferential treatment to those who consider themselves as members of their own group.

Manipulators take advantage of this tendency to control a group and preserve unity. Of course, the perpetrators of such abuse would continue to defend their own community members.

Moral luck: this is the tendency of people to blame or praise others, even though it is clear that they have little or no power over their acts or their consequences.

A manipulator may use this tendency to achieve support for a group of victims simply by gaining their approval for something not explicitly achieved by the manipulator.

Often, a manipulator may foster suspicion against someone who was not personally responsible for any wrongdoing.

Naïve cynicism: this is the belief that others will be more self-centered than themselves. Of course, most of us are equally egocentrically biased, but this prejudice is useful for manipulating a target into thinking they're more logical than those around them.

Therefore, a manipulator will establish in a victim the false perception that they are in full charge of a situation when they are not.

Perception bias: This is a propensity to believe unconsciously that others share one's current mental states, feelings, and beliefs.

It is also a means of transferring negative ideas, motives, impulses, and emotions onto someone else as a way to relieve the feelings of guilt of the subject itself. It provides a mechanism by which a person can protect himself from any otherwise repulsive feeling.

Chapter 49: Manipulation and Moral Question: Why Is Manipulation Important in Life

There are going to be certain times in your life when you will find that manipulation is going to come in handy. While you know that it is so important to practice in as many scenarios as you can, there are going to be ones that you will find manipulation will be the most useful.

Business Negotiations

When it comes to working on some negotiations in business, it is easy to see how you want to make sure that you can get your way. Getting your own way will usually mean that you want to close a better deal, one that is going to be highly favorable to your own company. Closing these deals and making sure that they are in your favor will mean that your company is able to get most, if not all, of the things that it is asking for and that you will barely have to deal with any inconveniences in the process to do this. There are a lot of things that you can negotiate during these meetings, such as better terms on the deals, better pricing on the services, and more, and if you use your skills in manipulation, you are more likely to get the whole thing to work in your favor. When you use manipulation in these efforts, it means that you are easily able to dominate the conversation without the other person even realizing it. When this happens, others in the negotiation are more likely to give in without even doing a fight, because they think they are getting something good out of it as well. Because of this, and all the good benefits that you can get from this, you should bring out the manipulation skills that you learn as much as possible when you are working with a business negotiation.

Closing Sales

If you are at all involved in a sales process at some point, then you know that it is not always easy to close sales. If you work in retail, for example, you likely notice that many of the people who come into your store are dreaming and looking around, and sometimes, they won't be prepared to buy anything. Because of this, it can sometimes be valuable to know how to manipulate people as you can encourage them to spend money that they did not otherwise intend to spend.

What this means is that when you get the other person to purchase something through your manipulation techniques, it results in more sales for the business. If you are the one who owns the company, you know how important this is. If you are an employee, you know that effective numbers of sales and good sales strategies means that you are more likely to be respected by your employer, and then you can make it up the ladder of the company.

If you are in a sales position that is considered business to business, then you know that manipulation is so important. People who end up going to a meeting with you are likely interested in what you are going to offer, but they could also be shopping around to a few different companies at the same time, and you need to find ways that will put your business ahead of all the other choices that they are considering.

Getting Prices That Are Better

You can use manipulation from the other side of the perspective as well. If you are the customer and knowing how to manipulate during this time can be highly valuable. As you know, many times salespeople have been given some room to negotiate with their customers in order to encourage sales. This means that if you are willing to use some manipulation and work with them, you can get a special and better deal. You are able just to take the price, but wouldn't it be much better for you to go through and get a better price if you are able to.

Leading the Desired Lifestyle That You Want

Each person has a goal about the desired lifestyle that they would like to have—but the lifestyle that you have right now, and the one that you desire, might not always be the same thing. However, the good thing about using manipulation is that you can use it to help you get to the desired lifestyle. There are a lot of ways that you can do this—you just need to learn how to make it work.

Let's say that right now you are living in a house that you are renting, and you want to buy your own home at some point—but right now, the types of homes that you are the most interested in purchasing are not within the price that you can purchase. However, with the right kind of manipulation, you may find that you are able to get a better deal, putting you into the home of your dreams sooner than you would like. This can work with any of the big-ticket items that you would like to purchase, such as cars.

Another way that this can work is with some of the relationships that you are in. If you are someone who would like to find a new group of friends, the friends who are going to help you reflect your new lifestyle, you may find that working with manipulation is going to help you out. You can also use the art of persuasion to convince others to become your friends and spend time with you—and from that, you will then have the friends that you need to live this new lifestyle.

Take this a step further and see how it can work with some of your intimate relationships. If this kind of relationship doesn't look like the one that you would like, then you can bring in some manipulation and see if it is possible to make the right changes towards a better relationship. If you want to have more romance, for example, you will spend some time with fancier places or people.

Getting Out of Things

Have you ever gotten into a situation where you were asked to do something, but you didn't have any want to do it? All the time we are going to be signed up for things, or given offers, that we aren't really that interested in—and sometimes, it can feel difficult to turn these things down in a polite manner. Depending on who is asking for the favor, you may feel obligated to help them out with it.

However, once you learn how to work with manipulation a bit more, you will find that this is not as big of a problem for you anymore. You may even find that this is a good place to start when it comes to practicing your manipulation. You can bring it up any time that you get.

You can use manipulation in any manner that you would like to make sure that you are able to live the life that you want. It can help you to get the business negotiations to work the way that you want, to help you get the friendships, relationships, and to get yourself out of the things that you don't want to do.

There are just so many different things that you can use manipulation with, and this can be a great way to ensure that you have the life that you have always dreamed about.

Work on Self-Esteem to Overcome Manipulation

To overcome manipulation, you have to examine your inner self. There is something about you that makes manipulators believe they can have easy control over you. Here's an example.

Stacy has learned since childhood that expressing emotions is a good thing. People will appreciate you more when they understand you, and if a person can't express their emotions, they will live a lonely life.

This is how Stacy was psychologically conditioned during her childhood, but as she got older, her personality becomes too vulnerable.

Stacy is now a very skilled advertiser, but her lack of confidence keeps you from being recognized. She hasn't developed confidence. Instead, she is emotionally vulnerable when she doesn't need to be.

She apologizes for everything, and she worries if she is liked by others. In fact, she has even asked her colleagues whether they like her. This is causing her to lose friends, which is the opposite of what her parents made her believe.

Some emotional vulnerability is great in relationships, but if you let it go too far, it leaves you open to manipulators. You must also have self-confidence or self-esteem. Having both emotional vulnerability and self-esteem will help you to know when it is safe to be vulnerable, and when you need to stick up for yourself. This makes it a lot harder for the manipulator to take control.

Self-esteem is the way in which you perceive and value yourself. It is your own beliefs and opinions about yourself, which are likely going to be hard to change because you have had them for so long. Your self-esteem can affect:

- If you value and like yourself
- If you can make decisions for you and assert them
- If you can see your positives and strengths
- If you are willing to try new things
- If you can show yourself kindness
- If you can move on from mistakes without unfairly blaming yourself
- If you take personal time
- If you believe that you are good enough
- If you believe that you deserve to be happy

There are many different things that can cause low self-esteem. Your self-esteem could end up changing suddenly, or you could have always suffered from low self-esteem.

Either way, it can be hard to notice that you have low self-esteem and make it hard to change it.

It doesn't matter what caused low self-esteem. A manipulator can use your low self-esteem to gain control over you.

Let's look at how you can improve your self-esteem to avoid manipulation.

Be Mindful

There's no way of changing something if you can't spot it and know it needs to be changed. Simply becoming aware of how you talk to yourself will start to pull you away from the negativity. You want to stop the self-limiting talk. When you notice yourself falling down the rabbit hole of self-criticism or doubt, take note of what is happening, and then tell yourself, "These are only thoughts and not the truth."

Change Your Story

Everybody has a story they have created about themselves. This story shapes our perceptions, which is what your self-image is based upon. In order to change it, you must know where it originated. Whose voices have you internalized?

Most negative thoughts that have become automatic were learned from somebody else, and that means you can unlearn them. What is it that you want to believe about yourself? Start repeating those things in your mind, and your story will start to change.

Stop Comparing

Accept who you are and stop comparing yourself to other people. Just because one of your friends seems super happy in their posts doesn't mean they truly are. Comparing yourself will only cause negative self-talk, which lowers your self-esteem. You are enough as you are.

Channel Your Strengths

Everybody has their own strengths and weaknesses. You could be an amazing chef, but lousy at singing. These things don't define your worth. Recognize your strength and the confidence that they bring you, especially if you are feeling down. When something doesn't go right, remind yourself of all the ways in which you rock.

Chapter 50: Negative Manipulation, Tactics and Recognizing

One of the main parts of learning about tricks is again figuring out how to protect you from it. Practically everyone in this environment has at least once have been altered negatively by some approach or another, and it never seems very good or pleasant. Everyone in this entire world simply just needs to satisfy their private necessities, but persons who work with detrimental tricks work with deceit and underhanded tactics to undertake.

In quality, they don't really care about your needs or desires and simply hope to help themselves. This is dependent on subtly influencing another person with violent, deceptive, or covered practices.

Indirect Hostility and Intimidation Tactics

Primarily, it may come across as flattering, user-friendly, and harmless, like that of a human soul, which has all your best hobbies at the center, but that is never the case with poor tricks.

Quite often, it is scarcely obscured hostility, and when an individual uses these abusive tactics, they hope to gain vitality over you. Sometimes you might not possibly realize that you are staying intimidated subconsciously. When you are employed to tricks by youth or elderly, it can end up being considerably tougher to acknowledge or understand what is happening, because it is familiar and might also come to feel healthy in some methods.

You may come to feel an instinctual angriness or soreness, while the manipulator uses fair, ingratiating, or pleasurable conditions that charm to your compassion or remorse. This causes you to override your turn emotions and not really learn how to respond.

Different Types of Negative Manipulation

Turning their Emotions Against Them

Approaches for mind games are vary widely. Manipulators can try out to get the emotions of others to do the job for them. They will make an effort to perform that by expressing issues that will be demonstrated as stir up fear, angriness, waste, remorse, or any other unpleasant sense. They might insinuate that if we don't follow through on their recommendations or orders, something horrible will result into.

Threats of Future Unpleasantness

They might also try to describe to you all of the several types of unpleasant scenarios that could arise if you do not carry out their demand. They might refer to any of our faults, responsibilities, or duty, applying ethics and morality to pressure us to arrive around their needs. Some persons will also chuck every technique at us, caution us of the implications of letting them down.

Common Phrases Used

They might imply to us that we can get a reward in return if we carry out what they wish us to carry out, or perhaps that we can try to make them very happy, and that can get them to like us very much. They may likewise employ words like "You want to…" or "You must…" or "You should…" as a method to subtly pressure you into being persuaded. They will claim those words and others, which insinuate wonderful implications if you do not follow the accountability they are supplying. The person practicing harmful manipulation does not give anything of benefit in return for rewarding the subject's hopes. Rather, the patient gets taken advantage of by a made ability imbalance.

Users of these Negative Tactics

Persons found in codependent interactions may possibly have a hard time getting assertive influence, leading to the application of adverse mind games to achieve their personal goals.

These types very often turn into narcissists or sociopaths. Violent or stubborn romantic relation seekers often work with these methods.

How to Recognize Negative Manipulation

There are a few tactics that every manipulator uses, and these are favors and gifts, flattery, more than the top apologies, fake sympathy, false concern, evasion techniques or avoidance, blackmail, making assumptions about you, playing with your mind, undermining your thoughts and feelings, bribing you, blaming you, faking innocence, making excuses, comparing, complaining, and guilt-tripping. Let us appear at a few of these approaches in depth:

Favors with "Strings Attached"

They will sometimes employ the strategy of shame either directly or in an implied way. They carry you out conditioned favors and, when time asks you to perform the string, they attached in disguise of the condition they applied.

Getting Power through Sympathy

Some unfavorable manipulators will deny agreements, conversations, or promises they made you. They might also intentionally start emotional or verbal battles and then blame you in order to gain an intellectual advantage over you by distressing you.

Bribery

Bribery is very commonly used by parents in order to get their kids to follow their instructions. For example, your parents might bribe you to go to the school they want you to attend, by buying you a new car. The evilest effect of bribery is seen in the underdeveloped countries of the modern world.

With Assumptions

Harmful manipulators will often try to make assumptions aloud about you or your beliefs or intentions, and you, in that case, are obliged to respond to those assumptions.

They will ignore what you claim to the counter as an approach to justify their activities and thoughts. They might also deny whatever you arranged or chose to successfully dismiss your objections on the subject matter.

Forced Reciprocation

The impact technique of reciprocation, where you present someone something little, which then follows up with something larger. This can end up being benign, but when it is utilized with pressure or guilt, that is when it becomes a bad treatment tactic. When you state no to their get, they will switch around and try to make themselves not to end up being the sufferer. It will end up being all about the manipulator and their personal problems, leading you to think defensively.

They will then bring up past incidences of you not fulfilling their wishes and lay a lot of blame on you to try to get you to agree with them. They do not care if it damages you at all. When it comes to a detrimental manipulator, they happen to be definitely covering factors or fasten strings when they give something to you.

False Concern or Blackmail

This is a tactic which relies on "well-meaning worry" that is intended to make you doubt yourself or to invalidate your choices. The harmful manipulator might as well function with disgrace, threats, intimidation, or anger procedures to receive you to bring out what they choose. They may disgrace you to generate negativity and think doubt and low self-esteem, probably covering this with an inappropriate confidence. Individuals who practice blackmailing might as well function with angriness to scare you; best graded you to adding your requirements and needs to bring out what they choose.

If this approach does not work on you, they might switch all of the sudden to an even more positive temperament and act great towards you. This could lead you to achieve satisfaction and become prepared to perform what they want you to perform. They may also deliver up shameful recollections from your earlier and threaten to inform others about it if you do not comply with them.

This may lead the sufferer of the negative treatment to think restless to express refusal. If they refuse, they will most likely face insults from the manipulator.

Submissive Manipulation

Some people, especially those who are on the shy side, use passive manipulation tactics, since most people with codependent personalities are not very assertive. They might act admissible on the surface, telling people what they want to hear, and then break their agreements. Instead of responding honestly to an issue that could lead to fighting or conflict, they rather make an effort to transform the subject matter or deny their fault by applying rationalizations and excuses. They are afraid to be wrong, and as a consequence they hardly find it difficult to raise conflict, they say yes even when they do not agree, and then follow up with complaints or remorse trips about how hard it will be to accommodate the other person. When somebody confronts them, they may come to feel waste and spend a hard time professing responsibility for their activities. Consequently, they create excuses, pin the consequence on others, or make an effort to "resolve" factors by apologizing, regardless of the fact that they actually do not mean it.

Also, these unaggressive methods, which are not evident simply because the methods of anger or shaming, are an approach for showing hostile thoughts. These could involve expressing yes indeed to a good submission and then forget to follow through it again, because you never required to be found in the primary place.

Self-Pity and Criticism

Unfavorable manipulators might use flattery and charm, offering to do good favors for you, help with something you need assistance with, or give you gifts in order to gain your love and acceptance. Then they will change around and employ manipulation methods like self-pity, remorse, and complaint to acquire others to abide along with their dreams.

The best way to figure out a security against manipulation is to know who you are working with and going up against. Every harmful manipulator features unique methods, and if they figure you out very well, they will know which trick to apply to get the best possible result from you. You should become mindful of their strategies for carrying out this and master realizing it when they glimpse to employ them on you. Build up your self-respect and self-worth, which will get your ideal security.

Chapter 51: How Psychology is tied to Manipulation

The act of manipulation goes beyond the idea that you want someone to do something for you. This is a desire that everyone feels, and it does not mean that you are necessarily a manipulative person. We all have wants and needs that can be fulfilled by other people; it is natural to crave this kind of connection. What makes the behavior manipulative is when you are actively getting the other person to do what you want, with no regard to their feelings or how it might impact them. This is when the behavior goes from a desire to an action. It is perfectly healthy and normal to crave certain things, but when you take the step of forcefully turning these things into a reality, this is when manipulation could be taking place.

Manipulation actually takes a lot of skill and understanding on the topic of psychology. In order to successfully manipulate someone, you must be aware of that individual's desires. By knowing this deep information, you will be able to use this to get what you want. For example, if you know that your partner does not want to go to a party that you want to go to, you can play off of certain fears. Explaining that people are going to question whether or not your partner is a good person if they do not show up to said party is a way to make them question their fear of being accepted. Convincing them that it would be best for them to make an appearance at the party would, in turn, get you to that party as well. It is a very slight action to take, but as you can see, it has the ability to completely change a situation.

When a person is already close to you, it is easy to manipulate them. Trust already exists, so you simply have to use it to your advantage. This is why cases of manipulation often appear in romantic relationships or close friendships. When you know a person pretty well, you already know what their triggers are.

You should have a basic idea of what will upset them and what will make them happy. In order to manipulate someone into making a decision that benefits you, the idea is to make them feel like they came to the conclusion on their own. While the reality of the situation is, you were taking actions along the way to lead them exactly where you wanted them.

Taking a look at the differences between what males and females want, you can see that there are likely going to be unique tactics when it comes to manipulation. Men crave perfectionism; they wish to improve on what they already know. If someone takes a jab at a man's ego, he is most likely going to feel a loss of self-confidence, whether he expresses this outwardly or not. Women want wholeness and security. Once this is threatened, she has the ability to crumble. Balance is generally a must for women, so anything that proves to throw it off will elicit a response of some sort. While these guidelines aren't applicable to everyone, they are a general outlook on how men and women operate.

With someone who enjoys the art of manipulation, it is likely not a temporary occurrence. These tactics are meant for the individual to have control in the long run. Part of what is so thrilling about being manipulative is that it gets easier and better over. Those who have been manipulative for extended periods of time will often perfect their strategies and approaches. It should seem effortless to a person who is experienced with manipulation.

It all starts with the offering of a "reward" of some sort. We are all driven by the things that we love, so when something is offered to us, there is a good chance that we are willing to go through the motions in order to obtain it. Most people do not like being told what to do, but when you offer the promise of something that they want in return, you'd be surprised at how quickly this mindset can change. A manipulator will then explain to the individual what needs to be done in order to get to the "reward." Because the focus is solely based on the positive outcome for the person who must act, a blind eye might be turned to the positive outcome that the manipulator will also experience.

Again, the goal is to get the individual to believe that they have arrived at the conclusion on their own. At the end of it all, they should feel satisfied, even if what they had to go through was inconvenient or unfair. The reward that is received at the end is enough to trick them that the experience was worth it.

This has the ability to become a pattern of behavior, one person jumping through hoops while the other does nothing but reaps all of the benefits. It is important for a manipulator to keep up this behavior in secrecy. One of the biggest parts of manipulation is the secret behind it. This is the part that will feel thrilling and worthwhile, making it difficult to stop the behavior. When someone does see past this disguise, they will be very quick to cut you out of their life. It is a pattern that can be very fulfilling until it all comes crumbling down. Because of this, manipulators are quick to fall apart. They are actually rather fragile individuals deep down inside.

The Distinction Between Negative Manipulation and Positive Manipulation

After reading about the behavior behind it all, you might be left wondering if there is such a thing as "positive" manipulation. The answer might surprise you — yes, this is relevant. This branch of behavior involves turning negative energy into positive energy, a simple concept. Most of us cannot associate the word "manipulation" with anything other than negativity, but it does exist on the other end of the spectrum. To positively manipulate a situation, you must use your mind to rid yourself of any negative thoughts that tend to creep in. This sounds like a fairly easy task, but it does take a good amount of effort in order to become efficient with it.

Instead of simply stifling the negative energy, the manipulation actually creates an appropriate place for it so that you are able to move forward. We have all experienced hardships, which lead us to feel like we were stuck in a rut. It can be healthy to sit with this anger or sadness for a certain amount of time, but it is essential that we begin the healing process soon after. You will never be able to move forward in life if you are stuck in a particular mindset for too long. Have you ever felt as though you would never get over a breakup or a betrayal done to you by a friend?

While these things can be a challenge to overcome, positive manipulation can help you.

Manipulation, no matter positive or negative, always starts from within. It is a conscious decision that you make and then back by your actions. The thing about manipulation is that nobody can force you to do it, so you must be wholeheartedly responsible for the actions that it can create. When you are trying to change the course of any situation, you must keep in mind that it won't always turn out exactly how you expect. What makes you great at manipulation is your ability to roll with the punches — you must always have a backup plan. Set forth with the confidence that you will get what you want.

Being able to positively manipulate a situation is a skillful display. It can benefit you greatly when you must face challenges, and it will also assist you in taking the next steps forward. A great example of positive manipulation comes from taking failure and turning it into a strength-building tool. If you got fired from your job, it would be a natural reaction to sink into a depression. Thinking about the time wasted and the money lost alone is enough to stress anyone out. Instead of becoming stagnant, you can apply some positive manipulation to the situation. Take all the feelings that would lead you to passive actions and then turn them into productive ones. You can use this time to boost your self-confidence; acknowledge that your company is missing out by not having you on board as a team member. Remember what your strengths are and make a pact that you will only work for a company that will appreciate what you have to offer.

Positive manipulation is nothing more than changing the way that you think. It is a very healthy action that allows you to grow as a person. Most of us tend to take on the feelings that are brought to the surface, those reactive feelings. While it is rightful to acknowledge them, it is also important that you know how to keep moving forward. Getting stuck in the moment is not going to help the situation or the way that you are feeling. Your actions can likely become skewed if a change isn't made. Consider this the next time you are going through something particularly difficult. By having a strong mind, you will be able to manipulate your way out of the situations that can hurt you the most.

Now, you have successfully learned that the word "manipulation" does not have a negative connotation by itself. To manipulate simply means to use skillfully. It is up to you to determine whether you want to use manipulation in a positive or negative way. No matter what you choose, know that it does take practice to accomplish either one. Once you have gotten the hang of it, manipulation can become habitual. You can use it to help you better manage your feelings or to stay motivated in life; the choices are unlimited.

Chapter 52: What to Do If You Get Caught

Many people fear that if they are using some of the techniques that come with manipulation that something bad is going to happen if the other person or their target figures out what they are doing. After all, the public opinion about manipulation is that the process is generally frowned upon, and most people are under the idea that manipulation is only going to be done when the manipulator is ill-intentioned. The idea of getting caught while performing these acts can sometimes be enough to convince some people not to use it.

Of course, your goal is not to get caught when you are using these techniques—it is a possibility at some points. This can happen at any time, whether you are brand new to using these techniques or if you have used them for some time. A simple slip up could be enough to get the other person to catch on to it—and if someone is already well-versed in how to spot manipulation, it is going to be even easier for them to figure out what is going on early in the game. The good news is that getting un-caught in what you are doing is really simple. It is a good idea though to learn how to do this and to get the right skills to get un-caught before you ever need it.

What Not to Do

The first thing that we need to understand is the things that you should not do when you get caught. If you are new to this game, you may find that it is easy to say and do the wrong things, which is going to make the situation so much worse. It is instinctive to go on the defense when someone catches on to what you are doing, and you may say something like:

- What are you talking about? I'd never do that.

- Are you kidding me, that's what you think?

- I can't believe you would think that of me.

These are all unhealthy types of manipulation that are meant to place some guilt and blame on the other person, and they are a sign of immaturity in this process. They are found in some processes of manipulation that are intended to take advantage or exploit the other person, rather than to bypass them simply, and it is best to find some other methods to help you get un-caught, rather than resorting to these. When you get caught, this can sometimes be your first reaction. Even if you are only going to use manipulation in order to encourage an honest and thought out answer rather than the predetermined no, you may still find that you are outraged and a little upset that anyone would think in a negative way towards you.

The point to remember here is that despite your initial reaction, you need to be able to find ways to override it.

Do not, under any circumstances, try to displace the blame, create any feelings of guilt in the target, or even deny what the other person is accusing you of. The first reason for this is that you would be lying if you did. If you were unable to reverse the situation completely, then this turns you into a liar and a manipulator—and the second thing, extreme defensiveness, is a bit sign that you are guilty. Even if you don't realize it, you are pretty much admitting that you are guilty of whatever the other person accuses you of, and this can make it impossible to defend yourself down the line.

So, even if it may seem like the right thing to do at the time, don't get defensive, and don't try to shift the blame over to the other person. This is just going to make things more difficult in the long run, will make it so that the other person starts to assume that you are guilty of what they accuse you of, and so much worse.

What to Do Instead

Now that we have talked about what you need to avoid if you don't want to arouse the suspicion of the other person, you may be wondering what you should do instead to get them off your trail. Instead of trying to blame the other person or trying to defend yourself, there are two things that you can do right after someone starts to accuse you of being a manipulator.

The first thing to do is stop every effort of manipulation that you were participating in before. Stop using persuasion, stop making requests, and stop doing anything else that you have been utilizing in order to manipulate the other person.

The thing that you want to strive for here is to make sure that there is no evidence for the target to link the manipulation back to you. Instead, you want to make it appear that the thoughts about manipulation were just in their head, and they were overreacting to the situation. If you keep using your manipulation tactics, then the target will see that you are actually trying to manipulate them, and they will stop being near you or paying attention to you.

You want to make sure that you are creating the illusion that the manipulation was just in the mind of your target. You may want to say something like, "I can definitely see how you think that. I am so sorry. That was not my intention at all." You want to apologize, but keep that apology short and sincere. Do not admit that you were manipulating them, but let them know that you understand where their concern and thoughts are coming from.

With this method, you do not agree with them that they were being manipulated. Instead, you are showing that you understand them. Your target is not going to expect you to apologize or agree for the behavior that you did, and they will decide that it was all in their mind or that they were overreacting to things.

When you completely stop doing everything manipulative that you did before, and you make sure to apologize for what they believed to be manipulation, you are going to get the target to doubt what they accused you have, and sometimes, there is going to be a level of guilt for even accusing you in the first place. In some cases, they are going to feel bad enough about the accusations, especially since you have now given them reasons to doubt what they had said, that they will want to find some way to make it up to you—and once this happens, you have the target right back where you want them.

So, to help you clarify this point, you want to go against your instincts when someone accuses you of being a manipulator. You don't want to get defensive, and you don't want to try and hide your trail.

Instead, you want to make sure that you get them off your trail. You want to make them start to doubt that you ever tried to manipulate them in the past.

How to Get Back on Track

Once the target is at the point of doubting their accusations towards you, and they may even feel a little bit guilty because they pointed some fingers at you, it is time to slowly and intentionally get back on track with the whole process of manipulating them.

Remember that you have to take your team here. The other person is already on the lookout for anything that seems odd. They may doubt themselves, but this doesn't mean that they have let you off the hook quite yet. This means that you don't want to jump right back in with full force. If you do that, the target is going to catch on to what you are doing, and they will walk away for good. Instead, you must take your time and work your way back up to manipulating them.

The good news is that you can just start back up with the three main steps that are needed to make manipulation successful in the first place. First, you will need to take some time to analyze the other person. Notice how your conversation is going, what the other person is saying to you, how they are responding to the things that you say, and what their tone is like. If the target has already pointed fingers at you and made some accusations, then you need to slow down and wait to rebuild some of that trust with them again before you get started with the manipulation again. The amount of time that this is going to depend on the individual you are working with; some are going to be easier than others.

Once you notice that the target looks a bit more relaxed and like they have started to open up to you again, then it is time to restart the manipulation. You want to make sure that the target has some time to trust you while being in a pressure-free zone that has no attempts at manipulation before you dive right back in again.

If you jump past this part too much, and you miss out on giving the other person enough time, then the other person, who is already on the defensive, is going to catch on to what you are doing and will put their defensive up again. If you have already been caught, it is important that you take your time. Being caught a second time means that you are going to lose out on that target, and who knows what other damage could occur to that relationship and to other prospective relationships that you may have in the future. Taking your time can help you get back on track once you are caught and will ensure that the other person isn't going to run off and make it impossible to manipulate them again.

Once you have been able to work on your analysis, and you are certain that the other person has had time to get comfortable with you again, and you notice that the conversation has begun to flow freely again, then you can start to introduce the manipulation back into the conversation. Take your time, just like with before, and try to be as subtle as possible with this.

Your goal here is not to tip the target off that you are working to win them over again, so tread with caution here. Go slowly and then build your way up to where you were in the past and where you would like to be in the future. This part of the game is not all about speed or a race of some sort to get back to the top. If you do this, you will end up losing the other person—and your goal of manipulation will be all gone.

Take your time and be patient. Try out a few of the techniques of manipulation, and see how they go. This can build up over a longer period of time, depending on how well you know the other person and how often you get to see them. If you take it slow and steady, you will get yourself back at the top, you just need to be willing to take your time, watch the cues that the other person is sending over to you, and learn when it is time to press forward and try a few more of the techniques that you know, and when it is time just to wait a bit longer.

Chapter 53: Employing Manipulation and Persuasion to Get What You Want

Manipulation literally means using something as a tool to suit your own purposes. The act of manipulating others typically involves using other people as tools. You can't have remorse or shame if you want to be a successful manipulator. You need to view people as pawns that you move around the board game of life. People are very useful; why not use them?

Manipulation has a bad reputation. It's a dark art because it involves making people act against their will or without their knowledge. Nevertheless, this does not mean that manipulation is always used for bad. Sometimes you might use manipulation for positive purposes, such as causing people to make wise decisions. It can benefit the person that you are manipulating as well as yourself. Sometimes manipulation only benefits only you, but it does not harm the other person. You don't have to use manipulation to hurt others, though it is certainly useful in that respect. Manipulation is a valuable skill to possess because it really helps you gain the upper hand and get what you want. It enables you to use people to their full capacity to further your own goals and aspirations.

It is crucial to be sneaky when you manipulate others. People hate being manipulated and made to do things that they do not consent to. But keep in mind that most people have manipulative tendencies, and manipulation is far from rare. You are simply going after what you want. That makes you powerful and even positive. Just make sure to hide your manipulation attempts and disguise your intentions. Otherwise, people will judge you harshly and get mad at you. You can lose friends left and right if you gain the reputation of a manipulator.

So let's delve into this fascinating and useful subject, shall we?

Make Someone Your Pawn

You can't just manipulate people with whom you don't share a rapport. You have to build a rapport and prime your subject before you can successfully manipulate him. This means that you need to form some sort of relationship with the person. Using a combination of psychological tricks, you can make a person weak for you. Your subject will be willing to do anything for you if you break down his mind and soften him to your attempts at manipulation.

Priming is best achieved through emotional manipulation. You want to play with someone's emotions. The first step is to make someone feel great around you. When someone likes you, he will be more open to your persuasive attempts and will want to please you. He will want to spend time around you because you make him feel good. This time enables you to get your hooks into his mind more successfully. So start with meaningful flattery. Observe your subject to see what means a lot to him. Then compliment him on the things that he values and cares about. For instance, if he loves sports and plays softball on the weekends, talk about sports with him and compliment his pitching techniques or his athletic physique. Over time, he will become increasingly attached to you.

Next, start the emotional roller coaster. As you get to know this person better and make him feel more and more attached to you, start to make him doubt his self-esteem. You can do this by finding things that he is guilty about or making him feel guilty about things that he does. Always play the victim and make him feel like a terrible person. It's possible to pout like a child, but it's even better to act like an adult and pretend to get very hurt about small things he does while telling him that you forgive him. You will look better if you pretend to be an adult who always takes the high road. He will become even more infatuated with you and may start to admire you.

Guilt is very powerful. But so is self-doubt. Plant seeds of doubt in his mind so that he feels insecure. Make him start to hate his friends and family by telling him about horrible things they do or say so that he doubts his social support network and his value to other people. Cause him to question his abilities and skills by saying things like, "You know that you're not good at that!" or "That's not one of your strengths." Tell him that you are simply opening his eyes to his inabilities so that you can protect him from the pain of failure or the pain of being around his hurtful loved ones. Then follow each little insult up with compliments. This will make him very confused. He will start to doubt himself, and he will believe what you say because he is attached to you. People are quite sensitive to suggestion, so this method works incredibly well. Meanwhile, he still feels like you are a nice person who cares about him. He won't be ready to end all contact with you just because you insult him from time to time.

You also want to provide him with multiple rewards for what he does for you. When he pleases you, show it and lavish him with praise or favors. Also, do favors for him and provide him with lots of services or support so that he is more open to doing favors for you. This is the basic principle of reciprocity, where people like to return kindness and favors that others do for them. You can use the things that you do for him as a bargaining tool. Call on him to return a favor sometime, and he will probably be willing to reciprocate. If he is not willing, guilt him by reminding him of a favor you did for him a while back.

The final part of priming is making someone doubt his sanity and perception. Tell him how he is wrong and come up with convincing arguments as to why. Inform him that he is making things up or misremembering things all of the time. Over time, this will chip away at his security and certainty in his own mind. This method is known as gaslighting, and it is one of the best ways that you can prime someone. Don't take gas lighting lightly. You can use it to totally drive someone crazy over time. It's actually a great form of psychological warfare against someone close to you.

Even if you care about someone, you can still prime him without hurting him. Make him dependent on you so that he never leaves your side. You don't have to be romantically linked to someone to accomplish this sort of dependency. Just offer him something that he can't get anywhere else. Make yourself very useful to him and bolster his ego so that he relies on you for his happiness, convenience, or even financial stability. Disable his other forms of support so that you become the only person in his life. You don't necessarily need to use gaslighting, guilt trips, and other such methods to hurt him; being nice is enough to gain a foothold on someone for persuasive methods. As a friend, lover, or even co-worker, you can accomplish this priming at varying levels. You can do it lightly to someone whom you want to manipulate only slightly. Or you can do it very heavily to someone whom you want to use for life.

Get a Good Read on Someone

There is another side to priming that you really need to take into account. This side is reading. To manipulate someone, you must get a good read on someone. Natural manipulators are adept at reading people at a glance. If you are not so good at reading people right off the bat, then you can use time and priming to get a good read on your subject.

Basically, you want to get to know the person very well. Listen to everything he tells you and glean his speech for potential emotional weapons to use against him. Anything he confides in you or accidentally reveals to you can be turned into a weapon at any time. Save these weapons in your back pocket for when you need to use them.

What are the best emotional weapons? Guilt is probably the most powerful one of all. People hate feeling guilty. So find out things that he feels guilty about.

Also find out things that he loves or cherishes. You can give him these things to make him happy and reward him for his work for you. Or you can cripple him by destroying these things. Love and passion give people power and a will to live. Taking these things away can crush a person. Try to become the gatekeeper of the things that he loves so that you can gain ultimate power over him. For example, bar his access to his loved ones and pitch a fit when he talks to people that you don't approve of, but let him talk to the people he loves whenever he does what you want.

Another way to use what someone loves against him is to trivialize things that he cares about. If he says how much he loves a dish, tell him how it is really not that good. Ruin the small things that he loves.

Then you can move on to bigger things. Also, trivialize his opinions. All people love and value their own opinions and believe that they are right. If you make him feel stupid for having certain opinions, then you will be able to chip down his self-esteem and make him doubt his rightness. Make him feel small by trivializing him in every way possible. Eventually, he will come around to your way of thinking and will love only the things that you love because you have made him abandon all that he loves. You will make him feel small and stupid, so he will look to you for validation and approval in order to repair his damaged ego.

Trust is a great weapon that you can use. Most people desire to be trusted. You can tell him that he is not trustworthy because of various things that he has admitted to. Then make him do what you want for the sake of winning your trust. Let's say you're dating a guy, and you want to manipulate him. Tell him that you don't trust him because he admitted to cheating on his ex. Tell him that you worry he will cheat on you. Or claim that you have been cheated on, so now you have trust issues. This way, he will want to win your trust. He will jump through hoops to make you trust him, including cutting off people you don't like in his life. You can make him cut off female friends and friends who encourage him to drink and have a good time without you around by saying that you feel threatened by these people.

You can also use his reputation to manipulate him. He wants to be liked by others, so you can use that as a weapon. Tell him, "If you do that, everyone at work will hate you. You don't want that, right?" Most likely, if he's a normal person, he will agree that he wants people to like him, so he will reconsider doing anything that might damage his reputation. Encourage him to do things by saying that it will gain him favor with different key people. One great way to manipulate co-workers is to give them "tips" on how to please the boss and possibly earn raises or promotions.

Chapter 54: Knowing Yourself

The key to being able to avoid manipulation is to know you. You will not be able to know yourself unless you experience failure in the world. Most people experience enough failure by the time they become adults to really know how they deal with it and learn how to keep going on. If you don't know yourself, you will be used over and over by people who don't care a lick about you. They are just more focused on their own goals. When you know yourself, you can know other people better. You will be able to tap into that voice that tells you this is not worth it, that you are being manipulated. If you know yourself, you are less vulnerable to deceit and lies.

This is because people are very self-repressed, and they don't learn about themselves. By not learning about yourself, you are opening yourself up to the worst of interactions and relationships. Relationships are shallower when you are like this. They lack depth and concentration. When you know yourself, you can analyze what is happening to you and other people. When you know yourself, you can protect yourself.

Analyzing people involves keeping knowledge of how we see the world and how we move in the world to be able to observe others. This is why knowing yourself is so important. It takes a lot of effort to understand how other people see you in the world, and this can cue you into their behavior.

One way to start this is to look at the Enneagram of personality and see what line up mostly with you. This can tell you about the drives that you have in your personality that you might not even realize. When you are trying to find out what type of personality you are, you are engaging in a self-reflexive behavior that will have you become a better person. It will help you to know yourself, and your intuition will be increased as a part of this.

Another way to know one is to participate in the art of watching or listening to art. A movie can tell us the story of a world. It is a way by which we understand the world. Each time you talk, you are telling a story, whether it is in words or in the way that you speak the words. This can help you realize the weaknesses and strengths that you have.

When you are reading a great novel, you become immersed in that manuscript, and you get to share a little bit of the writers' world in your imagination. The writer and reader create a continuum, wherein the writer's consciousness is being followed directly by another person. They say that literature is the art that most people can actually escape their world and get into another person's consciousness.

You start to learn the characters, and you start to predict what they are going to do. Characters in the story can be compared to people you know in real life, and the manuscript can give you ideas of how to behave and change the world through your actions. As you get into the story, you are experiencing a ride that is the most joyous way of expressing ourselves. This is art.

Art is a mysterious way that we participate in the world. Art has the power to incite wars and peace. It is a way that you can deeply disturb people, and you can keep them happy and calm. Art (we are talking here about the art with a big A, as to mean every category of art, from dance to film to sculpture) is a way that we are in the world that lets us start a feedback loop with the world, and it becomes a source of communication with the world and with others. This is a way that we can find solace and express ourselves to the world.

Art is also a way that we immortalize ourselves. Each human is subject to the lifespan that they are given on this planet, and when you realize when your life is going to end eventually, you start to realize that the world will move on without you. This means that you might be forgotten, at least according to our primal fear. So, we try to do things to counteract this. The most primal and animal way is to have children because then you'll live on in the world through the people who you have created to carry out their own goals and happiness in the world.

Having children is a primal way that people leave a legacy, and it is the ultimate creative act in the world. All other forms of art are underneath this one. That is because art comes from consciousness. That is why humans are not art. We are consciousness, we have the power of gods, and when we create another person, we are using our power as gods. We are also using our power of gods when we create art, but it is to a slightly lesser degree.

Art is a way that you can analyze yourself to deeper levels. Remember the Rorschach test, a way of analyzing people where we look at blobs of ink of paper and say whatever comes to mind first? Well, all art is sort of like that, as a creator and as a viewer. As a creator, when you are creating art, you are creating the ink blob. Sometimes it is very clear what the artist is talking about. When you look at a Norman Rockwell painting, you understand the scene that he has created because he is putting you right there in a scenario that you can recognize and understand. Other times, the artist is putting you in a place where you can't understand because you aren't meant to. This kind of art can help us to explore what it feels like for other people to experience tarts or fat world. Abstract art is not about telling you things, but rather gets you to think.

Many people say that literature is the way that you can most experience another persons' consciousness, out of all of the art forms. Think about the best manuscript you ever read. You were so into it that you couldn't put it down, and when you read it, you were nowhere else except in the world created by the writer. You were a citizen in his world, and there was nothing to do except to be there in the story and experience whatever was going on.

When you do this, you are experiencing a human mode called flow. Flow is when you are just in the moment, when you are only experiencing something that you are doing, like meditating, playing piano, running, driving, or something else. It is a state of focus and a state of creativity.

To know yourself, you have to be able to experience the extremes of life. You must have been able to understand the anger and express it. You must know when you feel angry and understand what that feels like to you. You must be able to experience joy at the highest level, for this is an extreme human feat. You must be able to take deep pain and failure and also accept the beauty in life. You must be able to immerse yourself in the manuscript and then go pay some bills that you have lying around, which is just menial work that you have to do. There are all sorts of things that you have to deal with that are big and small, and none are less important. It might seem that the small stuff is less important, and in many ways, it is, but the details are something that you can be vigilant with, and they are ways for you to let yourself really experience each part of life.

The number-one way to do this concretely every day and learn about you is journaling. You can journal every day but never write the same thing twice. Journaling doesn't have to be your homework. It can be fun, it can be creative, and it can be a way to release yourself from the shackles of what binds you.

Chapter 55: Why Is Manipulation Important in Life

As we have been talking about so far in this guidebook, there are a lot of different scenarios that you may use manipulation, and there are a lot of effects that can happen as a process as well, depending on how the manipulation is used. While we often think of manipulation as a bad thing, but there are actually quite a few benefits that are going to come with using manipulation in order to get what we want.

Just because we are getting what we want doesn't mean that we are going to always harm someone else. And this is the difference between regular manipulation and what is known as dark manipulation. It is an important distinction that we need to make. With regular manipulation, we want to get something, but we don't want the other person to get harmed or hurt in any manner, whether it is physical, mental, or emotional.

On the other hand, when it comes to dark manipulation, it isn't going to matter to the manipulator whether the other person gets harmed or not. They don't really care how much that person is harmed, and usually, there is going to be some kind of harm in the process. As long as the manipulator gets the thing that they want, they are going to be happy about the situation.

With that said, whether you are using manipulation in order to progress your own agenda while helping others (like in sales or getting some help on a group project), or you are using it to benefit yourself, and you don't care if someone gets harmed in the process, there are going to be some benefits that come with using manipulation on a regular basis. Some of the benefits you can look for will include:

Manipulation is often going to work. The idea here is that if I know what I want and I know how to evoke a feeling in the other person so that they are more likely to do what I want, then manipulation is going to be effective, and we are able to measure this effect as well. Think of how this works. Businesses are going to spend billions of dollars in research to do various marketing strategies to point to how well the manipulation that is found in their campaigns and their advertisements work, so we know that manipulation must be something that works.

Of course, you have to do things the right way. It is not enough to just put an ad online or on television and assume people are going to come in droves to purchase the product. There is just too much competition out there, and often we see so many advertisements that it is impossible to just see something and be manipulated by it. There has to be another level, and there needs to be some experience and expertise to pull it off, and that is what the research dollars of many companies are spending on.

The same idea can be said when we take a look at regular manipulation that an individual is going to use. It is not enough for us to walk up to someone and say, "Do what I want!" The target is likely going to take a look at us and just laugh and walk away. And you would do the same as well. You need to make sure that you are using the right techniques and that you really understand what the other person will respond to However, when you use manipulation in the right manner and with the right techniques, you will find that it actually works, which is a really cool benefit.

The next benefit that comes with manipulation is the idea that we can become pretty good at it. In fact, it is likely that you saw at least a few times when you have used manipulation in the past to help you get what you wanted, even if the answers ended up surprising you in the process. This manipulation is actually something that we have been practicing since before we were able to walk.

This is because there was a time when we were not able to talk, and we still needed to get things. We needed food, something to drink, to feel loved, to have clothes, to get baths, to get diapers changed, and more. Even though we were not able to talk and voice our opinions on our own, and we were not able to take care of these things on our own at this time, we were able to use manipulation in order to influence mom and dad to do the work for us.

Since we have been able to read others since a young age in order to help us get what we wanted as a baby up through adulthood, we are already good at reading others, often much better than we would think. And we can even find that, with a bit of practice, we are able to quickly guess the right thing to do to help us motivate that other person in the process as well. Of course, some of us are going to be much better at doing this than others, but it is still something that we can work on to improve and see some great results with influencing others.

Easier to get what we want. If you decided to come right out and ask the other person to give you exactly what you wanted, it is likely that they are going to say no. If you just ask about it, without using any of the techniques that we will discuss in this guidebook and the techniques of manipulation, then the other person really has no need to help you and won't feel guilty about doing something that they have no interest in helping out with.

However, if you are able to use some of the manipulation tools and techniques that we have been discussing so far and you are able to trigger some feelings in the other person, you will find that it is easier to get the other person to do what you want. They are going to feel some kind of obligation in order to help you, even if they are not sure what that is all about. And even if they are not fond of the idea of helping out with it, they are more likely to say yes.

This is going to be really great news for you. It means that you are going to be able to get the other person to say yes to what you want them to, without having to push too hard or worry as much about whether they are going to say yes or no to you. You will have already put in the work that is needed to convince them to work with you, and it is likely, especially if you spent time analyzing them and using the right technique for their needs, that they are going to agree to what you want.

And the final benefit that we are going to take a look at here when it comes to using manipulation and some of the different techniques that come with it is the idea of power. Since all relationships, whether they are with family, at work, or an intimate relationship, are going to have some element of power in them. All of us would like to have power over others or at least over someone at some point, and manipulation is going to be the tool that we need to ensure that we gain that power over our target.

Now, there are those who will take that power and go too far. This is where the manipulation is going to turn into abuse and some other problems as well. But the power that comes with manipulation can sometimes be as simple as having a bit of control over one person in your life, even your child, and it doesn't always have to be an abusive or negative kind of thing to work with.

The Negatives of Manipulation

Of course, there have to be a few negatives that come with manipulation. If there weren't, then everyone would use this technique all of the time, and we wouldn't have some of the negative connotations that come with it along the way either. The negatives of this are going to mainly occur when you are not versed well enough in using manipulation or if someone catches you in the act of manipulating them. Some of the different negatives that can come with using manipulation in your own life can include:

Manipulation is something that has the potential to backfire quite a bit. People are often going to have some kind of sense about when another person is trying to manipulate them. This is because we are heightened to the idea that because we want something out of another person, it is likely that someone else is going to want something out of us as well. When someone starts to sense that they are being manipulated, it is not going to end well for you, and it is often going to generate a lot of anger, resentment, and more.

If the target senses that the manipulator is trying to take control, or they feel that the manipulator is trying to take some power over them in a sneaky manner, it is likely that the target is not going to trust that person any longer. At this point, if the target feels like you have successfully manipulated them, they may withhold something from their manipulator in order to get even, even if it is not that big of a deal what you are trying to get. And if the target thinks that this manipulation has gone even further and feels like their feelings are being toyed with, then it is sure to bring out a big power struggle between the two people in this game, and the trust is going to head right out the window.

Another negative to be careful about is that we often are not going to think through the manipulation that we are doing before we do it. Before we even have a good idea of what we want out of the relationship, or before we start to evaluate the possibility of just coming out to the target and asking for what we want in a direct manner, we are going to head right over and start manipulating the other person.

The reason that we do this is because we are so eager to try out the techniques, we are eager to get what we want, or we just assume that the other person will say no to us, and we don't want to worry about the rejection in the process. However, this step is going to lead to some assumptions about you both that could end up corroding the relationship that you are in. Remember that once the relationship is gone and corroded, it is impossible for you to regain the control that you need in order to manipulate that person again.

There are a lot of different indirect versions of manipulation that can come into play, and sometimes they will become almost a habit in the relationship. Some of these are going to include options like guilt-tripping, abusive criticism, and complaining. And another layer of the power struggle is going to start showing up in the relationship when we use these techniques all of the time, even though that was usually not the intention.

Chapter 56: Financial Statement Manipulation

Manipulating financial reporting is a persistent issue in corporate America. While several measures have been taken by the Securities and Exchange Commission (SEC) to minimize this form of corporate failure, the management compensation system, the immense flexibility provided by the Generally Accepted Accounting Principles (GAAP), and the continued conflict of interest between the professional auditor and the corporate company tend to offer the ideal atmosphere for performance. As a result of these cases, consumers who buy specific stocks or bonds will be informed of the challenges, alert signals, and resources at their fingertips in order to minimize the negative effects of these problems.

Reasons Behind the Misuse of the Income Statement

There are three main explanations that management is abusing financial statements. First, in many instances, the remuneration of chief officers is closely related to the financial results of the business. As a consequence, they have a strong motivation to paint a rosy image of the financial state of the business in order to fulfill defined success standards and to increase their personal rewards.

Second, it's a pretty simple thing to do. The Financial Accounting Standards Board (FASB), which lays down the GAAP principles, includes a considerable deal of flexibility and definition of accounting regulations and procedures. For better or worse, these GAAP principles offer a considerable degree of versatility, making it easier for corporate managers to create a clear image of the company's financial situation.

Third, owing to the partnership between the impartial auditor and the business customer, it is doubtful that financial fraud would be identified by investors. In the US, the corporate auditing market is regulated by the Big Four accounting firms and a handful of smaller national accounting firms. Although such agencies are supposed to be unbiased auditors, they have a clear conflict of interest as they are paid, sometimes very substantially, by the same organizations they audit. As a consequence, auditors may be inclined to change the accounting laws in order to present the financial position of the firm in such a manner as to make the customer satisfied—and to maintain it in operation.

Why the Accounting Results Are Being Distorted

There are two common methods for managing financial statements. The first is to exaggerate the present period results on the financial statement by falsely inflating revenue and profits or by deflating existing period expenditures. That strategy helps the financial state of the business look stronger than it is in order to fulfill the standards that have been put out.

The second solution involves the very opposite method, which is to reduce current period revenue on the income statement by deflating profits or by inflating current period expenditures. It might sound counter-intuitive to make the financial situation of a corporation seem weaker than it really is, but there are several motives to do so: to dissuade future acquirers; to get all the negative news "out of the way" so that the business may look ahead more strongly; to throw bleak figures in a time where low results may be linked to the existing macroeconomic environment;

Clear Forms to Handle Financial Statements

When it comes to bribery, there is a range of accounting methods at the discretion of the business. Financial Shenanigans (2002) Howard Schilit discusses the seven key aspects in which business management manipulates the company's financial statements.

1. Premature or doubtful quality reporting of income

- Reporting sales due to the end of both facilities.

- You are reporting sales prior to the shipping of the drug.

- Reporting income for items not expected to be bought.

2. Recording of imaginary sales

- Reporting of advertising transactions that have not taken effect.
- Reporting investment gains as revenue.
- Reporting the income earned as revenue from the loan.

3. Increase profits with one-time earnings

- Raise earnings by selling properties and reporting sales as income.
- Increasing gains by classifying investment gain or dividends as revenue.

4. Switching current spending to an earlier or later date

- Price amortization is so late.
- Change accounting practices to promote bribery.
- They are capitalizing on regular running expenses in order to reduce expenditures by transferring them from the declaration of sales to the balance sheet.
- Failure to pay off or sign back damaged properties.

5. Failure to report or improperly minimize liabilities

- Failure to report costs and obligations as potential programs are in operation.
- Adjust accounting rules to enable fraud.

6. Move existing sales to a later date

- Building a rainy day fund as a pool of income to improve potential results.

- Keeping the money back.

7. The transition of potential expenses to the present time as a separate fee

- Acceleration in spending in the present period.

- They are modifying accounting rules to enable fraud, in particular by restrictions on depreciation, amortization, and depletion.

Although several of these methods apply to the analysis of the income statement, there is also a range of strategies used to control the balance sheet as well as the cash flow statement. However, also the wording of the financial management review and analysis segment may be distorted by softening the action vocabulary utilized by corporate managers from "may" to "might," "possibly," to "maybe," and "therefore" to "maybe." Taken together, investors can consider these concerns and complexities and be diligent when determining the financial situation of a business.

Financial Exploitation by Company Merger or Takeover

Another method of financial coercion can occur during the merger or acquisition phase. One traditional strategy is that management tries to raise support for mergers or acquisitions focused solely on the increase in the expected earnings per share of the merged firms. Let's look at the table below and see how this form of exploitation takes place.

Based on the details in the table above, the potential takeover of the target business seems to make perfect financial sense as the profits per share of the acquired corporation would be significantly improved from $5 per share to $5.83 per share. After the purchase, the purchasing business would expect a rise of $200,000 in client profits due to the introduction of sales from the target product. Moreover, despite the strong market valuation of the common stock of the purchasing business and the weak asset value of the target firm, the acquiring company would only have to sell an extra 20,000 securities in order to allow the transaction of $2 million. Taken together, a substantial rise in business profits and a small raise in 20,000 common stock issued would result in a more favorable profit per share.

Sadly, a financial judgment made solely on this method of study is improper and deceptive, because the potential financial effect of this transaction can be significant, immaterial, or even unfavorable. The profits per share of the purchasing business would rise by a substantial sum for just two factors, and there are no long-term consequences for any factor.

Protecting the Misuse of the Income Statement

There are a number of variables that can influence the consistency and precision of the data at the discretion of the user. As a consequence, analysts will have a good understanding of financial report research, with a clear grasp on the usage of internal liquidity solvency ratios, external liquidity marketability ratios, development and company productivity ratios, financial risk ratios, and business risk ratios. Investors will also provide clear knowledge of how to utilize various market metrics, through the usage of price/earnings ratios, price/book value ratios, price/sales ratios, and price/cash flow ratios, to gauge the reasonableness of financial results.

Unfortunately, very few institutional investors have the energy, expertise, and money to partake in and evaluate these practices. If so, it might be simpler for them to stick to investing in low-cost, diversified, actively managed mutual funds. Such funds provide investment research professionals with expertise, history, and experience to deeply evaluate the financial picture of a business before making an investment decision.

Conclusion

Can you imagine standing in front of your colleagues, able to eloquently deliver your amazing plan? You need not imagine any longer. Finally, everyone will see that you with authority and will naturally want to follow your lead and make you happy.

Others will be drawn to you as a person they can trust. Those around you will feel they really connect with you, even though it may only be the first time meeting you. As you gain experience and confidence with this new information, you will find ways to utilize it in your everyday situations and extraordinary ones, to get what you want and help others. It's amazing to think if you've already come this far and where you're going subsequent. You've been provided with all of the tools you need to achieve your goals, whatever they may be. The world is your playground. If you put your imagination to it, there is an opportunity in every single interaction you have, if you look for it.

A lot more is going on when two people meet for the first time than most people pick up on. Many people are so preoccupied with themselves and other thoughts that they would never notice the subtle cues that people are continually giving off, broadcasting their feelings and thoughts. When you know the tricks of the trade when it comes to picking up nonverbal communication and body language, you will be able to read a great deal about people before they even open their mouths to introduce themselves. When you can read the room and size people up, you already have an advantage over anyone else who might be trying to vie for that person's affection, political support, or sales transaction. It's all about taking the time it takes to learn and practice in the real world once you've decided to undertake the art of dark psychology. It's impossible to become comfortable with these techniques without observation and practice. You will find that the more confident you are with your strategies, the more comfortable and more natural they will happen, leaving your targets entirely in the dark about what's going on under the surface.

People tend to believe that manipulation is effective for different reasons. They have different ideas about what makes manipulation effective. In particular, there are three criteria involving the manipulator that must be met in order to ensure that manipulation is successful. Ultimately, it is the manipulator that is primarily responsible for the manipulation and determining whether it will work, though there are certain personality traits that tend to be particularly vulnerable to the attempts to manipulate. The three criteria that must be met to ensure successful manipulation are:

- The manipulator must hide the true intentions

- The manipulator must know the victim's most viable vulnerabilities

- The manipulator must be ruthless enough to follow through

Keep in mind that these three criteria being present are not a guarantee that the manipulation will always work. However, they must be present if they will work.

Some people out there will make you feel good because they genuinely love you. But it often takes time for such a relationship to build. If someone whom you barely know is suddenly super into you and trying to rush a relationship, become very wary. Don't let things move too quickly. Get to know the person first. Someone who wants you so badly right off of the bat is usually superficial and just trying to prime you into a victim. Don't fall for it. Normal people don't just jump into relationships or try to rush things. Normal people also don't start acting crazy about you in an unusually short period of time.

A manipulator will make you feel like there are butterflies in your stomach. You will strive to please him. Your biggest desire will be to make him smile. This is because he is already making you feel as if you owe him or as if you like him so much that you will work to please him. Beware of people who make you feel like a puppet. You should never want to bend over backward for someone so urgently. You need to have a sense of dignity and personal space, and value in every relationship. If you don't, something is off.